DON'T TREAD ON ME

Anti-Americanism Abroad

DON'T TREAD ON ME

Anti-Americanism Abroad

Carol Gould

To
my parents
Katherine Karash and Oscar Gould

British Library Cataloguing in Publication Data
A catalogue record of this book is available from the British Library

Printed and bound in the United Kingdom

ISBN 978-1-904863-35-9

Social Affairs Unit
314–322 Regent Street
London W1B 5SA
www.socialaffairsunit.org.uk

CONTENTS

Acknowledgements		8
PREFACE:	What is Happening 'Over There'?	9
Chapter 1:	Introduction to an Expatriate	19
Chapter 2:	Murderous Kenya, Bloody Pakistan and Sweet Iowa – Why America is Still a Beacon of Democracy	28
Chapter 3:	Carol Gould Returns to the USA	39
Chapter 4:	'Americans are So Stupid!'	50
Chapter 5:	Faith, Bush and Fiercely Secular Britain (a.k.a. Dawkinsland)	58
Chapter 6:	'Put That Flag Away and Talk Proper English!'	67
Chapter 7:	A Yankee in the Green Man Pub (and Condi Rice in Blackburn)	73
Chapter 8:	'Americans are Destroying the Planet and We Will All Die!'	76
Chapter 9:	But Aren't We Best Friends with Great Britain?	80
Chapter 10:	'Americans are Vile, Genocidal, Slavery-Loving and Illiterate Religious Fanatics'	84
Chapter 11:	The Myth of the Jewish Cabals	89
Chapter 12:	'The Jews Control the US Media and the Way Americans Think!'	91

Chapter 13:	'Is Good the Jew and Hindu Killed!'	94
Chapter 14:	The Hate-America/Hate-Israel Fests in London, Sponsored by the Police and Western Union	100
Chapter 15:	The Israel Factor – 'You People Invented Terrorism, and Israel is an Abomination Supported by the Other Terrorist State, the USA!'	104
Chapter 16:	When All Else Fails, Blame the Jewish Lobby!	112
Chapter 17:	The *Independent*'s Shameful 'Jewish American Flag'	115
Chapter 18:	'That Vile Expansionist Little Nation' and 'That Vile Imperialist Superpower'!	120
Chapter 19:	Sir David Hare and Rumsfeld	126
Chapter 20:	Harold Pinter and his 'America Obsession'	129
Chapter 21:	'How Can 57 Million People be So Stupid?'	135
Chapter 22:	From Greenham Common to Trident – The Small Matter of 'Red Ken' Livingstone	166
Chapter 23:	Ken Livingstone and Daniel Pipes in a Clash of Civilizations	172
Chapter 24:	Friendly Fire – Those Criminal American GIs!	178
Chapter 25:	Casinos Will Bring 'American-Style' Spent Needles, Thrown-Away Condoms and Prostitution to All of Britain	189
Chapter 26:	'You people killed Mountbatten!'	194
Chapter 27:	INTERLUDE – In Praise of MI5, the NHS, British Veterans and Some Wonderful Journalists	196

Chapter 28:	'Die, Glazer, Die!' – The Charming Reaction of British Football Fans to an American Tycoon	207
Chapter 29:	Mayfair Bans America, Now and Forever	211
Chapter 30:	You May Have to Walk Alone, Liverpool...but Avram Grant Will Never Walk Alone	215
Chapter 31:	The European View	223
Chapter 32:	My Diary Entries...	232
Chapter 33:	'Go Back to America!' Said the (Most Likely Illegal) Immigrant to Me	248
Chapter 34:	INTERLUDE – On a Lighter Note...	252
Chapter 35:	Dear Archbishop of Canterbury – Why I Still Adore America	254
Chapter 36:	Booing the 'Star Spangled Banner' – and Pumpkin Pie!	260
Chapter 37:	Americans 'Poison' British Soldiers – and I Finally Get Whacked!	266
EPILOGUE:	America Beckons Once More	270

ACKNOWLEDGEMENTS

My gratitude goes to Michael Mosbacher and Roger Kimball for liking the idea.

Dolores Claman, Peter Whittle and Sara Rogers helped make this project a reality. I would also like to thank the following people, without whose constant support, advice and encouragement during these recent and most trying years of my life this book would never have seen the light of day: Phyllis Chesler, Issy Benjamin, William Hoffman, Barbara Tennenbaum, John Ware, Lauran Stevens, Priti Shah, Stroma Hamilton-Campbell, Diana Morris, Sally Karwowski, Sue Kaye, Gretel Epstein, Ruth Meixner Bird, Douglas Murray, Hunter Steele, Vivien Lichtenstein, Glenmore Baird, Annie Price, Sandra Blackman, Laura Davies, Revd Susan Blue, Barbara Rosenblat, Felicity Trew, Susan Brooks, Ruth Winter, Milli Kosoy Gervasi, Barbara Pope, the Little Venice Medical Centre, my cousin Amy Novek, my sister Susan Gould and the rest of my family.

And a final thank you to Joyce and Don Rumsfeld, whose warmth, humour, humility and inspiring faith made me feel so welcome when we were neighbours in Washington.

Carol Gould, London, July 2008

PREFACE
WHAT IS HAPPENING 'OVER THERE'?

Just as I was putting the final touches to this manuscript, I had two experiences in rapid succession that, though unpleasant, could be regarded as a 'gift' to an author. In my case, I am somewhat put upon, because there is a small coterie of expatriate Americans and Hampstead *Guardian*-reading Anglo-Jews who insist that I just imagine the verbal garbage I have heaped on me, and who maintain that there is no anti-Semitism or anti-Americanism in the United Kingdom. So to have *two* experiences that I sincerely did not 'imagine' is something of a gift.

The first encounter was with Robin Oakley, the London bureau chief of CNN, in the run-up to the 2008 US presidential primaries. He told me that anti-Americanism had reached such a pitch abroad that in some locations his crews had to remove the CNN logo from their vans. What Robin then said was sad, but at the same time music to my ears: his colleague, the respected broadcaster Walter Rodgers, had left London after having had his fill of anti-Americanism. He apparently used to bound into the London office of CNN and bombard Robin with the latest unpleasantness he had endured, Robin having to calm him down. Finally, after many years based in the United Kingdom, Rodgers had had enough and had returned to the United States. This story from Robin Oakley made me feel vindicated: if a tough old veteran journalist like Walt Rodgers can feel cornered in a hostile London, then I am not alone.

My second encounter came in late 2007, when I hopped into a taxi in central London. The elderly cabbie was obviously very agitated, so I asked him if he was alright. 'No,' he replied, 'as a matter of fact, I'm not.' He then told me that he had had to collect an American couple from the Marriott in George Street and take them 'someplace where we won't be yelled at'. He then told me that this couple had arrived and taken a walk along Edgware Road, near their hotel. There they had been on the receiving end of verbal abuse wherever they had ventured. He said the 'icing on the cake' was that they had been spat on in a coffee shop. They had packed their bags, checked out of the hotel and asked the cabbie to find them a part of London where they would not have abuse hurled at them. He was visibly upset and said he never thought he would live to see the day when 'Yanks would not be welcome in this country'. He went on to regale me with stories of his having been an evacuee during the war, of the kindness his family had received from African-American and white GIs and WACs,* and of Americans always having been 'the best tippers and the most courteous'.

Readers must understand that visceral anti-Americanism in various sections of society goes back to before the days of Abu Ghraib, Guantanamo or the Iraq War; it has been a feature of my life in Britain over 30 years. It has now reached epic proportions, with the head of the Anglican Church, Dr Rowan Williams, launching into a lengthy tirade against 'imperialist' America in a London-based Muslim magazine, *Emel*. (This episode is covered in detail in the chapter on 'The European View'.)

I want to set the record straight right at the start: in recent years, I have been on the receiving end of more verbal attacks than I can count, but am often told that I imagine or exaggerate these confrontations. So, in order to validate my viewpoint from now to the end of this book, I would like to share with readers a remarkable story related by Rosemary Righter, a senior journalist for *The Times* of London and the *Spectator* magazine. In an article entitled 'Why It is Right to Join America's Fight' (*Spectator*, 16 March 2002), she tells of the

* Members of the Women's Army Corps.

night of 11 September 2001, when she went to have dinner with some old London friends. One of the guests asked for a lift home. She was driving fast, when he said: 'Rosemary, isn't it marvellous to think that the arrogant bloody Americans have finally got it in the neck?' She braked. Hard. She goes on to say that European and British anti-Americans have got their priorities wrong, and that readjusting their view would be advisable.

On 9/11, my London neighbours arrived home from work and said exactly the same thing as Rosemary's passenger: 'America got it in the neck.'

Having just visited the graves of 3,800 American airmen and the wall of the 5,100 American missing at Madingley Cemetery in Cambridge, I would suggest America think twice before it sticks its neck out again for anyone. The 8,900 commemorated at Madingley and the 9,600 buried at Omaha Beach 'got it in the neck', too.

As this manuscript nears completion, there are also three current stories in Britain that reflect the feeling of resentment towards anything and everything American and that belie the theory that anti-Americanism is due to utter hatred of the Iraq War. Dolly Parton arrived in Britain in December 2007 to promote her highly successful scheme to provide every underprivileged child with a monthly book. Her planned meeting with Rotherham Council caused consternation amongst some council members because their regular meeting time had to be moved. There were the usual jokes in the media about her presence here.

In the same week, Donald Trump was prevented from building two golf courses and 1,500 houses in Aberdeenshire. (He is not a Bush man by any means, so the hostility to his presence here had nothing to do with Iraq.) What was so interesting for me – and this might explain why, for so many years, my smiling, enthusiastic and sometimes overly driven demeanour has landed me in deep trouble in Britain – is the comment made in the *Guardian* (6 December 2007) that he has the kind of face you want to punch – 'well-fed, smug ...imbued with infuriating sense of entitlement'.

The Trump affair has a lot to do with damage to the Scottish rural environment, but the griping and mud-slinging about the American tycoon have been painful to watch.

This book is my journey from what was, until 9/11, a settled life as an expatriate in the culturally rich London I so loved, and in what I felt had become my adopted country, back to my homeland, the United States of America, in a state of fear and hurt. It is a wake-up call to Americans that they still live in the dark about the true nature of 'anti-Americanism'.

Interestingly enough, John Gibson, in his excellent book *Hating America: The New World Sport*, sees this phenomenon as dangerous and frightening. Whilst some may say that I make it up or exaggerate, I find the recent tirades directed at me by those who used to be friends intimidating. They verge on physical confrontation. Anti-Americanism, which, as I will explain, is often tied up with hatred of Israel, is a wake-up call to American Jewry: the comfort and security it enjoys in the greatest nation on earth are a world removed from the resurgence of hatred that is consuming Europe and Britain – hatred directed at their small, decorous and relatively unprotected Jewish communities.

In recent years, anti-Americanism has hurt me financially: a London-based business venture of mine is in ruins because of the rage amongst the people I had approached for finance, one of whom accused me of being 'one of those Americans who come here and relieve old ladies of their money and scarpers back to America with their cash'.

Anti-Americanism, coupled with its sister hatreds of anti-Zionism and anti-Semitism, is not just the crazy imam exhorting his flock on a Friday in Pakistan, but the pinstripe-suited businessman in Hertfordshire who wishes more Jews were killed when suicide bombers strike, and the middle-class, elderly Scotsman in a studio audience who exclaims that he hopes the next 9/11 will see 3 million, not 3,000, people killed inside America. Anti-Americanism, often wrapped inside a sheath of anti-Semitism, is the Barbour-jacketed middle-class lady from the shires who joins in with the burning and stomping of the Stars and Stripes in Trafalgar Square during the American president's 2003 visit. The smoke rising from the pile of American flags on that autumn evening merges with the screeches of 'Down with Israel! Free Palestine!' from young, otherwise sweet-looking Britons.

Why is it important for Americans to understand anti-Americanism? We have been told that 9/11 was one of the worst intelligence failures in our history. Indeed, I have joked to Washingtonians that I could pick up better intelligence in a smoky café in London's Edgware Road than could all the thousands of civil servants staring at screens in concrete-clad government agencies in rural Virginia.

It is important for Americans to understand this phenomenon, because it has begun to affect the way we do business in the world and it feeds the flames of hatred that lead to terror. Who was singled out on the *Achille Lauro*? American Leon Klinghoffer. Who was singled out to be tortured for hours in front of other passengers and then shot on a hijacked aircraft in Athens and his body flung out onto the tarmac? US navy diver, Robert Dean Stethem, on TWA flight 847 on 15 June 1985. His wounds were so terrible that his remains were almost unrecognizable to his loved ones.

Whose nation's soldiers were massacred as they slept in Lebanon? America's. I remember, way back in the 1980s, as a drama executive with Anglia Television, being terrified to travel because I held an American passport. Anti-Americanism is huge and scary and dangerous and, most of all, has nothing to do with Dubya or Rummy.

On 5 May 2005, George Galloway, whose extremist views had caused him to be spurned by the mainstream of the Labour party, won election to the British Parliament as a member of the virulently anti-Israel Respect party. Apart from a fly-on-the-wall video on C-SPAN, the American media barely covered this story. Yet it was a major event in British political history. Galloway roused the citizens of Bethnal Green and Bow to turn against the incumbent MP, Oona King (half African-American, half white British, with press reports that her mother was Jewish), and to vote for him as a representative of the 'enraged' Muslim community that he believes has been demonized since 11 September 2001. I watched C-SPAN in horror, as Oona King tried to speak at a rally, only to be drowned out by furious crowds. A reporter noted that residents of that borough had been warned that, if they kept a picture of Oona King in their premises, they would be 'burned down'.

In 2000, after a career as a television network drama script editor in England, I became so alarmed at the level of anti-Semitism and anti-Americanism that I was hearing on the street, on television and on radio – and even from neighbours, colleagues and 'friends' ('Carol, I hope the next war in the Middle East will annihilate your brethren in Occupied Palestine...') – during the al-Aqsa Intifadah that I decided to start writing about this frightening phenomenon. Since 2001, I have written scores of articles chronicling the increase in attacks on Americans and Jews in the UK and Europe. Like my much-loathed but celebrated colleagues Melanie Phillips and Julie Burchill (at the pinnacle of her career, she quit the *Observer* because she, a non-Jew, could no longer tolerate the anti-Semitic talk in the office), I feel it is vital for Americans to know that we have a long and bitter struggle ahead. Sad to say, the populations of European countries harbour such a deep loathing of America and Israel that there will come a time when we are absolutely alone.

This loathing affects the US economy. Here is a tiny example: I rang an old friend in London in April 2005 and suggested he take his family over to Washington to enjoy the glorious spring and the cherry blossom festival.

He said: 'Are you kidding? Have you left reality, Carol? Your country is the most unpopular on the planet. People here simply despise America. To be honest, I am not about to spend my money there. It'll just go straight to the Israelis.'

I will wager that, at this moment, sleeper cells are busy planning their next terror atrocity inside the United States. They are aided and abetted by thousands in Europe and the UK who see Israel and the USA as dispensable. American Homeland Security Chief Michael Chertoff announced, in

January 2008, tighter controls on British visitors to the United States, but for a decade I have been of the belief that the mightily appeased Jihadists who enjoy unlimited freedom in the streets of Britain are a major threat to security inside Britain and further afield.

In 1998, I was making a documentary about the three monotheistic faiths. When it came time to film at the Central Mosque in Regent's Park, my cameraman, a Libyan exile, pleaded with me, the producer, not to go to the mosque. He said he would supervise the filming, but if I went I 'would be killed'. This was when Bill Clinton was president, there was relative quiet in the Mideast, and there was no Rumsfeld to blame for everything. I protested, but my well-meaning cameraman reminded me that, if I went, there would be an international incident similar to that in April 1984, when WPC Yvonne Fletcher was gunned down outside the Libyan embassy. I would have been killed in my own neighbourhood of London because the worshippers at my local mosque regarded an American as a legitimate target. When I told neighbours about this, their response was: 'Well, you Americans helped start that provocative Israel in 1947 because of the Holocaust and frankly it is still a ghastly provocation.'

In 2000, I wrote to the *Independent*, warning the editors that the relentlessly inflammatory tone of the British media would one day inspire an attack on humans and buildings that would totally overshadow the Taliban's blowing up of the Buddhas. Little did I appreciate what a prophecy that would turn out to be...When 9/11 unfolded, I was not surprised. The British and European media love to depict Israel as an apartheid state, bent on genocide and supported by an America jammed full of crazed Evangelicals and billionaire Zionists.

In what I like to call the 'Dixie Chick Syndrome', one of the most disturbing manifestations of America-hatred comes from its own citizens. Amongst the notions promulgated most often by Americans inside the USA is that they live in a police state, and that 'Europeans' are so enlightened and civilized. I suggest they listen to London football fans yelling 'Yiddo!' at

Jewish supporters and players, or witness the shameful Spaniards, made up in blackface, shouting obscenities at Afro-Caribbean British motor-racing genius Lewis Hamilton, to understand why America is light years ahead of Europe in race relations. For years, I have heard the accusation that 9/11 brought a police state to the USA. Have any of the people who articulate these notions ever lived in a real police state? I love those police dogs sniffing the Amtrak car I am boarding.

Americans living outside the United States often use the opportunity to defame their native land in strident tones. An incident that is indelibly etched on my memory occurred one evening in February 2004, at the Charing Cross Hotel bar, when several fellow members of Democrats Abroad were loudly condemning the Bush regime and the Iraq War. They had a right to their opinions, but their hysterical shouting was profoundly embarrassing. Suddenly a burly Englishman got up and told them to shut up. It transpired that he and his family, along with most of the other people in the bar, had been to Whitehall to see Defence Secretary Geoff Hoon. And why? Because their sons had just died in Iraq. I wanted to climb under the table. In succeeding years, I began to find the rhetoric of so many expatriate Democrats so wildly aberrant – dare I say bordering on treason? – that I decided to jump ship and join Republicans Abroad. My parents would be revolving in their graves, but I will not be screamed at (and many did just that) by Americans who denigrate their country whilst abroad.

Back in time to September 2001: the hate-fest known as the United Nations Conference on Racism had just ended in Durban, South Africa, and Shimon Peres and other Jewish and American dignitaries had had to run for their lives from hysterical crowds whipped up by pro-Palestinian groups. The conference, led by the former Irish president, Mary Robinson, was a terrifying example of the way media bias against Israel and the USA can whip up huge crowds into a near-violent frenzy. To this day, throughout conservative circles, 'Durban' is a euphemism for the worldwide movement to bring down Israel and the USA. The 9/11 atrocity happened three days after the close of Durban, and I was not shocked, because only recently I had been sitting at late-summer dinner parties being berated about the crimes against humanity perpetrated by the United States and Israel.

One of the incidents that inspired my decision to venture back to my native land occurred a week after 9/11. My dear friend and fellow film producer, Aida Young, had encouraged me to leave my shock behind and go to a BAFTA screening of *Moulin Rouge*. Unfortunately, the violent and noisy short film before the main feature upset me so much that I left the screening theatre and went to recover my composure in the lobby, where a receptionist brought me a stiff drink. A few days later, I ventured out to a screening of *The Royal Tenenbaums*. I told a BAFTA member – call him Tony – that I had been so traumatized by 9/11 that I had had to leave a previous screening in a state of discombobulation. He suddenly became a maniac, screaming at me that Britons had lived through five years of the Blitz and nobody had made a fuss, adding all sorts of insults about America and Americans. It was agonizing enough at that time to be outside the United States and away from family and old friends, but to be tormented this way made me realize I might no longer be 'at home' in England.

In 2002, after a dressing-down by a friend I had known for a decade that left me with chest pains, I decided to start my long road of return to the United States. Her remonstrations had been specifically focused on the 'ghastly' tradition of Americans having flags on their houses. She saw this as a form of Nazism, and when I repudiated this she became so agitated and began to rail at me with such bizarre ferocity that I thought she was going to strike me. And so it was that, on 8 September 2004, I arrived at Dulles International Airport. And when the immigration officer said, 'Welcome home, hon' and I saw the giant Stars and Stripes on the wall, I burst into tears. Americans who live inside their own shores all year round cannot imagine what it is like to see the flag in one's own land after years of being hated abroad with such venom.

These are my writings. Please take them to heart. I urge the leaders of the United States to heed the words of writers who are taking risks to expose the dark cloud that has fallen across Europe. We may end up without allies, but, from my perspective, we must be prepared to go it alone.

As this goes to be typeset in autumn 2008 and the world moves on apace, I continue to be reminded of my American origins...

* * * * *

When I see that the overworked and under-equipped ticketing system at Victoria station means I will miss my train to Canterbury, Matthew – eyes so full of hatred that I feel like a Jew in the line-up for the gas chambers – says: 'I don't help bloody Americans!'

* * * * *

The viscerally anti-American *Candide* devised by Robert Carsen at English National Opera – cheered by capacity audiences on their feet for every cruel and often wildly inaccurate swipe at anything and everything American – makes me feel distinctly uncomfortable.

* * * * *

Barack Obama, John McCain, Joe Biden and Sarah Palin – each represents a slice of me and a slice of America: a generous and diverse nation so misunderstood and, as I explain in this book, undeserving of the hatred it generates.

CHAPTER ONE

INTRODUCTION TO AN EXPATRIATE

WHO AM I?

It is vital that readers know something about me, in order to put into context the narrative of my 32 years in Great Britain. To understand why I embarked on a book about anti-Americanism, you have to understand that three decades in Britain have done nothing to dampen my pride in the country that made me who I am.

My grandparents emigrated to the United States in the early 1900s to escape the staggering levels of persecution besetting Jews in Russia and in what is now Lithuania and Poland. If you have seen *Fiddler on the Roof* (and millions of non-Jews have seen it without making the connection of why Israel still means so much to so many Jewish people of my generation), you will appreciate that the conditions under which Jews lived in the Pale of Settlement in Tsarist Russia were grim. They were regularly beaten to death in murderous pogroms. Passover was dreaded, because the Christian hordes threw bricks through the windows of Jewish homes and generated terrifying mayhem.

The *shtetls*, from whence over a million Jews emigrated, were conurbations of impoverished scholars, whose wives toiled to put a meagre meal on the table, but whose large broods of children never got into trouble; boys were devoted to *cheder*, or Torah studies, and the girls were happy to become their brides. I am reminded of a posh lady at the Cambridge summer school of the Centre for Jewish–Christian Relations, who announced on day one that she was 'horrified' at the idea of Jewish children being force-fed Torah from the earliest age and having to do 'that ghastly bar mitzvah' ritual. That was a red rag to a bull, and I duly delivered a stern rebuke about Hebrew School keeping Jewish boys and girls away from drugs, crime and hooliganism. Some start to Jewish–Christian relations on a cold, wet English summer's day...

In the Russia and Lithuania in which my grandparents starved, studied and still had the energy to make love, young men were conscripted into the Tsar's army, which for Jews was a life sentence. That is, a life sentence that lasted only a few years, because more often than not they were ill-equipped to survive the brutality meted out to them. Today, when I see an Israeli soldier – who, to my British dinner-party circuit is a 'genocidal murderer', to Tom Paulin is an SS guard, and to *Guardian* bloggers a Nazi – I experience an involuntary, uncontrollable wave of pride, realizing that, in just 50 years, from the horrors of the Russian pogroms arose a formidable army of tough young Jews who have faced countless Arab armies in war after war and have triumphed.

Somehow, my grandparents made it to the USA on crowded and filthy ships. When they arrived at Ellis Island around 1907, they were processed and checked for disease and lice. My grandfather, Charles Karash, who had piercing blue 'Karash eyes', already had relatives in the USA – my cousins who had emigrated in the early 1800s to South Carolina, where they had made a living in local crops. My family tree shows one prolific Mr Karesh (same family, different spelling) in the 1800s who had oodles of children, and that is why I seem to encounter a blue-eyed cousin wherever I give a lecture. It is noteworthy that my maternal grandparents, Celia and Charles, were the children of two of the most revered rabbis of Bialystok. So, a hundred years later, when I am shouted at in London by Britons who insist that Americans are innately dumb, I am not too happy...

My paternal grandfather died in 1929, leaving his wife, my grandmom, Rose Gold, alone with two youngsters to raise – my father, Oscar, just 12, and my Aunt Isabelle, just five. She did everything she could to put food on the table, never remarried, and worked her fingers to the bone to make sure these two children went to school. My father worked during the day, attended night school and New York University, and went on to become a distinguished naval architect for the marine design division of the US Army Corps of Engineers. I have little sympathy for the millions of scroungers and whingers who have made a lifetime career of blaming everyone else for their lot in life. My grandmother did not have the best command of English, was a poor Jewish woman widowed during the Great Depression, and yet she managed to raise two children who never committed a crime and who led respectable lives.

My mother Kay's father became a cantor in Philadelphia, and she says her parents fought a lot because they were so desperately poor. My mother was so malnourished that her first teeth were black. Yet all three of her sisters and her brother went to school and survived life with dignity. My Uncle Lou was a much-loved dentist, who looked after scores of poor people in West Philadelphia during the Great Depression.

My parents were highly educated and deeply principled. My late mother was an intellectual who instilled in my sister and me a foundation that included music, theatre, opera and strong political awareness. She was a graduate of the Philadelphia Normal School, which will mean nothing to anyone who is not from that great city. Normal School produced some of the finest teachers in the United States. She also worked for the DPA,* as a case worker who visited the impoverished residents of Philadelphia's black ghettoes. I remember her shame and fury at the appalling conditions of their rented accommodation and at the rotten meat sold to them by white butchers. My mother had a close friend in Harry Jackson, who worked next to her at the DPA, and in today's world they would have married. But in her day, a Jewish girl did not 'marry out' and nor were there many interracial unions. To

* The DPA was a welfare organization, unique to Philadelphia, created during the Great Depression by a small group of mainly Jewish and black social activists. It eventually became a major force in welfare rights, but was disbanded in 1947.

this day, I am convinced that she would have had a happier life with Harry than with my father, whom I adored but who was completely unsuited to marriage. But that is another book...

My childhood was dominated by trips to the Philadelphia Orchestra concerts, to the theatre and ballet and to the Free Library. This is a huge structure on Benjamin Franklin Parkway, and from an early age I loved going there. My parents were not affluent, but somehow they managed to expose Susan and me to every conceivable cultural activity going. My sister was a brilliant young pianist.

Recently, a London friend, shouting at me (as do most Britons these days the minute I open my American mouth), insisted it was not 'normal' for most Americans – or, for that matter, most Britons – to attend concerts, opera, theatre, ballet and art exhibitions on a regular basis. I did finally shut this friend up when I explained that the Philadelphia Orchestra children's concerts and Leonard Bernstein's incomparable New York Philharmonic children's events were attended by the poorest, as well as by the wealthy, and that a construction worker's son could be found sitting next to the daughter of a professor. One of the accusations that have been hurled at me for 30 years is the dearth of cultural life in the United States. My parents had scant funds, but the wealth of cultural activity afforded to my sister and me in Philadelphia was nothing short of miraculous.

My mother regaled us with stories of plays that had premiered in our great city. During my life in England, I was reminded of the 'lack of intellect' in America; but my mother's tales of attending the opening nights of Arthur Miller, Tennessee Williams and Clifford Odets plays left an indelible impression on me. I wish to tell my British critics that the city of Philadelphia was so rich with educated and discerning audiences that, if a play bombed there, it did not make it to Broadway. My mother's close friend, Sophie Adams, whose daughter Jody Weisbrod is now an eminent judge, told breathtaking stories about seeing Rex Harrison's Philadelphia opening night in *My Fair Lady*, when electricity filled the legendary Erlanger Theatre.

My parents also lived through the McCarthy era and the execution of the Rosenbergs. This was a time that shook many Jewish Americans, because the attraction of socialism had been strong, and in turn the ruling classes of the United States had decided to rein in the 'Jewish Bolsheviks'. It is no coincidence that many who were blacklisted by McCarthy were Jews.

My parents were liberals in every sense. My father had marched in Harrisburg, the capital of Pennsylvania, to allow blacks into civil engineering. My mother had talked at great length of the disgraceful behaviour of Philadelphia transit workers during the Second World War, when black men were being hired to replace whites who had been sent to war.*

My mother idolized Franklin Roosevelt. She said she had been as devastated by his death in April 1945 as by that of her own father. I have a theory about both men. My grandfather died very suddenly in the summer of 1936. I believe he was already getting mail from Karash family members in Europe, who were reporting the first anti-Jewish edicts handed down by Hitler. He literally came home from synagogue, told my grandmother he felt unwell, lay down and died. Franklin Roosevelt died of a massive stroke the day after the liberation of yet another concentration camp. No doubt he had known for some time about the death camps, and some feel he did nothing because he was an anti-Semite. My mother's inclination is that FDR was so profoundly shocked by the reports that came in on 12 April that he sat down in his favourite chair and just died. (Nowadays when I am screamed at – and I mean screamed at – by Anglo-Jewry about the 'Nazism' of FDR, I am well aware of the resentment many harbour for Roosevelt's lacklustre reaction to the Wannsee Conference

* In August 1944, there was a crippling strike by white transit system employees in Philadelphia because a small number of black workers had been promoted to take the jobs of white men sent off to the war. Federal troops had to be called in to restore the system and prevent riots. It is said that Eleanor Roosevelt was incandescent with rage over the white riots and disturbances across the USA when blacks were given jobs to replace those of wartime servicemen.

and the Final Solution* and to entering the war in 1940, but he was a heroic figure to my parents' generation, having brought them out of the Great Depression and having initiated the Works Progress Administration† and social security.)

My young life, before I went to England, was filled with music, violin lessons, drama productions at school, and the magic of attending the splendid Philadelphia High School for Girls. This fiercely competitive academic institution for high-achievers was second to none, and to this day I become consumed with rage when friends in Europe and Britain ridicule my education. In my entire lifetime in the UK, the workplace contained many gifted women, but none had gone to school beyond the age of 16. I doubt many of the women I encountered in 30 years in the UK could have got through the gruelling curriculum of Girls' High. It has a long list of outstanding graduates who inhabit the halls of academia, the judiciary, government, the arts and sciences, and I am proud to be a graduate of that still-great American school. I was a Phi Beta Kappa‡ graduate of Temple University, whilst my sister achieved distinction at Barnard (Columbia) and Villa Schifanoia in Italy.

* Wannsee: This is a huge issue even today amongst Jewish historians and rabbis: my reading of modern accounts – of historians like Richard Overy and Martin Gilbert – is that the general belief is that FDR toyed with the idea of entering the European war in 1940, but it was actually Henry Morgenthau, secretary of the treasury, who downplayed Wannsee, as he was bending over backwards not to make it look as if he was angling for war to save his fellow Jews.

† Established by Congress and President Roosevelt in April 1935, it generated millions of jobs for the poor; they worked on construction of magnificent new public buildings and the money was also channelled to jobs in the arts and music. It fed children, distributed millions of books and clothing, and provided comprehensive literacy training nationwide. It was disbanded in 1943 due to the wartime boom in the American economy.

‡ Phi Beta Kappa: established in 1776 during the War of Independence by five students at William and Mary College in Maryland, this is a prestigious academic distinction and was set up to honour a tiny percentage of university graduates who each year achieved exceptionally high

The defining moment of my childhood was the assassination of President Kennedy on 22 November 1963. My parents, like so many middle-aged and younger Americans, felt he was a new hope for a troubled nation – a nation still steeped in racial prejudice and Cold War tensions. 'For one brief shining moment', the line from Lerner and Loewe's *Camelot*, America had had its own elegant Court. Pablo Casals and other cultural icons played at the White House, and Jackie Kennedy brought unprecedented style to Washington. All this ended that horrible November day, and the years that followed were painful and turbulent. My high-school years were dominated by political earthquakes: the Six Day War in Israel, the assassinations of Martin Luther King and Bobby Kennedy, the anti-Vietnam War riots, the violence of Mayor Daley's police against demonstrators at the 1968 Democratic convention in Chicago, the shooting of Governor Wallace (this assured Richard Nixon a victory in the November 1968 election), the slaying of students at Kent State University, and the protracted race riots across the nation, summer after summer. Even at Girls' High there was racial friction: I can still remember, as if it were yesterday, black students standing on a table in the cafeteria shouting 'Black Power! Black Power!' At one stage, my parents, liberal as they were, deliberated moving to Livorno, Italy, where there was an American base (my father had been offered a position there). But we stayed and my parents eventually grew old in an America that somehow managed to hold itself together.

My years before England were full of rich experiences at Temple University, where I encountered some brilliant scholars – most particularly Dr Annette Levitt, whose genius

academic results, and were also highly talented as writers in philosophy and the arts. Today, only 10 per cent of American universities are allowed to have Phi Beta Kappa lists and then 10 per cent of those selected by each institution will be inducted by PBK. Famous Phi Beta Kappas have been Presidents Wilson and Franklin Roosevelt, Stephen Sondheim, Mark Twain, Leonard Bernstein, Benazir Bhutto, Condoleezza Rice and many Supreme Court Justices and members of Congress and the Senate.

has affected me to this day. She taught William Blake to perfection, and I was, in turn, inspired to write a comparative essay on the personalities of Beethoven and Blake. Her scholarly writings, and those of her husband, Mort, are important and will endure. She is still a friend. Throughout my time in England, up until his death, I kept in touch with Dr Benjamin Schoenfeld, my Constitutional Law professor. He was heartbroken that I did not pursue a career in law and eventually Congress or the Senate, and he died bitterly lamenting my 'bizarre adventures in that hive of anti-Semitism, Britain'. In 1975, I had to choose between a job at the Turtle Bay Theater Company in Manhattan, with lodgings in the house next door to Katharine Hepburn's residence, or London. I decided to go to the London campus of Temple University to do a postgraduate course in Theatre Studies. I often wonder what my life would have been like had I lived it out in the United States; but destiny landed me in Harold Wilson's Britain.

It is no small wonder that I went into shock when I first came to London and people constantly berated me about the 'hillbilly wasteland' from which I had sprung.

I had an interesting encounter when I arrived at Heathrow in January 1976. I was carrying my violin, and the immigration officer immediately assumed I was here to find work and not to study. On the same flight was David Kanter, the head of the celebrated Ambler Music Festival at Temple University. He intervened with the immigration officer, pointing out to him that I was a 'pipsqueak' (at that time I was five foot two and weighed about seven stone) and I was given leave to enter the United Kingdom. It transpires that David Kanter had, earlier in his life, intervened to bring refugees out of Europe. At that time, I would not have called myself a refugee from the United States; but arriving in tranquil Britain was a far cry from race riots, students being shot and Watergate.

It must be pointed out that I am one American expatriate who has never, ever hated the United States and who has never engaged in derogatory rhetoric about my native country. In fact, when I saw footage of furious Britons and

Europeans, with utter hatred in their eyes, in massive demonstrations outside American installations in Europe and Britain, I immediately bought a 'POW bracelet' and signed up to keep a vigil for an American airman missing in Vietnam. When I had spent time in Washington in 1973, I had been taken under the respective wings of Vice President Ford and Senator Jim Abourezk, who were at opposite ends of the political spectrum. Both were incredibly kind to me, leaving me with a passionate love for the city of Washington that is matched only by the admiration felt for it by the British historian Andrew Roberts, who rightly says that that splendid city embeds itself in one's soul and cannot ever be extricated.

So, I arrived in Britain with mixed feelings. There is much about Britain that has become part of my heart and soul, and there remains nothing so glorious as London in the height of summertime. I stand and get a lump in my throat when I hear 'God Save the Queen' and am always moved to tears by 'Jerusalem' at the Proms. But the unique experience of being born in magnificent Philadelphia and raised an American is something I cannot shed; after three decades abroad, I have never lost my undying affection for the United States. From tirades directed at me about imported grey American squirrels decimating poor British red ones, to vicious and sustained diatribes about the ugly, murderous American military, I have come under sustained attack in every imaginable sphere about my native country, to the point that I feel I am being trodden on. I am deeply proud of the nation that gave the world Jefferson, Franklin, Lincoln, Wilson, FDR and Martin Luther King. No Yank will be trodden on.

Hence this book.

CHAPTER TWO

MURDEROUS KENYA, BLOODY PAKISTAN AND SWEET IOWA – WHY AMERICA IS STILL A BEACON OF DEMOCRACY

I have decided to focus on the single accusation that has been hurled at me more often than any other in my 32 years in Britain: that the United States is a cesspit of violence and racism. The following is my response.

DIARY: 7 JANUARY 2008

There is a weird synchronicity to the events of this week: elections in three countries, thousands of miles apart and spanning three great continents, have caused major political earthquakes.

The assassination of Benazir Bhutto in Pakistan has thrown that nation's election agenda off course and the country has been on the brink of civil war since the 27 December murder in Rawalpindi.

The synchronicity – to wit, irony – of the American presidential primary race, set against the murderous violence in Kenya, is the story that intrigues me to the core of my being.

For years, many Britons on both the Left and the Right have thrown at me the legacy of racism and slavery that forms part of the history of my native United States of America. Recently, accusations of racism and of the USA being an uncontrollably violent society have dominated the conversation in social situations; I try to remind my London critics that the tragic massacre at Virginia Tech was an isolated case in a huge nation with thousands of peaceful university campuses. I also remind Londoners who think I come from the most racist nation in the world that Colin Powell was chairman of the joint chiefs of staff at the Pentagon 17 years ago, and that

Britain does not have anyone in public life of the stature of Condoleezza Rice, and nor has it produced a Martin Luther King, a Jesse Jackson, a Bill Cosby or an Oprah Winfrey. (If the USA is so relentlessly racist, how did Oprah become a billionaire, and how have so many black entertainers and entrepreneurs become internationally esteemed?)

In 2007 Britain, there was an unprecedented rise in teen crime and homicides. The *Evening Standard* recently listed 257 gangs operating in London and the Home Counties. Race relations are not good in Britain.

And so it was that, on 3 January 2008, Iowa, one of the whitest states in America – perhaps second only to snowy Vermont – voted with overwhelming enthusiasm to elect Barack Obama, an American with a Kenyan father, to be their Democratic party's choice for the American presidency.

There was, for me, an immediate irony to all this: there was Kenya in the same week, coming apart at the seams in – dare I say it – tribal violence that had been pent up for generations. The riots and bloodshed, culminating in the burning alive of 50 souls in a barricaded church, were, to all intents and purposes, inspired by the belief amongst opposition supporters that their candidate, Raila Odinga, had won the presidential election and that the incumbent, Mwai Kibaki, had stolen the election. As of this writing, 350 are dead and 250,000 homeless in a rapidly escalating humanitarian crisis.

Many Britons asked me in 2000 why America had not erupted into near-revolution when the 'hanging chads' debacle had unfolded in Florida and the Supreme Court had essentially decided the outcome of the presidential election. Why, they asked, did Al Gore not call for a million-person march on Washington? Why had the people of the USA not come out onto the streets to protest and even cause violence and mayhem? Indeed, my Democrat friends were beside themselves with fury that the Republican-dominated Supreme Court had been allowed to decide the outcome of a presidential election. (At the time, Christopher Hitchens had reported in the *Evening Standard* that Justice Sandra Day O'Connor had vowed not to retire until she was sure a Republican was in the White House.)

The last time the United States erupted into full-scale civil unrest was during the Civil War in the 1860s. The anti-Vietnam War riots at the Democratic convention between hard-hats and demonstrators in Chicago in 1968 and the inner-city summers of what James Baldwin called 'the fire next time' were the closest the country had come to large-scale civil disobedience. When four students were killed by national guardsmen at Kent State University in Ohio in 1970, I remember wondering if the country would erupt into full-scale street warfare. It never happened. America went on functioning and Americans focused on the life cycle and the Thanksgiving turkey. As Donald Rumsfeld said during one of his sorely missed press briefings, Americans have a strong centre of gravity.

It is, therefore, fascinating for me to sit here in London and watch the television screens fill with discord and violence in Pakistan and Kenya, whilst happy Americans, in states as radically divergent as New Hampshire and Iowa, make their aspirations heard with order and discipline; their voices say they want a president who has humble origins and is a fresh face in the crowd. Mike Huckabee and Barack Obama fit this mould.

For me, the powerful irony is the Kenyan background of Barack Obama. On our television screens over the past few days we have seen endless tableaux of brutal violence between Kenyans. One wants to reach out and shake them and shout: 'Look at what one of your brethren has achieved in the United States! Look at how peacefully white America has expressed a revolutionary change in its attitude towards race! Look at this state filled with white people voting for this son of Kenya!'

Who was amongst the first to fly to Kenya this week to try to mitigate the rise in violence? US Assistant Secretary of State for African Affairs Jandayi Frazer met President Kibaki on Friday 4 January. She, a supremely confident black woman, brought with her the self-assuredness personified by America at its best. Can the Britons who berate me for the lack of ethnic minority leadership in the United States tell me how many European minority men and women have the power and influence of the Powells, Winfreys, Rices and Obamas of this world?

About 30 years ago, a stunning film, *The Autobiography of Miss Jane Pittman*, was broadcast on American television. In a *tour de force*, Cicely Tyson played an ancient African-American woman, born in slavery, who had lived almost a century without seeing a true leader emerge who was worthy of being called a Messiah for her people. Whenever a new black baby was born, she would look at him and murmur: 'Is he the one? Is he the one?' The film was searing and moving. It was made at a time when black–white relations were at a miserable low. The babies were born, but there was no hope. The film left me in tears. The events in Iowa this week have brought its message full circle.

At the end of my 2004 play, *A Room at Camp Pickett*, about my late mother's experiences as a WAC at a segregated Virginia army encampment, performed in a one-off tryout at the Africa Centre in London, the narrator makes the following observation:

> Today Camp Pickett is a Fort and museum. In Florida some votes still seem not to count. As Al Sharpton has said, 'We were promised forty acres and a mule. I'm still waiting for my mule.' But African American commanders train raw recruits. A black General commands the world stage. Things are not perfect. But with leaders like Barack Obama on the horizon there is hope and a rainbow left behind for us by the departed young souls of Normandy.

Obama has struck a chord with Iowans that may very well resonate across the huge American expanse. He has stressed American-ness, rather than race or creed. He makes crowds feel that he cares about them. He comes from a background to which more and more Americans relate: he was not born into wealth, and indeed his mother ended up a single parent.

I saw Barack Obama speak in Philadelphia in 2004, just a few streets away from Independence Hall, where the Great Experiment* had started in 1776. He told a story that shook me to my foundations. He said that he had witnessed burly white men campaigning for him in Illinois, wearing Obama buttons and cheering him on the stumps. A mature citizen had told him that those same men had been young, bigoted rednecks 40 years before, but were now passionate supporters of his. He told the story with charm and without bitterness. He made us feel he held no grudges about Jim Crow, but wanted all of us to be part of the dream of Jefferson, Franklin and the Founding Fathers.

Looking at Obama from the viewpoint of the Right, his meeting with Kenyan opposition leader Raila Odinga in August 2006 was seen as an indication of friendship with a fellow Luo tribesman who has evinced sympathy for the inclusion of sharia law in Kenya. Many in the United States worry that Obama may even be hostile to Israel, and may dismantle the USA's alliance with that country. These are real concerns that exercise the conservative wing of the American electorate. But his high profile cannot be matched by any European country that rushes to label America 'racist'.

There is a distinct possibility that Michael Bloomberg will be drafted in as an independent. Unlike the British media, which revel in 'Jewish' and 'Zionist' labels the minute a Jew enters politics, the American press will dine out on Bloomberg's great successes, rather than on his Jewish connections. Like Obama, Bloomberg does not dwell on his ethnic origins, but sees all New Yorkers as his family – just as Obama sees all America as his. Then there is Mike Huckabee, the son of impoverished hillbillies, but a man who has struck a chord with what is emerging as a new America.

In 2006, something happened that the British media missed. In fact, there was virtually no coverage of the midterm elections in November 2006, so Britons knew little of the

* An umbrella expression used to describe the American Revolution and the drafting of the Constitution.

revolution that took place then. Not only did the Republicans lose control of Congress, but Bernie Sanders, a 'democratic socialist', was elected junior senator from Vermont. He is the son of Polish-Jewish immigrants and a former member of the anti-Vietnam War Liberty Union party. A socialist in Congress? This is not the stupid, Zionist-driven, reactionary nation described over and over again to me at London and Cambridge soirees.

Whatever the outcome of the primaries, the dynamism of the television debating process far outshines any public discourse leading up to British elections. Kenya and Pakistan have been convulsed with violence because of elections, yet the United States is bounding along with dignity and energy, as it shows the world how the democratic process is meant to evolve. Hopefully this magnificent sequence of events will at last silence the voices who love to make me feel I come from a violent, uncouth and unintelligent nation of racist nincompoops. Whoever wins the nomination, be it Italian–American Giuliani or Kenyan Barack Obama or blueblood Hillary Clinton or Jewish Michael Bloomberg, this year will show the global community that the melting pot of America is thriving and evolving, and can only be a beacon of hope to the rest of the world.

DIARY: LONDON – 4 FEBRUARY 2008

It did not escape my eye that in the same newspaper, on Monday 4 February, photographs of racist Spaniards covered in blackface appeared alongside images of Barack Obama rejoicing in the clamouring rainbow that is the American electorate. On Super Tuesday, lily-white folks in Idaho, North Dakota and Minnesota came out in their droves to sweep him to victory in their respective states. Meanwhile, in Spain, land of the Inquisition and Franco, medieval men and women chanted hideous epithets at ace Formula One driver Lewis Hamilton, a black person as dynamic as Barack Obama, Tiger Woods and Condoleezza Rice. In the United States, so often reviled in the European press as a bastion of racism, 21st-century citizens of every ethnic origin prepared for a Super

Tuesday in which a man of colour, a son of Kansas and Kenya, was the projected front runner.

As I gazed at the pictures of Spaniards taunting Hamilton, I thought of my mother, who had worked in the 1930s for the Department of Public Assistance in Philadelphia alongside her black colleague, Harry Jackson, trying to better the lives of the poor. I thought of my father, who had skirted baton-wielding mounted police when he marched in the 1930s for the right of a black civil engineer to join his union.

For 32 years I have had to swallow hard when Europeans and Britons have berated me about the 'racism' of the United States. I would posit that things have moved on since the days of Jim Crow, but I do not see this progress manifesting itself in Europe.

It was, therefore, all the more galling to read a *Guardian* column by Gary Younge on Monday 4 February, entitled 'In This Great Meritocracy, Only One Thing Matters: Who is Your Daddy?', in which he postulates that family connections and entrenched wealth have shaped the destiny of America, with little room for the oppressed and disenfranchised. If I am to understand the theory promulgated in the Younge screed, only white aristocrats drive the American infrastructure, through what he calls 'a web of wealth and family connections'.

It is nothing short of astounding that Younge, a liberal black man, laments the success of the sons of the Rev. Martin Luther King Jr, Jimmy Hoffa and Richard Daley, complains that Nancy Pelosi is the daughter of a congressman and moans that 5 per cent of senators are the sons of men who held the same office. Why does this constitute a grievance in the eyes of the British columnist? Is there no culture more steeped in family dynasties than that of Great Britain? The expression 'Bob's your uncle' evolved from the legend of favours granted by Robert Peel to his benighted nephew.

To complain about the rise to power of Nancy Pelosi is an absurdity: her rise to Speaker of the House is a triumph of everything Emma Lazarus extolled in her poem that adorns the Statue of Liberty: 'Give me your tired, your poor, your huddled masses yearning to breathe free...' Pelosi is the personification of the American dream and of the new spirit of 2008: she is the descendant of Italian immigrants, has risen to the top of her profession and broken the glass ceiling of Capitol Hill. Was Betty Boothroyd's career achievement an aberration? I think not. It should also be pointed out that the progress of women into national politics in the United States has been a long struggle, not a thing of privilege. Bella Abzug, Maxine Waters and Eleanor Holmes Norton did not spring from a dynasty.

Many commentators have pilloried Hillary Clinton's candidacy as an outgrowth of a dynastic trend in America. To equate her rise to prominence with that of George Bush is absurd: she is her own woman and comes from the Rodham clan, which, so far as I know, has had no members in public office. Her paternal grandparents were immigrants from Britain. Osama bin Laden also warned the American people about dynasties – he placed the Bushes in the same basket as the kings and princes of Saudi Arabia; one could say the many pundits who accuse the Clintons of being part of a conspiracy to fill the halls of power into eternity are as daft in their assessment as the malevolent Osama.

It is interesting that, in late January 2008, Yasmin Alibhai-Brown became agitated on *Dateline London*, a BBC television political programme on Sundays, because she was incensed that a 'little Missy' had pretensions to the American presidency. Thankfully, the other panellists, from various countries around the world, leapt at her for saying this. She argued that Hillary Clinton had been a little Missy standing by her man, had made very few marks in her political career and had accomplished very little. Her claim to fame was her marriage to a president. Alibhai-Brown's assessment put Hillary Clinton in the same bag as Laura Bush. The rage of the other journalists was gratifying to behold, and I shouted at the screen: 'Yasmin, what about your fellow Muslim women – are they authoring legislation, flying on the space shuttle and piloting aircraft as do American "little Missies"?'

Invited to appear on a television debate, I set about researching Hillary Clinton's background. Her record in the

Senate since 2000 has been exemplary, and her accomplishments prodigious. I watched her grill Secretary of Defense Donald Rumsfeld with the relentless determination of a seasoned trial lawyer, and knew then that she could take on any world leader. Before the Senate, she was an activist First Lady, and before that a much-noticed First Lady of Arkansas, where she had been a formidable attorney. At Wellesley she was the first student ever allowed to deliver a valedictory speech, because she was regarded as one of the most brilliant women ever to attend that college.

Younge's editorial makes out that college admissions depend on family and wealth. Yes, it costs a fortune to attend university in the United States, but brilliant students have a wide choice of scholarships to apply for. Then there are the students like Bonnie Greer, who informed the BBC *Question Time* panel last week that she – like me – worked in several jobs to pay her way through college. Her comments came during a discussion of the 'McDonald's A-Level', a concept Amanda Platell finds offensive because it impedes progress in literacy. Bonnie said she had flipped many a hamburger whilst earning a fine degree. Inasmuch as commissioning editors at certain stolid British institutions have informed me that they had been 'sat' reading my work, and one of them told a trainee of mine, 'You done it wrong, innit?', I suggest a McDonald's education might benefit them.

Having just watched the American Super Bowl, played in a magnificent Arizona school stadium to a capacity crowd of sober, good-natured 'folks', and heard a succession of highly articulate professional American footballers being interviewed, it occurs to me that Gary Younge should visit an average American high school or college, where he will see that hundreds of thousands of children, often from impoverished backgrounds, can receive a good education with a sports or ROTC* scholarship, or both combined. When I was on the *Any Questions?* panel and the subject of anti-social behaviour orders (ASBOs) came up, the audience applauded my

* Reserve Officer Training Corps.

American viewpoint: over 500,000 children are afforded superb sporting opportunities each year, and some go on to careers in politics, the sciences, law, academia, medicine and business.

But let's get back to this idea of political ascendancy and educational privilege being dependent on one's pedigree. If a British journalist living in America asserts that there is some sort of dynastic phenomenon that drives politics, it indicates that he has not stopped to read some history. Amongst the many presidents who rose from abject poverty to distinction were Andrew Jackson, Martin Van Buren, Abraham Lincoln and his successor Andrew Johnson. Benjamin Franklin, a genius who did not seek office, came from a humble background, as did some of the signatories to the American Declaration of Independence. Presidents Woodrow Wilson, Harry Truman, Richard Nixon, Lyndon Johnson and Bill Clinton came from anything but privileged or aristocratic stock.

I spend a lot of my time defending the academic achievements of Americans, so here I risk being hoist with my own petard: in my decades in Britain, the natives have constantly chastised me for defending a country of 'hicks', 'slobs', 'idiots', 'trailer trash' and 'vulgar morons'. Now we have Gary Younge telling *Guardian* readers that you cannot get anywhere in America unless you are part of an Ivy League-educated dynasty. Thankfully, *The Times* of London lists Princeton, Harvard, Yale and MIT amongst the greatest places for education in the world, so I am vindicated in my assertion that the USA is not heaving with morons. On the other hand, it has to be said that many 'hicks' from the backwoods have made their way from the log cabin to the White House.

Finally, as a proud graduate of the prestigious and academically gruelling Philadelphia High School for Girls, I take issue – just short of apoplexy – with Gary Younge's gripe that children of the alumni of distinguished institutions account for 21 to 25 per cent of freshmen. Again, Gary understands so little about American academic traditions. When I collide with a middle-aged woman in Edinburgh or Paris or Cape

Town and discover she is a 'Girls' High girl', the first thing we do is find out if our mothers and grandmothers were Girls' High graduates. Sometimes I come across a Temple University graduate and we have the same conversation, that institution having been established for the children of humble immigrants. My late mother remembered being held atop her father's shoulders in Connie Mack Stadium in 1915, when Russell H. Conwell, in a legendary speech, called Temple and its less than affluent student body 'diamonds in your own backyard'. Most Girls' High girls come from humble backgrounds and often from poor homes, but the criterion for entry is academic brilliance. That's it.

And if Gary thinks it is aberrant for Americans to cherish family connections to schools and colleges, has he looked at the dynasties in Britain that boast generations of Old Etonians and Harrovians?

Younge's description of Bill Clinton as a 'bruiser with the generous Rolodex and secret service protection, race-baiting his way around the campaign trail' is stuff and nonsense. The reason why so many African-Americans still adore the Clintons is that he was regarded as 'America's first black president'. Gary Younge cannot begin to comprehend how American blacks trusted Bill Clinton, and how he, in turn, had a deep empathy with their struggle. If the Tories or Labour could produce a Clinton, Roosevelt, JFK or Woodrow Wilson, Britain might see itself out of the ASBO-filled mess we are in. Perhaps, rather than denigrating it, it would be of more benefit to Britain at this worrying time to emulate the American democratic process, which has seen considerably more rags-to-riches stories than disasters in the aristocratic dictatorship Gary imagines.

CHAPTER THREE

CAROL GOULD RETURNS TO THE USA

DIARY: OCTOBER 2004 (MY FIRST TRIP HOME IN TEN AND A HALF YEARS!)

Something remarkable has been happening to me in the past 19 days. Wherever I go, no one launches abuse at me. When I open my mouth to speak, I am received with civility and the occasional 'Have a good one.' I am not attacked or intimidated to the point of utter fear and loathing. Where have I been visiting for the past two and a half weeks? And where do I live? I am not Dorothy in Oz. I am in the greatest nation on earth, or, as I like to call it, God's own country.

The crux of it all lies in a conversation I had with my sister in a charming ice-cream parlour in Philadelphia's historic Suburban Station this afternoon. I looked up from my dessert and said: 'My God, I've gone for 19 days without anybody – not taxi drivers, shop clerks or waiters – launching an abusive tirade at me.'

I live in Tony Blair's Britain. Tony is loathed by the majority of the population because of his loyalty to George Bush. Interpreted by the media, this means Tony and George doing what best helps Israel. The 'Zionist neocons' in the US administration drive its policy, and 'lapdog' Tony follows along. The 'axis of evil' neocons are seen as a bigger threat to world order than the plethora of rogue states around the globe, some of which are active United Nations members.

The paradox is that we have Islamic extremists in our midst in Britain, preaching all manner of mayhem and holding 'festivals' to celebrate the 'magnificent 19 of September the 11th'.

There are some 260,000 Jews in Britain and more than 2 million Muslims, but at dinner parties all one hears about is the 'birthplace of terror, Menachem Begin's Israel' and the 'world's number one terrorist state, the United States'. Last November, when President Bush visited the United Kingdom and London's mayor, Ken Livingstone, boycotted the state banquet, ordinary folk gathered in Trafalgar Square to burn and stomp on the Stars and Stripes.

Frankly, I don't like what is happening in Britain and am shocked and dismayed at the level anti-Americanism has reached in recent months. Does anyone say 'George W. Bush' or 'Donald Rumsfeld' or 'Dick Cheney' when they fly into these tirades? No. In fact, the visceral, hurtful and in-your-face America-hatred goes back long before the days of the 'Bush-43 regime'. When Bill Clinton was in the White House, I attended a human rights conference at my local synagogue in St John's Wood. During the tea break, I asked a man at one of the booths for a leaflet. When he detected my accent, instead of welcoming me and asking for a donation, he launched into a loud and red-faced screeching session about the evils of the American Empire and of the 'Nazism' and 'fascism' promulgated by the United States. A black man came over and began shouting about America having 'invented slavery', and soon a delicate elderly lady joined the fray to bellow about the Zionists running America (did she mean Robert Rubin, Dennis Ross, Sandy Berger? – after all, it was the pre-Wolfowitz/Perle time zone) and the 'genocides' perpetrated by Americans since the days of William Penn. I remember wondering why I had ventured out on a Sunday to be with like-minded people concerned about human rights issues, only to be reduced to a gibbering jelly as the ugly, strident and deeply uncivil crowd soon grew around me. (Remember what it was like being surrounded in the school playground at break time by all the bullies?) The English are not known for public displays of fury (except, perhaps, at soccer matches), but there is something about an American accent that brings out their pent-up rage.

I hesitate to blame my own profession, the media. However, the *Guardian* ran a lead article by Faisal Bodi in January

2001, entitled 'Israel Simply Has No Right to Exist', and, on a daily basis, Robert Fisk, whom many of my British friends and colleagues think is God, runs an *Independent* column that is brutally critical of the United States and Israel. I have stopped attending meetings of my trade union, the National Union of Journalists, because I cannot listen to its incessant vitriol about the crimes of my native country, the United States, and of Israel when we should be dealing with the problems unions are supposed to address. I often talk of Israel and anti-Semitism; they are inextricably linked in social discourse when the United States and its 'imperialist crimes' are discussed. One of the many things that inspired me to start writing about this phenomenon was the narrative to which I listened most nights some 28 years ago, when a dear friend, who had starred in a play of mine, was performing in *Evita* in London's West End. She would cry down the telephone at me most evenings, and after matinees, about the taunts she had received because she happened to be Jewish. At the time, I thought she exaggerated, but her tears were real and I lamented the fact that, even in show business, the hate-Israel-hate-America-hate-bloody-Jews syndrome had crept into the workplace.

Yes, the Sharon government is the one I have loved the least; and yes, there is much to worry about in present American policy. But how many American unions spend hours devising resolutions to censure their most trusted and valued ally? How many Americans invite expatriate Brits to their dinner table, only to abuse and intimidate them, especially if they are Jewish? If someone can find me a Broadway production that relentlessly baits a Jewish cast member... Well, anyway.

Another mantra thrown at me daily these days is that the United States is one giant Fundamentalist Christian nation, with raging Bible-pounders on every street. I have had otherwise enlightened colleagues tell me that the USA is 'running wild with religious extremism that threatens the world far more than bin Laden'. As I am also informed, coupled with the religious fervour is the 'dangerous fact that America, Carol, has no culture to speak of, and that is a lethal mix'.

My hunch is that the daily dose of relentless America-bashing in the European media, combined with the abundance of criticism of Israel – some of it justified – has created an atmosphere of anger and hostility that, for the first time in my lifetime, makes me fearful for my safety in my beloved adopted country, Great Britain.

So, what does this all mean in the grand scheme of things? I have lived in Europe for all of my adult life and, from the day I arrived as a youngster, have been aware of an often blatant anti-Semitism and resentment of Americans amongst the 'chattering classes'. (These comprise the 'Hampstead elite' who, in their teens, went on *kibbutzim* and revered socialist ideals, but who now reject Israel as a fascist satellite of the United States.) What is significant about this rage is that it emanates not from the great unwashed, but from the educated and intellectual classes. At the time of writing, we all know about the academic boycotts of Israeli scholars, approved by the council of the British Association of University Teachers on a Friday night and eve of Passover, when virtually no Jewish academics were present to vote. Poor Philip Lader, former US Ambassador to the Court of St James, was reduced to tears on BBC's *Question Time* on 13 September 2001, as the moderator, David Dimbleby, sat and dispassionately watched as a crazed studio audience stomped its feet and shouted anti-American epithets two days after the Trade Center and Pentagon attacks.

What I find so frightening is that, increasingly, many Americans cannot conduct business or even take a taxi ride in London, Bournemouth or Edinburgh without a scathing tirade about the scurrilous Yanks. In May 2005, the New York Convention of Travel Executives made anti-Americanism a topic for discussion: we are hated abroad, hence no one wants to spend their euros or pounds inside our shores. I see it as an irrational hatred, whilst liberals see it as a 'reaction to shameful American behaviour'.

The day after 9/11, I was obliged to keep a consultant's appointment, and the minicab driver informed me that the 'yellow Americans' on the four hijacked planes were typical of the way 'the Yanks do battle' – they chicken out and let the Brits do the dirty work. I was in such a state of shock from the events of 9/11 that I could not find an answer, and he continued with a further lecture about the cowardice and stupidity of Americans and their pilots when they are threatened, adding that, had Brits been on those planes, not one would have come down.

In late summer I was travelling on a bus when a well-dressed woman boarded with her equally respectable son in his school uniform. Ahead of her was an elderly American woman, who said: 'I beg your pardon, I didn't mean to bang into you.' This prompted a tirade from the Englishwoman – let's call her Lady E. – that resembled a verbal assault by a Brown Shirt against a hapless Jewish pedestrian in 1933. The American – call her Mrs A. – sat down and cowered as the tirade continued: 'I rejoice every time I hear of another American soldier dying! You people all deserve to die in another 9/11. You are destroying the world.' Mrs A. fought back: 'I personally am NOT destroying the world.' This only provoked Lady E. more, and, as the bus driver and passengers laughed, she screamed into the American's face: 'I wish every one of you would leave this country and not set foot in it ever again.' Mrs A. winced and started to cry: 'Thank you for ruining my day and my trip.' At this point, Lady E. lunged at the American. I shouted at the top of my voice for the driver to stop and for her to leave the woman alone, prompting Lady E. to come over to me: 'Another bloody American accent! You come here and think you can strut about. Well, you are scum.' Thankfully, the woman next to me pushed her away. I left the bus as the American woman sat sobbing.

Did I imagine this? No. Was the Englishwoman crazy? No.

This brings me to an incident that was one of many watershed events that turned me towards a return to the USA. I went over to my favourite tape-duplicating shop to have copies made for the actors who had appeared in the video of my new play in London. I handed the master tape to the proprietor, whom I have known for some 10 years. He seemed unusually agitated and flushed. He looked at the material and snarled: 'Is this another one of your Jewish Holocaust things?' I was speechless. He scowled and continued: 'You know, Carol, I want to get something off my chest that I've been dying to say to you for years. Number one, just don't say Israel to me. Number two, you people should look at yourselves in the mirror and wonder why, every so often, there is a Holocaust or massacre or pogrom. You bring it on yourselves. Just look at the way you are and then figure out why the rest of the world wants to flatten you. Number three, America throwing money at Israel has to stop, and hopefully all hell will break loose. Israel is not a country. I just hear the word and I turn puce.'

By this time his anger was so visceral that I wanted to head for the door, but I had to take a stand. 'Let me tell you,' I said, 'if the USA or Israel came under threat, I know many Americans who would die for either country.' To which he replied: 'Israel is not a country. The Jews have no right to a country. What makes you people think you have a right to a country?'

Me: 'There are over a hundred Christian countries and 55 Muslim countries.'

He: 'The Jews have no right to a country.'

Me: 'What, a strip of land the size of Wales?!'

He (grinding his teeth and close to hitting me): 'Just say Israel, and I can't be depended upon for the consequences of my actions, Carol.'

His litany of offences committed by the Jews, Americans and Israel continued for another 20 minutes or so, and I came away realizing that a man who had always greeted me with genteel, cheery sweet nothings was actually a rabid Jew-hater.

Where will it all end? I know Jews – including Anglo-Jews – who have ceased socializing because of the abuse they receive from old friends. The much-loved British actress Maureen Lipman and her eminent playwright husband, the late Jack Rosenthal, attended an Israel Solidarity Rally in London, much to the astonishment of her fans. In her long career, Lipman had never been political; but one suspected she felt as marginalized as the rest of us who turned up for the rally (it was severely hampered by pro-Palestinian demonstrators with loud-hailers).

It is impossible to convey to Americans inside the United States, or to American Jews, the open loathing of both groups that has begun to dominate daily life outside the United States today. Without doubt, the Iraq War and the right-wing government of Ariel Sharon have inflamed the hostility that lay beneath the surface. What is so disturbing to me is that so many Americans and Jews are no longer accepted at face value in daily encounters. If the media set out some years ago – even before Bush-43 – to turn the public against America and Israel, they have done a magnificent job. I have stopped counting the number of unfair accusations hurled at both nations in the course of a day on the airwaves or in the print media. Long ago I stopped wearing a flag pin (how wonderful to be able to wear one as I walk down a Philadelphia street, without fearing for my life) and just the other day a friend had a tongue-lashing from an old acquaintance about the 'appalling flags the Americans put outside their homes, like Nazis all over again'.

Imagine what it is like these days to emerge from one's home to attend a dinner party or tea and be browbeaten about 'Zionists' running America, as if it is a criminal offence to be 'passionate' about Israel. And, dammit, despite the dark days of the Sharon–Arafat standoff, I remain passionate about the remnant of my people who made a go of it after the Euro-generated Holocaust. Lord Gilmour quotes a Blair aide making the other accusation that is hurled at Americans abroad these days: 'the only special relationship is between America and Israel'.* Well so be it.

* In a recent review of James Naughtie's book, *The Accidental American*, Lord Gilmour in the *Guardian* (18 September 2007) asserted that the 'neocons' or 'axis of evil' who comprise Cheney, Rumsfeld, Wolfowitz, Feith, Bolton, Libby, Abrams, Perle and others are 'not only passionate about Israel, they are Likudists to a man'. He adds that the American 'Likudists' are happy to let Sharon create more 'apartheid settlements'.

I am aware that some Americans are leaving their homes abroad and returning to the USA after decades in foreign countries. Notwithstanding the loss of universal healthcare enjoyed in their adopted countries, they can no longer endure the daily abuse and the ugly posters and stickers that proliferate across European cities. When the many anti-war rallies were held in February 2003, young people in European cities were seen wearing headbands with slogans wishing death upon Jews, Americans and Israel.

I went to hear Seymour Hersh speak in Washington, and he suggested that Americans with dual nationality value the other passport and 'keep that villa in Italy' if Bush-43 is re-elected. I see it, dear Sy, from a different perspective: Europe created the Holocaust, the Inquisition and other genocides. Anti-Americanism and anti-Semitism proliferated long before the Bush administration came onto the scene in 2000. Anti-Americanism is not a result of Abu Ghraib or of a Rumsfeldian pronouncement. It is a disturbing and hurtful form of psychosis that is rapidly eroding the all-important special relationship.

At present, I do not yet fear for my life in jolly little St John's Wood; but it sure is heaven strolling around the artists' studios at the Torpedo Factory in Alexandria, Virginia, and being greeted as me, not as a bloody American or an accursed Zionist.

DIARY: END OCTOBER 2004

Images of America – one month on

One month on, after much time spent in various states, several cities and many remote rural villages, the images are even more powerful. The overwhelming affection with which Americans of every colour and creed hold the United Kingdom and the British people is palpable. This makes it all the more painful that the sentiment is not mutual in the streets and pubs of London and elsewhere. What is remarkable is the unconditional love Americans express for everything British: from our prime minister to our quirky food to our television drama.

Admittedly, there have been a few less-than-cordial encounters since I've been here. Trying to get anything, be it a driving licence or a simple train ticket, requires ID checks that are stringent and often strident in their execution. Without doubt, since 11 September 2001, individuals in authority have acquired a coldness that runs counter to the 'have a nice day' cordiality that was the trademark of American business. The 19 hijackers were likely to have been wished a nice day and cheerily whisked through the departure gates with a good-natured 'this way, hon'. But no more. Even a bespectacled, middle-aged woman is now asked for ID and told 'How do I know it's yours without seeing your card?' when she rattles off her social security number from memory.

In sleepy rural Vermont, an irate customer at a filling station argued with an even more irate cashier because he wanted to pay with a $100 note. I really thought the argument would result in a murder. The cashier said: 'I will be fired if I take that from you.' And eventually the matter was settled with small change dug out of the customer's pockets. But one's illusions about a nation filled with cheery folk were slightly dashed.

But just for a moment.

In four weeks, the huge majority of Americans met on this journey have been the warmest, most generous and cordial human beings one could ever hope to encounter. At the twilight concert at the Smithsonian Museum, held to mark the opening of the new American Indian Museum in Washington DC, under a glorious sky and in the shadow of the Capitol building at one end and the Washington Monument at the other, the women on either side of me were eager to know me. Soon the husband of one joined us and promptly went to fetch food to share. As Buffy Ste Marie and Rita Coolidge sang tribal lyrics, circular clouds formed overhead and audience members spontaneously left their seats and danced with strangers. When my new friend's husband arrived with the food, the sun had set and the crowd had swelled to capacity. Atop the Capitol dome, the light signifying a congressional vote was flickering, a curious sight in the milieu of an overwhelming hurt and sadness in the sounds of the singers' chants: the words were strange to us, but the women's chants stirred thoughts of the truly ancient history of these much-trodden-upon peoples. My new friends gave me their addresses and telephone numbers, and this became a pattern throughout this trip. Like Israelis, Americans have an immediacy that is endearing, and their generosity is genuine.

In Washington, the warmth of new acquaintances, as well as the generosity of colleagues met only through e-mail, was a continuing source of wonderment. In Philadelphia and New York, the same phenomenon occurred. An eminent writer, with whom I had only corresponded by e-mail, promptly invited me to stay overnight. We watched the vice-presidential debate amid a spread of food and drink, and I felt as if I had known the hostess for decades. At the outdoor street party held for Philadelphians who wished to watch the presidential debate on a large screen, I was dismayed to see a burly and hostile veteran not letting anyone pass who wore a Kerry button, citing what he saw as the candidate's betrayal of his comrades in arms when he formed the Vietnam Veterans peace movement. The presidential campaign engenders extreme emotions at present, and this is one area of American life in which 'have a nice day' is not in the equation. In turn, an electoral registrar on a main street bitterly complained that a colleague had inflamed a prospective new voter by denigrating President Bush and expressing displeasure that the prospective registrant wished to be a registered Republican.

Notwithstanding the dark cloud hanging over the political scenario, a long journey on Amtrak from Philadelphia to Northern Vermont resulted in an exchange of cards with a delightful and fascinating train companion, who has made me promise to stay with her in North Carolina; once in the Green Mountain State, I was hosted by yet more first-time acquaintances and driven all over the Northeast Kingdom with not one complaint. Meals were cooked for me and doggy bags made up for my long journey back to Philadelphia.

As I was boarding the train in Vermont, a woman exclaimed: 'You were on the train coming up!' And once again I was engaged in an absorbing discussion of presidential politics and world affairs. This encounter brought to mind a tirade I had witnessed in a restaurant just after 9/11, when an American couple was berated by a group of diners at the next table about the world's evils being the result of the 'worthless educational system' of the United States. Aside from the fact that the Americans' meal was spoilt by the relentless shouting of one particular individual, it was embarrassing to hear fellow Britons accuse them of being 'idiots', when I could see that all of the Americans wore college rings. In Britain, we still accept it as routine that young people can be 'school leavers'. Yes, it is true that in the United States any Tom, Dick or Harry may attend Podunk College if he can catch a football, but in Britain our literacy problems remain a blot on the landscape. Were it not for the appalling deterioration of our grammar and punctuation skills, Lynn Truss would not be a millionaire from her book of English usage lamentation, *Eats, Shoots and Leaves*. The highly enlightened and well-informed people I have met, even in the most remote of American villages, bear no resemblance to the 'idiots' so many Europeans perceive walking the streets of the USA.

I am nearing the end of my journey through the northeastern United States, and I have a heavy heart. It would be a dream to stay here. This vast and beautiful nation has always been a magnet for immigrants, and after four weeks here I can well understand a physicist being willing to work in a bakery just to remain in the United States. The American experiment has had many ugly moments and is in the grips of a disturbing chapter in its history, compounded by the unsavoury fact that some 45 million citizens have no health insurance. Nevertheless there is an energy that emanates from its city streets and village paths, and a warmth that is infectious. I am humbled by it, and will not let the next 'America-basher' pass by me without a fierce rebuke.

CHAPTER FOUR

'AMERICANS ARE SO STUPID!'

America-bashing is a pastime in Europe and Britain. It can erupt at any time.

The top 10 accusations I will not let pass without a rebuke are these:

1. Americans are all fat, hugely obese slobs.
Have you been on holiday in Britain of late? Does Britain have millions of supremely fit young men and women playing varsity, high-school and college sports at such a high level that their games are televised in prime time (as is the case in America)? Is there ever any trouble at these games? No. Despite the preconceived notion that American youth go around toting assault rifles, I will swear on my late mother's Bible that these kids go home and drink a glass of (semi-skimmed) milk.

2. Americans are all violent and are running around shooting one another.
Columbine, tragic as it was, is not America: British Home Secretary Jacqui Smith told the nation in January 2008 that she could see how frightened people could be going out at night in Britain.

3. Americans are racists.
Yes, the United States has a disgraceful history; but how many countries have waged a civil war in which hundreds of thousands of white men fought to the death to make the other half of their country slave free? How many European countries

have given the world such staggering cultural achievements as those emanating from the American black community: jazz, ragtime, blues, soul, and the scores of fine actors, writers and entrepreneurs?

4. Americans are polluting the world.
Sure, but if the USA is causing 25 per cent of world pollution, what about the other 75 per cent? China, Russia, India?

5. Americans are so, so stupid.
Sure, tell that to *The Times* newspaper, which compiles an annual list of the world's top universities. Morons teach and study at MIT, Harvard, Princeton, Columbia, Bryn Mawr, Brandeis, etc., etc. Then there are the other inarticulate, school-leaving morons, past and present, like Thomas Jefferson, Benjamin Franklin, John Adams, Abraham Lincoln, Woodrow Wilson, Franklin Roosevelt, Jonas Salk, Albert Sabin, J. Robert Oppenheimer, Bill Gates, etc., etc.

6. America has no culture to speak of and is a vast wasteland of pap.
See above, plus cultural detritus: Aaron Copland, Mark Twain, Ernest Hemingway, Pearl Buck, James Michener, Jerome Kern, the Gershwins, Sinclair Lewis, Theodore Dreiser, Upton Sinclair (still being made into movies starring such actors as Daniel Day-Lewis), Arthur Miller, Tennessee Williams, Clifford Odets, Rodgers and Hammerstein, Stephen Sondheim, etc., etc., etc.

7. Americans inject farm animals and eat contaminated products.
Perhaps, but I'd rather eat an American turkey that costs $25, raised in immaculate and stringently regulated conditions, than a British organic one that, for some reason, costs $80–160.

8. Americans have no dress sense.
Has anyone who makes these comments seen the chic, power-dressed professional men and women on their one-hour,

alcohol-free lunch breaks decorating the streets of Philadelphia, Washington, Boston, Chicago or New York on an average day? Has anyone seen country folk in Suffolk in their jumpers that have not been washed since rationing and Barbours that stink of dog's breath and cat pee?

9. Americans never get to see news and know nothing about the world.

The news cycle that starts at 6pm Eastern Time outshines anything available on British television. The level of debate and the calibre of the presenters is impressive and carries on all evening, through to midnight. Britain has nothing like the three C-SPAN channels, which give a 24-hour cycle of political coverage, the likes of which are not available to the British public about its own political system.

10. Americans do not bother to get passports because they do not care about the rest of the world.

Americans get two weeks' vacation a year.

Number 11 should be 'America is run by Jews and Zionists', but that is for another book.

Inasmuch as England, not Germany or Spain, invented the very first blood libel;* expelled its Jews in 1290 after having spent a hundred years killing them; had the horrific York massacre; did not readmit them until the time of Cromwell; staged 'Jew Riots' at the very whiff of Jews being enfranchised; and then continued to bar them from university until Jeremy Bentham founded University College – I suggest Britons belt up about the Jews, as they now have a much more sinister threat to their Barbour-jacketed tranquillity: Jihadists in every town and hamlet.

One of my favourite encounters was with a white-haired minicab driver, who spent a very long journey berating me for the stupidity of my fellow Americans. He even imitated, in an

* To wit: Jews drink the blood of Christian children and use it to make matzos.

exaggerated manner, the 'appalling' Americans he had driven from the airport. He told me that my compatriots 'never know where anything is' and that they do not even know that Scotland is north of the border. I tried to reason with him about the many intelligent Americans alive on the planet today, but he got so angry that he began shouting at me.

What is so amusing about this encounter is that, in 30 years, I have met precious few Britons who know where my birthplace, Philadelphia, is; and I delight in being told that I must miss the beach, the skiing, the Jewish delicatessens or the cowboys. A young student who was working at my local beauty salon said she had been telling people that I was about to emigrate to Alaska. During a previous visit I had told her all about Nebraska, the Indian reservations, Mount Rushmore and the prairie, but she had registered 'Alaska'. I can safely say that even university-educated people I have met in Europe and the UK have virtually nil concept of the geography of the United States. But I bet no American cabbie would think them 'appalling' when they visit.

Throughout the post-9/11 year, I had a series of astonishing experiences on a par with those of Chelsea Clinton, who encountered cruel anti-American rhetoric at Oxford University during her first semester there in the weeks immediately following 9/11.

On one occasion, several friends and I went out for a meal, and the conversation turned to my educational background. I was asked what I had thought of my high-school chums 'going to Israel' for a semester when they were 17. The question baffled me, as none of my friends, nor for that matter any friends of my sister's or parents', had ever entertained the slightest notion of a 'gap year' in Israel or anywhere else. My mind was cast back to the tensely competitive days of my teens, when we had already experienced the convulsions of the civil rights revolution, the assassinations of Malcolm X, Medgar Evers, President John F. Kennedy, Martin Luther King and Robert Kennedy, as well as the terrible Chicago convention riots, the Kent State University killings and the shooting of Alabama Governor George Wallace. Add to this the

Vietnam War, and it is a wonder anyone of my age was able to complete high school in one emotional piece.

As we finished our meal, I tried to explain to my friends that the young women with whom I had attended the fiercely competitive Philadelphia High School for Girls were already focused on their university careers by the time we reached tenth grade at the age of 15.

One of the people at the table, Liz, said: 'Ah, well, the American students who came to Israel had to take an extra year to catch up with the other students!'

When I asked her to explain (I was thinking of all the geniuses from Girls' High who have gone on to glittering academic and professional careers), she said: 'Well, in America you take so many subjects in high school that you have proficiency in none!'

With great authority, friend Sheila added: 'Surely you appreciate that no human being is capable of having any useful education if they dabble in scores of subjects in high school! Here we study three subjects and are well ahead of Americans at the same age.'

Having lived abroad – outside the United States – for nearly 30 years, I am a seasoned debater when it comes to attacks on my academic qualifications; but this was a new concept that, to use the colloquial expression, 'I couldn't get my head around'.

The people at the table were aggressive and arrogant, shouting so loudly at me that the entire restaurant was staring at us. What I found most astounding was their absolute conviction about every fact they 'knew' about the lamentably inferior American educational system. It was not possible at that table to defend myself, because they kept interrupting me and berating me for 'creating a fantasy' about the excellence of my education, but here are some points I tried to make:

1. Girls' High girls are a breed apart. My contemporaries were privileged to have been taught by the last generation of graduates of the Philadelphia Normal School, of which my late mother was a proud alumna. From Dr Esther Meixner to Helen Johnston to Katherine Skelton, the faculty was a

formidable collection of brilliant scholars who demanded a punishing discipline and excellence from the student body. Some of the most outstanding women in public life in the United States are Girls' High graduates. (I learned recently that Shirley Franklin, the dynamic African-American mayor of Atlanta, is a Girls' High graduate.)

2. Although it is 34 years since high school, I have a dim memory of studying the standard curriculum: History, English, Maths and Science, with one foreign language. I was also in the renowned Treble Clef Choir, directed by the eminent baritone William Murphy, on the editorial staff of the *Iris* leaflet and annual *Milestone* publication, and still I found time for orchestra and drama. On graduation, I received the Vera Schenker Prize for Diversity of Artistic Gifts. This was nothing unusual, as Girls' High girls were expected to excel in every department. My sister, also a Girls' High graduate, is an eminent music journalist, a brilliant linguist, a gifted artist, an opera coach and a concert-level pianist. She 'dabbled' in the subjects offered in high school and is the formidable product of that system. In all my years in Britain, I have yet to meet a woman as brilliant as my sister. The women with whom I worked had 'left school' at 16, and even those who went on to higher education are painfully dull company.

3. I have no experience of high-school education across America, but my impression is that we are not thrown a salad bowl of courses that amount to a row of beans and that condemn us to a mire of ignorance.

* * * * *

There is a certain arrogance amongst non-Americans that has always bemused me. Many years ago, a senior British military officer at a dinner party looked me straight in the eye and said: 'It is a great pity you Americans haven't any culture.' I proceeded to reel off my list: Mark Twain, Ernest Hemingway, Eugene O'Neill, Tennessee Williams, James Michener, Sinclair Lewis, etc., etc. But he chuckled and said: 'Oh, a few names on a list mean nothing.'

Jokes about George W. Bush abound, but I would love to wake up one morning and not hear a British-educated television presenter referring to a guest being 'sat' on the sofa. How wonderful it would be not to have to spell my name and address three times over the telephone, nor to hear 'You was holding for someone?' when I ring a British company or a London colleague's office. Over the years, people in my neighbourhood have asked me to 'write a letter' for them because they are unable to spell or write a complete sentence. Some have even been generous enough to say: 'You're clever for a Yank; I can't string a sentence together.'

If the British educational system is so vastly superior to the American equivalent, why is Britain not in the forefront of every industry? Why is it not leading the world? Why is the West End theatre bursting with American-written musicals and no significant British new plays? Why has London Mayor Ken Livingstone had to lament the fact that IT consultants from abroad are being encouraged to come to Britain to fill gaps?

* * * * *

Getting back to the friends in the restaurant: Liz and Sheila refused to back down and were still shouting at me at the top of their voices when the manager reminded us that he had to close, as it was nearly midnight. (They had started berating me about my inferior high-school education at 10:30pm.) As I walked them to their car, I could not help handing back a dose of sarcastic arrogance in return: 'I am sorry to come from a third-world country that has achieved nothing in 200 years.'

This scene repeated itself on two further evenings in 2002 with, respectively, male companions and elderly friends, as if Britain had suddenly been gripped by a desire to show how brilliant it was and (as a taxi driver had pointed out to me on 12 September 2001) that *it* would never have allowed 9/11 to happen. As I say in the chapter on MI5, perhaps the British intelligence services are still the best on earth, but 'intelligence' is not, by any means, in short supply in the land of Harvard, Yale, MIT, Microsoft, Boeing and NASA.

Footnote: Bill Clinton is said to enjoy telling a story about being invited back to Oxford University, where he had been a Rhodes Scholar. He had had a fairly miserable time and, when he was asked whom he would invite to join him from his university days, he said 'the janitor'. He must have had some mighty run-ins with those who thought he, too, needed to 'do a year over to catch up' with the British students in order to do well. He did well, indeed.

CHAPTER FIVE

FAITH, BUSH AND FIERCELY SECULAR BRITAIN (A.K.A. DAWKINSLAND)

Throughout my life in Britain, I have been aware of a growing contempt amongst the chattering classes, and even amongst the blue-collar population, for organized religion. Before the reader closes this book and puts it into the bag for the next trip to the charity shop, be advised that those who comprise the surviving remnant of world Jewry, even those who eat bacon and work on Saturdays, value the fact that there are synagogues left standing in the world after *Kristallnacht* and the years of the Third Reich. In recent years, with the advent of President Bush's born-again Christianity, contempt and ridicule have turned to anger. Go to a gathering in Britain and you can be sure that someone will launch into a tirade to the effect that the Evangelical Right – not Wahhabism or the Kassam Brigades – is causing the downfall of the civilized world. It never fails to amaze me that people who lived through a world war (and the possibility that Hitler could have brought his own form of religion to these shores) can dismiss with considerable fury the choice many have made to have and sustain a faith. Hence this chapter.

One of my heroes, the late Rabbi Dr John Rayner, delivered a sermon at the Liberal Synagogue in London some years ago. It was one of those discourses that remain in one's memory for all time. Those amongst you in the fiercely secular nation of Great Britain who are in the tiny minority that attends religious services will know what I mean by a sermon that wakes you from one of those very unholy mind-wanderings on credit card debt, the blocked kitchen drain and one's dying hydrangea.

Rabbi Rayner, who was part of the *Kindertransporte* and whose parents perished in the Nazi 'Final Solution', said he was often asked by young Jews why they should adhere to Judaism – or in fact to any faith – when the so-called Almighty had allowed the Holocaust to happen. He told the congregation that he had no magic answer to this terrible dilemma, and that each person must seek out his or her own path to spiritual peace, although he hoped that those same seekers would end their search in adherence to a Jewish way of life. He did not expect them to be devout, but he did hope they would perpetuate Jewish values in their daily lives – those values being a thirst for learning, ethical behaviour in all aspects of life, and attention to the suffering of others. In this regard, John Rayner was often a fierce critic of Israeli and American foreign policy. He was a man of deep faith, but he could also be critical of his own coreligionists.

John had arrived in the United Kingdom in 1938 with a string attached to a cardboard number slung around his neck, speaking only German, frightened and alone. He was adopted by a Christian clergyman, William Stannard (later Bishop Stannard), and was soon proficient enough in English to attend university and go on to rabbinic studies. He served in the British armed forces and became one of the Liberal Jewish movement's most erudite rabbis.

Near the end of his life, Rabbi Rayner and I exchanged writings; he often provided me with his critiques of my own articles and sent me essays for my website. He knew I was right-wing, but we enjoyed a lively discourse. Where we agreed was on the issue of where men and women of faith and decency should intervene in political affairs. His favourite quote from Scripture was from Isaiah: 'the people that walked in darkness have seen a great light'.

Another great man of belief, the late Rabbi Hugo Gryn, devoted his life to faith, despite the unspeakable horrors he had experienced in the Holocaust. He told a story about his starving father in the Lieberose concentration camp in Upper Silesia saving a tiny, precious ration of margarine and commemorating the inspiring story of Chanukah and the miracle of the oil that lasted to see the ancient Maccabees through terrible turmoil. Hugo said his father reminded him that a man could survive for a few days without water and food, but he could not survive one moment without hope. When Richard Dawkins and Christopher Hitchens, who never once in their lives could have experienced the hell that Hugo Gryn described, dismiss religion as a waste of time, I think of Hugo's Chanukah story.

Much has been written in outrage and fury about the born-again Christianity of George W. Bush. Notwithstanding the accusations currently circulating around the world courtesy of Professors Mearsheimer and Walt that the committed Christians Bush and Rumsfeld were driven to war in Iraq by a group of Jewish neoconservatives, the reality to me (because I got to know some of these very people so demonized in the media) is that they had a vision for the Middle East. Lest we forget that Bill Clinton spent eight years tirelessly working for a solution to the Israel–Palestine conflict, and that born-again Jimmy Carter brought Sadat and Begin together. Rev. Martin Luther King brought his people out of bondage. Woodrow Wilson, a man of faith, wanted more than anything for the First World War never to happen and died heartbroken over the failure of the League of Nations. Some will assert: 'But Bush was not a man of peace; he shocked and awed Iraq.' I sincerely believe that those who planned the overthrow of Saddam expected American-style parades and candyfloss and gratitude from the people.

I will assert that President Bush's deep Christian faith, like that of Donald Rumsfeld, informed his desire to turn the region into a little America with Tastykake cupcakes, Geno's* steaks, baseball and hot dogs – well, *halal* hot dogs – and Thanksgiving turkey. (Incidentally, at most places one goes for baseball in the USA, the hot dogs are Hebrew National. I am surprised that Mearsheimer and Walt did not pick up on this as another example of the Jewish lobby dominating American thought and policy.)

As Madeleine Albright states in her book, *The Mighty and the Almighty*, throughout the past hundred years or so

* Sic: Joey Vento, who runs the restaurant, had to change the name because the burger chain Gino's demanded it!

America, in its wisdom, has assumed that others want to live as we do. When I came to the United Kingdom 32 years ago, my gas fridge leaked because I kept running out of shillings to put into the slot; I had no central heating, and kept being plunged into darkness and hypothermia because of the shilling crisis. After about four days here, I wept down the phone and begged my parents to send me the fare home, but they demanded that I tough it out. Soon I discovered that I could not find water bagels, cream soda or knishes, and that there was no air conditioning anywhere. Perhaps this has less to do with Bush's desire to turn the Middle East into the 51st state than my having been a Jewish Princess, but I mention this because I do believe successive administrations have felt that Americanizing the world would make us all happier and safer. The evil intentions of the USA, as depicted in John Pilger's films and writings, fail to reveal that there has always been a well-meaning down-home kinda naivety about America's broad aspirations for the rest of the world.

For example, in recent months, I have been subscribing to a cable channel called NASN, a new network of 24/7 American sports, geared to European and worldwide consumption. I had forgotten how high-school and college boys and girls devote so much time to organized sport and go on to fine careers. In the past year, 400,000 former sports scholarship recipients have completed qualifications in professional careers, including the law, aeronautical engineering, business management and the arts. I watch those capacity crowds across America and see not one hooligan or lout, and very few police, because massive forces are not needed at sporting events over there. Then I think: 'Wouldn't it be nice if all European and British sport were like this?' The vast majority of the people attending the events, along with the young competitors and cheerleaders, come from traditional, churchgoing homes. That is the global image the Bushes of this world would like to see, rather than strife.

This brings me to a crucial point: the United States – whose head of state invariably drives world affairs – is a deeply religious country. There is nothing bad about this. Indeed, perhaps, if the Anglican Church would spend less energy tearing itself apart over the ordination of Gene Robinson and more time working out how American churches – including gay congregations – get capacity attendance every Sunday, Britons would begin to attend church again and understand the power of the Scripture in one's life. Three years ago, the *Atlantic Monthly* magazine did a long report on the effect the churches had had on reducing street crime. African-American inner-city parishes had made a concerted effort to bring disaffected youth into church on Sunday. Soon many of them were visiting the sick and elderly, learning how to make videos, singing in Gospel choirs and setting up enterprises.

For 32 years, I have tried in vain to explain to my British friends and colleagues the lively religious life that exists in the United States. Britons who have recently watched the World Series on Channel Five will be mystified by the players who cross themselves before coming up to bat. This is not some form of crank fundamentalism, but one of many manifestations of the freedom of religious expression that was the cornerstone of the earliest colonial venture of William Penn.

In his new book, *The Stillborn God: Religion, Politics and the Modern West*, Professor Mark Lilla's narrative emphasizes the impact of the 'Great Separation' between Church and state, on which the American nation was founded. Yet no Christian country is more pious than the United States. The incumbent president is seen on TV most Sundays going to church. In the recent presidential debates, even the traditionally liberal and anti-war Democrats are enthusiastic churchgoers. This is something my British friends cannot 'get' – the idea that a friend of mine, who is a liberal, registered Democrat anti-war campaigner and art history professor, will visit me in London and want to set aside Sunday for multiple church services. Those presidential candidates are easy about expressing their religious devotion, and that does not make them freaky Evangelicals. When Hillary Clinton talks about her vision of universal healthcare, she cites Jesus as the Shepherd, holding a small child. Imagine a British prime ministerial hopeful saying that – it would be on the cover of *Private Eye* the following week. My parish in

Washington DC houses a large, beautiful Episcopal church, which is packed on Sundays. It also happens to be one of several gay churches. The congregation are men and women who hold mostly liberal views and march on the Capitol on various issues. But their faith is central to their lives.

In a recent essay on the turmoil in Burma, Henry Porter in the *Guardian* (30 September 2007) reminds the world that the fall of the Berlin Wall was the result of a mass candlelit prayer meeting that grew to 400,000 people, urged on by Pastor Führer of the Nikolaikirche in Leipzig. Porter stresses the power of the monks in Burma. In another piece, James Mawdsley (*Daily Telegraph*, 1 October 2007) says it was his belief in Jesus and remembering the suffering on the Cross that sustained him for a year in a Burmese torture centre appropriately named Insein Prison. Sam Leith writes in his column (*Daily Telegraph*, 29 September 2007) that the Burmese monks 'present a problem for the militant secularist in the Dawkins or Hitchens mould'.

Hitchens says religion 'poisons everything', but Leith asserts that it is faith that helps the monks stand firm – a faith he deems 'uniquely powerful'.

This takes us to the issue of faith and foreign policy. Adolf Hitler wanted the 'Christian tenderness burned out of the Hitler Youth'. Mao Tse Tung squelched creativity and originality. Stalin had hundreds of thousands murdered in the name of communism. Hitler and Stalin detested traditional Judeo-Christian faith. These were men who led their own people and the world into darkness and slaughter.

And this brings us to the central issue of George Bush, Guantanamo, extraordinary rendition and Abu Ghraib. Never in the history of the US military has its reputation come under such scrutiny as in the days after Seymour Hersh and Dan Rather reported on the events recorded by a young soldier filming in Abu Ghraib. Like the character portrayed by Jake Gyllenhaal in *Rendition*, he was overcome with remorse. How could a nation whose foundations were based in the most ethical aspects of Judeo-Christian values behave thus? My response is that the world after 9/11 – a day that, if more successful, could have been a kind of Armageddon – has changed irrevocably. If the American leadership feels that it is in a battle against a movement that seeks to destroy whole nations and even its own people, then Bush's Christian zeal wins the day for me.

Madeleine Albright relates a story about a speech she delivered to Yale Divinity School in 2004. This invoked the ire of the eminent theologian Stanley Hauerwas. He felt her record in government had been anything but honourable; she represented the military establishment, and no American who supported armed engagement could claim to be a Christian. Albright responded that non-violence is not always the best course. Had Roosevelt remained neutral, she, a Catholic of Jewish ancestry, would not have been alive today.

I am old enough to remember the unfortunate American Navy lad who happened to be a passenger on the flight hijacked in Athens by the PLO and the aforementioned Leon Klinghoffer tragedy on the *Achille Lauro* cruise liner. Hundreds of American servicemen, trying to bring stability to the Middle East, were blown up in the Khobar Towers; and countless others, Britons Ken Bigley and Margaret Hassan to name but two, have been tormented in protracted capture and then murdered in the most humiliating way on video, in the name of extremism. Some who say that Muslim radicals are as dangerous as George Bush need only read the excellent insight by Con Coughlin in the *Telegraph* into Iranian President Ahmadinejad's bloody vision for the world as it prepares for the return of the Twelfth Imam. It is a vision of mass murder and mayhem, and includes the death of millions of Ahmadinejad's own people.

During the Second World War, my late mother was a WAC stationed at Camp Pickett, Virginia – a huge holding camp for Italian and German POWs. She said the Axis soldiers had prayed that they would be captured by the Americans, because they would receive the kindest treatment. Indeed, though Camp Pickett was not exactly a country club, there were cinemas and recreation rooms and numerous dining facilities.

Now, in 2004, the reputation of the United States as the most decent of all nations in the way it treats POW prisoners was seen by many to have been shattered by Abu Ghraib and Guantanamo. Until 9/11, Americans had, for the most part, enjoyed a reputation for decency under the Geneva Conventions. But if George Bush and Donald Rumsfeld felt that moving the goalposts was the only way to stop another 9/11 and to confront not just al-Qaeda but radical movements that think nothing of castrating young non-combatants – as was done by the PLO in 1972, in Munich, according to the testimony of the widow of one of the Israeli Olympic athletes, Josef Romano – then so be it. Yes, Rumsfeld and Bush are men of deep faith, and one could argue that Christianity repudiated torture decades ago. Yes, waterboarding was used during the Inquisition. The new attorney general of the United States has, as I write, just been approved by the Senate on condition that he ban the practice. But in the case of men who would otherwise commit mass murder against people of their own faith, as well as of other faiths, if extreme methods of interrogation can prevent tragedy, then governments will have to exercise these methods. Khalid Sheikh Mohammed confessed to killing the American journalist Daniel Pearl, and provided a long shopping list of planned atrocities that would have effectively caused the painful deaths of millions around the globe.*

In his book, Professor Mark Lilla talks a great deal about what he calls 'political theology'. He goes on to say that modern Christian society looks at radical Islam and sees a turbulent, bloodstained universe such as it left behind centuries ago. Sadly, modern liberal Christian society is not equipped to deal with the phenomenon of radical global Islamic extremism; but perhaps a western fundamentalist is needed to confront this death march head on.

* It is accepted as fact that a variety of state-sponsored and 'movement-driven' radicals commit and have committed the cruellest atrocities against both military and civilian captives, and despite former hostage Brian Keenan's relentless criticism of Israel, his Hezbollah captors were not angels. *Wall Street Journal* journalist Daniel Pearl was mutilated, but apparently after his beheading on video.

I was not moved, and nor were my views changed, by the recent film *Rendition*. In the film, the character portrayed by Meryl Streep says that 7,000 souls in London were saved because of the extraordinary rendition of a terrorist. However, the CIA interrogator played by Jake Gyllenhaal is so moved by his conscience that he arranges for the captive to be smuggled away to safety. They were principled individuals, and I had sympathy and admiration for both. But I would still prefer to live in a universe envisaged by Americans of faith than in a world according to Ahmadinejad.

CHAPTER SIX

'PUT THAT FLAG AWAY AND TALK PROPER ENGLISH!'

Some of the most unpleasant anti-American encounters I have had in recent years have been with members of my own sex. It is notable that the brilliant feminist writer and teacher Dr Phyllis Chesler has suffered confrontations with female audiences.

On 9 September 2007, I attended the BBC Last Night of the Proms in Hyde Park. The early pieces were an endless stream of musical medleys, written almost exclusively by American composers. I had brought with me, as I do every year, an American and a British flag. It is traditional at the Proms to wave one's national flag during the grand finale. When it came time to sing 'Land of Hope and Glory' and the other anthems, I waved both flags. A group of women stomped over to me and shouted: 'Put that flag away!' I was nonplussed. 'This is a British event, not an American one!'

I reminded them that for most of the afternoon and evening in the park they had been entertained with music by American composers, but they continued to berate me. I moved away, schlepping my picnic hamper and chair elsewhere. No sooner had the next anthem started than I was once again chastised and told to 'put that American flag away'. Readers may think I was being arrogant and provocative, but there were scores of Danish, Italian, Canadian, Australian and German flags being waved throughout the park.

Three days later, I decided to go to Grosvenor Square to pay my respects at the 9/11 pagoda, a tranquil wooden memorial to the British dead of the Twin Towers. It was nearing 1:45pm and I wanted to close my eyes and say a prayer at the exact moment of the first impact. As I did so, a piercing voice asked: 'Are you family?' I opened my eyes and there stood a rather angry, middle-aged British woman who most definitely did not want me anywhere near the memorial, although technically I was standing within the grounds of my own Embassy of the United States of America. She continued: 'If you are not family, I must ask you to LEAVE!' I really thought she was going to drag me off. I said: 'I am sorry, I knew someone who lost a loved one on 9/11 and I really wanted to say a small prayer at the exact moment he lost his life.' She was not moved, never mind the fact that the 'exact moment' had now passed me by. She snapped: 'Well, alright, but when you are finished, please leave.'

Well, I thought, what a strange way to behave on the anniversary of this tragedy that supposedly brought our two countries together in grief. What struck me most was that, had Great Britain suffered a 9/11-level attack and had an expatriate Briton turned up at her own embassy in Washington to pay tribute to the dead of both nations, not in my wildest dreams could I ever imagine an American chasing that person away.

A few days later, I was at BAFTA, the British Film Academy. At the bar, a number of members came over to make their usual sarcastic comments to me about America and Americans and my accent and quirky things that make Yanks the source of endless British mirth. I told them I was writing a book about being a put-upon American, and one woman launched into a discourse about how much she was dreading an upcoming trip to Texas. When I asked her why she was dreading it, she said: 'Oh, those people are so ghastly!' When she revealed to me that she had never actually been to the United States, I asked her how she KNEW Texans were ghastly. 'Oh, come on, my dear, you know how ghastly those people in that part of the world are.'

I could feel my blood beginning to boil. I told her I did not go out of my way to visit certain parts of Britain and Europe, but that I could not think of any part of America that was not warm and welcoming to visitors, especially Britons. She continued her tirade about Texans, and then I happened to say I was tired of slurs being hurled at Israel and the USA. She turned ashen. 'Israel? Are you JEWISH???' I said: 'Yes, I was born into the Jewish faith...' And – yes, dear reader, in 2007 – she growled 'Yechh!', scowled at me and walked off.

One night after a performance and video recording of a play of mine at a workshop in Covent Garden, one of the producers and her husband joined me for dinner. They had already had a uniquely Northern European-level alcohol intake at lunch, but nothing could prepare me for the loud tirade she offered, about everything horrible one could conjure about Americans. From global warming to genocide of the blacks and Native Americans to the 'ghastly fascistic flag-waving', I really got it in the ear. She shouted, her husband nodding, her voice rising with each litany, about the disgusting Zionists, Evangelicals, 'those stupid and violent people' (that's all 300 million, I guess) and the police state that encompasses every aspect of life in the 50 states. What is so odd is that the play she had produced was unremittingly American in subject and style, but she ploughed on with her rant, moving inexorably on to Israel and the Jewish neocons and the genocidal Israeli army supplied by the obscene American military machine. She shouted and roared for some time.

What motivates this bilious hatred? Why do so many Britons do this? Why do Americans never do this to Britons? In his review of the book *Old World, New World* by Kathleen Burk (*The Times*, 20 October 2007), the former ambassador to Washington, Christopher Meyer, comments: 'It is almost beyond the modern imagination to grasp the fortitude...of those 17th-century settlers, who managed to survive disease, starvation, hostile Native Americans and a ghastly two-month Atlantic crossing.' I think it is the very fortitude of Americans that engenders such anger and hatred. We plough on with energy and enthusiasm – and drink a bit less than our British cousins – and manage to remain cheery and smiling and wishing everyone a nice day. According to Meyer, Dean Acheson had noted that the 'special relationship' had never actually been affectionate. In her book, Burk notes that, in 1866, the *Spectator* wrote: 'the United States is a power of the first class, a nation which it is very dangerous to offend and almost impossible to attack'. Inasmuch as the latter observation became invalid on 11 September 2001, it also occurs to me that the increase in verbal putrefaction thrown at me since then comes from an emboldened Briton or European who secretly rejoices that finally the impenetrable Satan has been attacked on its own soil and is vulnerable. We unlucky expatriates are on the receiving end of the said rejoicing.

A few days ago, I went to my local mailbox and discovered, to my delight, that it had been 'unsealed' after a protracted national postal strike. An elderly woman came up to me and said: 'Don't mail that! It will never be collected.'

I told her that I had heard on the radio just before coming out that the strike was over and that the backlog was being cleared. She snarled: 'I have heard no such thing!'

I said: 'Well, maybe Mr Brown is lying to us, as some said Mr Blair did.'

She shouted: 'Are you accusing my country of being led by liars?'

I said: 'No, but that is what every British newspaper has been saying for four years now.'

She repeated: 'Are you saying British leaders lie?'

I said: 'I am British, too.'

To this she harrumphed: 'You! You could never be British.' And she walked on.

I then made my way to the chemist to get a prescription filled and she was there. She announced to the (Asian!) pharmacist: 'She purports to be British. They come here and badmouth this country but are very happy to sponge off the NHS.' That is a red rag to a bull, and I am afraid my cheery American temperament evaporated. I tore into her about the decades I had spent as a taxpayer and sometime employer here, but the hatred in her face just simmered on and on.

On a lighter note, there is another aspect of being an expatriate American in Britain that is, at times, infuriating and does not happen to expats in Europe or elsewhere; it is unique to Britain. This has been my 32-year battle with Britons on what is 'right' within our common language. For example, I simply cannot say 'Durr-em' when confronted with 'Durham'. No matter how hard I try, 'Dure-um' comes out. I guess this is on account of the first 22 years of my life having been spent in the United States, where the names of its great cities were part of my childhood. Only last night, as I was putting this manuscript into final form, an enraged friend nearly crashed his car when I said I had been to Dure-um Cathedral. He was apoplectic when I said I could not get my mouth around 'Durr-em' and seemed to think I had committed some sort of treason against the Crown by not 'saying it correctly'. Dear reader, I am happy to learn to say it the right way, but could you ever imagine an American screaming in a very nasty way at a Briton in the United States? I have expatriate British friends in Philadelphia and Washington, and could not conjure up any scenario in which they would be brought down in a merciless tirade about their way of saying things.

Considering that so many regional accents in Britain are impenetrable, even to fellow citizens, my occasional Americanisms should not provoke tirades.

Perhaps the next time the BBC and ITV export television drama to the rest of the world, they might consider subtitles for the truly incomprehensible speech of Yorkshire, Scottish and Geordie characters.

On an even lighter note, for 32 years, whenever I am introduced at parties or dinners, and even in the course of business, I have been greeted with: 'YOU HAVEN'T LOST YOUR ACCENT!' Readers may wonder why this has always irritated me, and I have concluded that it is because I come from a nation in which one's immigrant origins are accepted and not brought to one's attention the moment one opens one's mouth. Imagine what would ensue if every cab driver in Manhattan was greeted with: 'You haven't lost your accent!' When, after some years, I had risen to a senior position at Anglia Television, I was still introduced as 'the American girl' and was always asked by new colleagues, in a tone as if only

Fulbright scholars or perfectly formed beings ought to be let into the UK, 'What brought you here?'

My American expatriate friend Lauran had a priceless answer to that one: 'An airplane'.

CHAPTER SEVEN

A YANKEE IN THE GREEN MAN PUB (AND CONDI RICE IN BLACKBURN)

'Condoleezza Rice should be sent to Iraq, tried as a war criminal and executed.'

Demonstrator from the Muslim community of Blackburn, 31 March 2006

March 2006 was not an easy month to be an American in Britain. In newspaper columns, Francis Wheen referred to an audience in Florida he had never actually met as 'ghastly', and Nick Cohen said the arrival of 'United States style casinos' in Britain would herald rampant prostitution, crime, money laundering and drug trafficking. Somehow I cannot see the ladies who daily pack the casino buses to Atlantic City skirting those hordes of hookers, crackheads and money launderers...

Then, the mayor of London said the United States Ambassador to the Court of St James, Robert Tuttle, was behaving like a 'chiselling little crook' because his embassy owed congestion charge fines. Mayor Ken Livingstone had announced that he would pursue the guilty parties at the American embassy all the way to the courts, but did not make any poisonous pronouncements about the 54 other embassies and consulates that owed thousands in congestion penalties, which many diplomats regard as a tax. Legations in Washington DC are exempt from the District's taxes, so, they argue, why should they be taxed in London?

Then came the late March/early April 2006 visit of US Secretary of State Dr Condoleezza Rice to the Blackburn constituency of her British counterpart, Foreign Secretary Jack Straw. He was returning the hospitality she had provided in her Southern home town during Straw's recent visit to the United States. Whatever liberals and Democrats may think of her, the angry protests and the surly children at the school she visited simply left observers with an impression of a miserably rude and churlish British populace behaving like a medieval mob. One Muslim representative called for her execution. Small children shouting mean epithets and carrying confrontational placards, and youngsters inside the school hanging their heads and refusing to talk to Dr Rice, were shameful moments in Anglo-American relations.

Let's face it: as Dr Rice commented recently, there are no western governments that can boast of having had people of colour in their senior cabinet and joint chiefs of staff for years, as has the United States. Find me a British woman who, like Rice, is an accomplished classical pianist, a linguist, a scholar and diplomat, who also adores sport; instead of sending their little girls out to screech abuse at Condi Rice, the people of Blackburn might have considered exposing their children to this remarkable woman as a role model. When I suggested as much to a fellow journalist, who is also a supporter of the anti-war movement, he said he would not have his children sit in the same room as a war criminal.

What was so admirable about Dr Rice's visit was her ability to keep her dignity and to rise above the ugly scenes that plagued her visits to Liverpool and Blackburn. Lord Mayor of Blackburn Ysuf Jan Virma greeted her and then went outside to the demonstrators and waved his arms to goad them on. His encouragement led to their shouts drowning out the press conference she was trying to hold with Jack Straw. The fury of the crowds in Liverpool and Blackburn was palpable. It was ugly and repugnant. The crowds in Birmingham, Alabama, had given Jack Straw an ecstatic welcome wherever he went. Why could this generosity of spirit not have been reciprocated?

This chapter opened with a comment about being an American in the UK. On 28 March 2006, I had an experience I will not soon forget. It ties in with the Condi Rice story. Having just had a close call in Edgware Road during a freak mini-gale, when a falling glass store sign had narrowly missed decapitating me, I decided to go into the Green Man pub to recover my composure and have a drink to celebrate my narrow brush with the Grim Reaper. For some reason that I still cannot fathom, the portly publican refused to give me the time of day and treated me as if I were a black trying to purchase food in a Mississippi diner in 1955. I asked him why he was being so unfriendly to me, and he continued to scowl at me, muttering something to the effect that he did not have to talk to me at all. I tried to chat to some other mature Englishmen in the pub, but got the same hostile looks. Wow! Is this what the world can expect when it pours into London for the 2012 Olympics?

What would possess an Englishman, whose establishment is there to serve the public, to treat a well-dressed, cheerful and dignified middle-aged woman, a cross between Dawn French and Victoria Wood, with such deplorable contempt? Perhaps the pub landlord thought I looked Jewish. Perhaps he thought, despite my mid-Atlantic accent, that I sounded like an American who would be demanding. I thought to myself: 'This is what it must have felt like being an African-American in the Deep South in the 1950s.' Whatever that beastly publican thought, his behaviour would be unthinkable in any bar across the USA in 2006. I will not soon forget this incident. If this is what Britain is becoming, we have a serious problem on our hands.

Tony Blair addressed the Australian Parliament in March 2006, and made an impassioned plea to Britons back home to curb the wave of anti-Americanism that he called a 'madness'. It is hard to be an American in Britain with the daily hail of ridicule about how bestial, stupid and idiotic we are, but having just sat through a stunning documentary about the Hoover Dam – 'it will last another 2,000 years' – one proposes that a bit more humility and a bit less arrogance might suit London before 2012 is upon us. That is, if the London Olympic stadium ever gets built in time.

CHAPTER EIGHT

'AMERICANS ARE DESTROYING THE PLANET AND WE WILL ALL DIE!'

One of the crosses an American has had to bear in Britain during the era of 'global warming' – as I sit near my scorching radiator in my London flat in July and frigid Wimbledon is, as usual, rained out – is the refrain, whenever pollution is mentioned in the media, that 'America is producing 25 per cent of greenhouse gases'. What I always ask is: 'But what villain is producing the other 75 per cent that is sure to kill us all?'

When I made my BBC radio debut on Jonathan Dimbleby's *Any Questions?* live broadcast in November 2006, I made myself the Enemy of the People by reminding the audience that China, the former Soviet Union and India were, in my measured opinion, responsible for a goodly amount of raw pollution.

It is never, ever articulated in British chattering circles or in the media that Americans work punishing hours and get just two weeks' holiday per year. Europeans and Britons get up to six weeks' holiday per year (and fairly lenient sick leave allowances). I have worked with enough Britons to know that the wine bar, pub and 'hols' are a major part of adulthood, and that they do not kill themselves to advance in their careers. Perhaps that explains why the USA does have environmental problems. Look at those pictures of Manhattan, the City that Never Sleeps, or any great American city at night; this is the teeming activity of advanced societies. Yes, there are a lot of bulbs burning and air conditioners groaning away.*

* Donald Rumsfeld, whilst American defence secretary, pointed out over and over again at his memorable press conferences that North Korea is pitch black at night. This is not due to intense environmental sensibilities. Would the environmentalists like to live as North Koreans do?

That brings me to another point.

Since 2000, there have been several very hot summer weeks in Europe and Britain. In France, old people have been left to pile up in morgues, whilst the August *vacances* were had. In London, actors in the West End, where some theatres cannot be air conditioned because of historic listing status, were collapsing from dehydration. I went to see *My Fair Lady* at the Theatre Royal Drury Lane, and sat pouring water over myself from a small bottle; the following evening, the *Evening Standard* newspaper said it had been into several theatres with a thermometer, and the temperatures had been near 100 degrees Fahrenheit. Some will say: 'Aha! Global warming!' I say: 'Isn't it about time Europe and the UK came out of the dark ages and installed air conditioning – a technological advancement Americans have enjoyed since the 1940s – in even the most basic places of public assembly? The summer of 2007 was cold and wet; but in 2006, Londoners sweltered in unbearable and completely unacceptable conditions in the tube and on fleets of brand new buses because of the absence of air conditioning. I had to laugh when it was reported that the mayor's office had asked the public for ideas on 'cooling down buses'. Dropping ice from helicopters, maybe?

Yes, it is possible that the millions of air conditioners groaning away across the USA from May to September have contributed to environmental damage; but what are the factories, chemical works and other unregulated industries belching forth poisons in Russia, China and India doing to the world's future?

When one is under the cudgel of anger from Britons about 'America destroying the environment', one hears about millions of Americans driving around in SUVs, polluting the atmosphere. Yes, cars pollute. Americans, who have the pitiful two weeks' vacation mentioned above, try to get in a short holiday with the kids and mother-in-law by driving from Vermont to Tennessee, or from Nebraska to Seattle, and before they blink it is time to get back to work the following Monday. So, does this mean that the millions of increasingly affluent Britons scooting around the UK in their Porsches,

Audis and Range and Land Rovers – not to mention the recent plague of stretch limousines across the British Isles – are somehow the Virtuous of the World?

I remember my father, as far back as the 1960s, trying to find a car that was energy efficient. When I was growing up in the 1960s, we had American Ralph Nader, the consumer pioneer, haranguing industry, whilst Britons were still putting shillings into meters to power gas refrigerators and those ridiculous 'electric fires'. (Talk about energy inefficiency! I could not believe my eyes when I arrived in the UK in 1976 and saw these primitive things, which guzzled electricity and were a hideous household fire hazard.)

There have been freak heat waves and cold fronts and floods and droughts and hurricanes since the beginning of time (what would the Torah and Shakespeare have been without the various weather-related calamities?), and, though it is generally accepted that the temperature of the globe is rising, why is this the fault of those Americans in their SUVs? If they contribute only 25 per cent to this problem, why do audiences rage on BBC debates? I recall attending a conference on human rights at a local synagogue in 2000 and visiting the stall of Greenpeace. The otherwise mild-mannered young man attending the stall suddenly became agitated when he heard my accent. He began to berate me, not tell me about the evils done to the world by the USA. His anger was scary. I could not reason with him. He really hated me – the kind of hate you see on those newsreels of Nazi thugs kicking old German Jews on the streets of Munich. (Another highlight of that day at the conference was having an elderly woman come over and screech at me about the genocide of American Indians and African slaves. Yes, all heinous acts, but do British people ever reflect on their own long history?)

So, whilst the British media and audiences castigate the United States for plunging the world into Environmental Doomsday, Americans Ralph Nader and Al Gore have been leading on environmental and consumer issues. If global warming has been harming us for so long, where are the European and British Gores and other pioneers? The United

States has had its Environmental Protection Agency for decades, and indeed factories and gasworks are strictly regulated. Are they regulated in China, India, the former Soviet Union and other parts of the billion-plus-populated, not-quite-Second World? I think not.

Lest we forget, Arbor Day (akin to Israel's Tu b'Shvat (New Year for Trees)) was established in Nebraska in the 19th century and soon became a national day of environmental awareness and work: thousands of trees are planted each year on this day.

It is interesting that a well-meaning article by Will Hutton in the *Observer* ('The Greening of America', 7 December 2003) reminded readers that the United States has the most dynamic and well-organized environmental programmes in the world, dating back many decades. He lists the Sierra Club, Earth First, the Environmental Defense Fund and other pressure groups that have convinced 29 states to adopt measures that conform to the Kyoto Protocol. He even says that 'smug France, Ireland, Spain and Denmark' outstrip many American states in carbon emissions. Indeed, Hutton's article was written long before Al Gore's Oscar-winning film and Nobel Prize. What I find most interesting about Hutton's impassioned defence of America is that the *Observer*'s title assembler chose the subheading: 'Some of the boldest environmental decisions are now coming from the world's most reviled country.' (Yes, and for any of you out there who doubt how much I am forcefully told on an almost daily basis that the USA *is* reviled, there it is in print!)

America is not the world's biggest polluter. Get off its back, world, and get to work fixing yourself.

CHAPTER NINE

BUT AREN'T WE BEST FRIENDS WITH GREAT BRITAIN?

Anti-Americanism goes back long before the era of Abu Ghraib and Guantanamo, long before the IRA and the late entry of the United States into the Second World War. After all, it was the shedding of the British yoke that saw the birth of the world's most powerful nation. Throughout the 19th century, Britons viewed their errant child with a combination of disdain and admiration. Charles Dickens marvelled at the bright and clean facilities available to the general public in the America he visited – a far cry from the abject poverty, deprivation and squalor he had left behind in teeming London. In the same century, visitors puzzled at the brash and often vulgar world of both rural and cosmopolitan America, so different from Victorian England.

The American Civil War very nearly saw the young country disintegrate into chaos, but the remarkable leadership and prose of Abraham Lincoln impressed the world. By the early 20th century, the United States was gaining in size and was absorbing millions of immigrants, the largest contingent from Italy. Already populating the emerging new towns were German and Irish arrivals, and Jewish immigration of 1900–05 from the persecution in Tsarist Russia changed the face of America forever. Soon Jewish immigrant songwriters were bringing entertainment to Broadway, while black music and jazz were being played in Europe and Britain. As Europe seethed in what has always seemed to me 'perpetual tribal turmoil' (without which Shakespeare would have had nothing to write about), America was celebrating the moving picture, the motor car and the Wright Brothers' flight. It is this very dynamism, this 'I can do anything!' attitude that has always engendered resentment and jealousy. I remember going to work at a London charity in my early days in the UK and the boss complaining that I 'was generating far too much work' when, in no time at all, I had organized several fundraising events. 'One a year is enough', I was told, as she sloped off to the wine bar for three hours.

Anti-Americanism since the Second World War has, in my view, stemmed from a deep feeling of sadness in Britain at loss of Empire. Palestine became Israel, and the USA took it under its wing. Nothing is guaranteed to provoke greater fury in polite company than for me to utter the word 'Israel'. This has nothing to do with the present conflict, but everything to do with the lynching of British soldiers and the blowing up of the King David Hotel in Jerusalem during the formative days of the Jewish state. The fact that the United States has been a firm friend and protector to Israel causes deep anger amongst people I know in Britain. Having grown up in the USA, where Jewish culture, food, music and literature are all-pervasive and greatly loved by a majority of the population, one of the most hurtful aspects of my life in Britain has always been the hatred spewed forth by even the most enlightened people about the Jews, as if they are some sort of scourge that poisoned the minds of Americans into supporting Israel.

The delayed entry into the Second World War by Franklin Roosevelt resonates to this day in Britain, and the Suez Crisis of 1956 did nothing to help Anglo-American relations. How many times in my decades in Britain have people lost their composure, accusing 'Americans' of supporting the IRA? Too many to count. I cannot deny this calumny; but again, as with the Jews, the relationship Americans have with the Irish is vastly different from the way the Irish are perceived in Britain. The Irish are amongst the most beloved of American immigrant groups.

Richard Nixon's House Un-American Activities Committee, which saw Alger Hiss sent to jail and Helen Gahagan Douglas and Jerry Voorhis publicly humiliated, and then Senator Joseph McCarthy's anti-communist witch-hunts created anti-American sentiment around the world. In the 1960s and 1970s, the Vietnam War and civil rights struggle, including the shameful fire-hosing of black demonstrators, turned much of Europe and the United Kingdom against the United States. The assassinations of Bobby Kennedy and Martin Luther King in 1968, the Chicago convention riots and the Kent State University shootings* in 1970, and then Watergate and a presidential resignation – all this made the world think the Land of the Free was about to implode. This was not so much a time of America-hatred, but of immense worry around the world that the lynchpin of democracy was now a long way from what had been envisaged by the Founding Fathers. I remember being an intern in Washington and meeting Gerald Ford, who was soon to become president. More than anything, he wanted to heal the wounds of a battered country; and he succeeded in doing that. Since his time, the United States has seen progress in the advancement of African-Americans and stunning success in the arts and sciences, and it has established itself once more as a formidable democracy. I like to tell people that, in the years of the turbulent time after the assassination of President Kennedy, perhaps a hundred Americans died. No other nation could have gone through the monumental struggles of that era without considerable bloodshed.

How can one explain anti-Americanism? Perhaps it is America's ability to bounce back smiling from catastrophe, and then produce movies and music and the polio vaccine and a man on the moon that so infuriates the rest of the world. I know, having lived in the United Kingdom for 32 years, that, at times, I have been unable to comprehend the utter hatred

* The Vietnam War had so enraged the youth of America that a national student strike ensued around the time of the My Lai Massacre in November 1969; this atrocity engendered worldwide condemnation. Student unrest continued for months, further fuelled by the American invasion of Cambodia, culminating in a confrontation at Kent State University in Kent, Ohio on 4 May 1970. National Guardsmen opened fire on students. Four were killed and nine injured. One of the slain was an onlooker who was an ROTC man (reserve officer) actually preparing to join the military upon graduation.

shown to me by otherwise sensible individuals, who splutter with rage about American food, cars, music, movies and Evangelism. In 2004, when I visited the USA for the first time in over a decade, I saw a magical land filled with cheerful, optimistic citizens and a new generation of Americans wanting a positive and productive future.

So, the following chapter's compilation of the sentiments expressed in newspapers in Britain about the USA will perhaps provide some insight into the hostility that, wherever I go these days, jumps out at me as soon as I open my mouth. But if you are British and are reading this, be assured – you will be loved in the streets of the USA as soon as you open your mouth.

CHAPTER TEN

'AMERICANS ARE VILE, GENOCIDAL, SLAVERY-LOVING AND ILLITERATE RELIGIOUS FANATICS'

What are the papers and the chattering classes saying in Britain? Why did my closest friends suddenly start closing in on me, on Israel and on America? Why does the crash in British church attendance go hand in hand with hatred of Israel and loathing of churchgoing America? How can the Monty Python nation that now abhors religion and never reads the Bible understand American values? I have come to the following unhappy conclusions...

In the years after 9/11, I have attended numerous conferences, seminars and one-day events presented by the anti-war movements and by a Palestinian organization in London.

The climax of all of this has been the televised investigation of the 11 September terrorist attacks being held in Washington. Dignitary after dignitary appears before this august commission, squirming and skilfully evading the incisive questioning.

Watching Madeleine Albright, Colin Powell, Paul Wolfowitz, Bill Cohen, Donald Rumsfeld, George Tenet and Sandy Berger being interrogated, I am moved to despair.

Were I an Islamic, ETA, Colombian, New IRA or Abu Sayaf terror chief, I would be chortling. Here is a group of immensely civilized westerners, raised and educated in the Judeo-Christian tradition, supplemented by the unique experience of Thanksgiving turkeys, 4 July fireworks, the Macy's Parade and Veterans' Day, being pummelled by fellow westerners of the same tradition. They are trying to figure out why a bunch of 'folks' flew airplanes into the World Trade Center and the Pentagon, and nearly demolished the White House and much of Capitol Hill.

Almost weekly on the BBC we hear stories such as that of an 11-year-old Palestinian boy who burst into tears when he was stopped by an Israeli checkpoint soldier. His backpack contained a mass of explosives. He had been sent to kill Jews by men old enough to be his father. The army is reported to have performed a controlled explosion on the backpack, and it created a sizeable crater. It would have killed the little boy and many others. What sort of people send a child to do this? If one watches the scenes of massive crowds in Gaza and the West Bank, one notices the robustness of the men and women marching and their attractive clothes. If they are starving under occupation, how do they have the resources for hundreds of smart uniforms and masses of guns and hand-held missile launchers? Cynics have said to me that disgruntled Israeli soldiers are supplying Palestinians with lethal gear, and that Israel even encouraged Sheikh Yassin, in order to isolate Arafat. Other rumours suggest that a Palestine Authority member is taking kickbacks on the construction of the 'Apartheid Wall'.

A commission could sit for a hundred years and not achieve anything, because it is not possible for the western, and most particularly the American, mind to comprehend how to prevent a repeat of the acts being investigated. Notwithstanding the tongue lashings I have received in recent months from British peace campaigners about the utter evil of my country, the United States (genocidal, racist, Zionist-inspired rogue state, etc.), I cannot see Americans, even those as astute as the array of leaders testifying to the 9/11 Commission, being able to predict and prevent the bizarre and cruel acts of the new generation of terrorists.

The European media's obsession with Israel's killing of Sheikh Yassin in his wheelchair ignores the obscene tragedy of the death of Klinghoffer, an elderly Jewish American on holiday in October 1985 with his wife on the *Achille Lauro* cruise liner, singled out by the PLO hijackers of the ship and thrown overboard in his wheelchair after the terrorists had forced a waiter and ship's barber to shoot him. (His wife died four months after – needless to say of a broken heart.) Unlike Sheikh Yassin, he had never in his life ordered the death of innocent souls.

Suffice it to say that I was chilled to the marrow by the speech delivered by Dr Azzam Tamimi, chairman of the Muslim Association of Britain (co-sponsor of the Anti-War Coalition), at a 2004 seminar given by the Friends of al-Aqsa. Dr Tamimi worked himself into a near-frenzy, explaining to the audience of mostly berobed young British-born Muslims that the world cannot exist with Israel in its midst. He wishes Jews no harm, but Israel must be dismantled. Why does my blood freeze at this thought? There are scores of Muslim and Arab countries, as well as several that are rapidly reaching a Muslim majority. Why must a tiny strip of land, devoid of oil and natural resources, be *Judenrein*?

How long will it be before such 'spokesmen for the anti-war coalition' are demanding the dismantling of the USA and the disenfranchisement of its Jews? The United States could have been brought to its knees by 9/11. Is this what the 'anti-war' leaders want?

Harold Pinter, the eminent British playwright (more of him anon), sent a message to an anti-war event at St James's, Piccadilly, in March 2004, saying that America, the perpetrator of a litany of crimes he listed for the huge and adoring audience, had essentially had it coming on 9/11.

I am reminded of a talk I attended in London in December 2003. The speaker was a Jewish member of the peace movement. He said that Americans were sitting in their living rooms, scheming about who they wanted to kill next. I had to cut in: I reminded him that it was December and that Americans, including President Bush, were sitting in their living rooms on the edges of their seats, waiting to see who would win the Super Bowl.

Despite the endless streams of crimes I have heard levelled against my native (and dare I say beloved?) United States of America in three years of seminars, demos and day events in

London, my assessment of the situation is that the Big Country is not just misunderstood but viscerally hated. Likewise, the Americans appearing before the cameras at the 9/11 Commission hearings will never understand terrorism (oh, how often I have heard about 'American state terror' these past few weeks from fuming Brits!) and will have to become much meaner and more ruthless if they are to prevent further 9/11s.

My overall impression of these varied conferences is that, in the UK, the United States is hated more than Israel by a large number of people of all ages and backgrounds. In a recent newspaper poll, 15 per cent of white Britons said they would happily be suicide bombers in Israel. Nevertheless, my impression of the mood of the anti-war groups whose symposia I have attended is that they feel an even deeper hatred of the USA. The little grey-haired ladies, cheering at the endless stream of America-bashing entertainers and speakers in the Piccadilly church, made me feel physically ill. (By the way, the jokes were not all about Dubya – there were even obscene turns about how overly upset the hysterical Yanks got about 9/11 and of how other victims of violence do not have mobile phones to leave impassioned messages for their loved ones.)

There is a mistaken concept here in Europe that 'Zionists' run the American government. This may be at the root of the current wave of anti-Americanism. Whatever the cause, it is disturbing and painful, and all I can say to the good people in whose land I live is that I have yet to find one American who hates Britain or the British.

It is notable that Dr Richard Perle, who spoke in London at the end of 2007, feels the tip of the iceberg has barely been scratched in the American quest to stamp out radicalism in the Muslim world. I take this observation a step further and say that in Britain and Europe – where radicals have for decades found a tranquil home, and the perception by the radicals is that the native populace and media to a considerable extent sympathize with their hatred of the USA, Jews, Americans and Israel – the job is near impossible. If every day on the media and in the newspapers there are calls to stamp on America and Israel, why should Muslim schools and mosques curtail their radical teachings?

For American expatriates, these are troubling times. For the Americans on the 9/11 panel and their distinguished witnesses, all of whom have little idea of how much their nation is venomously detested worldwide, there will, I fear, be trouble ahead.

CHAPTER ELEVEN

THE MYTH OF THE JEWISH CABALS

In the 2007 film *Kike Like Me*, British journalist Richard Ingrams tells director Jamie Kastner that it is indeed true that he gives short shrift to letters from people with Jewish-sounding names. Sound familiar? But this is tea-drinking, Royal Blighty!

Going way back to 2003, in an interview in *Vanity Fair*, British parliamentarian and 'Father of the House', Tam Dalyell, referred to a cabal of Jews driving American foreign policy. Here is my letter to the great man.

> The Honourable
> Tam Dalyell MP,
> The House of Commons,
> Westminster,
> London SW1.
> 7th May 2003
>
> Dear Mr Dalyell,
>
> I cannot remember when I last wrote an MP but your comments about Jews must be refuted by every decent human being of my generation (I having been born a while after the Nazi Holocaust).
>
> There are so many things I would like to say but having spent the evening with an elderly Jewish South African veteran of the anti-apartheid movement my thoughts have gelled onto one theme.
>
> Mr Dalyell, are you aware that the huge majority of anti-apartheid campaigners – Joe Slovo, Ruth First,

Helen Suzman, Ronnie Kasrils etc – were all a 'cabal of Jews?'

A cabal of Jews wrote the Talmud, the Midrashim, the Zohar and other monumental tracts as well as having been involved in many of the great revolutionary movements and the rise of modern psychiatry. Every other great Broadway composer has been a Jew; they have dominated the world of violin and piano virtuosity, symphony conducting and films for decades.

Having lived in the USA and seen the splendid contribution Jews have made to that remarkable country it is utterly appalling to me that you could single out Jews as having in some way negatively influenced Bush. What about the evangelist Franklin Graham or the right-wing Christian ideologues like John Ashcroft, Gordon Liddy, Oliver North and Newt Gingrich? Or for that matter WASPs Cheney, Rumsfeld, Card and Rove? President Bush works closely with Dr Condoleezza Rice, and it is a running joke in Washington that she is 'the last person he speaks to before retiring for the evening'. Is she part of a cabal of Jews?

Bill Clinton was surrounded by Jews, as was Margaret Thatcher. They win heaps of Nobel Prizes, rarely become intoxicated and have an enviable tradition of family and domestic stability that rivals no other segment of society. A cabal to be admired.

Your comments have shocked me. If this country continues to contribute to the world the thoughts of David Irving, the late Dowager Lady Birdwood, George Galloway and Tom Paulin – and now your lamentable views – we are far worse in spirit than the much-maligned French and Germans of 'Old Europe'. Lest we forget that England was the birthplace of the Blood Libel and the custom of expelling Jews for hundreds of years.

Yours sincerely,
(Miss) Carol Gould

CHAPTER TWELVE

'THE JEWS CONTROL THE US MEDIA AND THE WAY AMERICANS THINK!'

Moving on to 2007 in the 'has time stood still?' mode...

I was invited to a rare event in Cambridge as Advent 2007 commenced: the delivery of a new paper by Professor Peter Avery, a world authority on Persian history based at York University. Now 85 years young, the professor's lecture was indeed a treat, presented to an invited audience in the elegant private rooms of the provost of King's College. Though I was nursing what was to become a near-pneumonia-level bug, I was captivated by his discourse on the evolution of factional Muslim infighting that has led to today's 'war on terror'.

What was of particular interest was his emphasis on the dismay a variety of modern-day Muslim leaders feel towards Osama bin Laden, and how many of these heads of state yearn for the United States to dispose of the leader of al-Qaeda. His captivating talk enumerated the occasions in recent history in which western bullying and military aggression have so badly damaged Muslim-world relations and pointed out that the Middle Eastern temperament harbours a long memory in the wake of defeat and humiliation.

I was struck by the fact that Professor Avery never once mentioned Israel. After his lecture, he asked for questions and I raised this omission. I asked him if the wrath and perpetual turmoil that seems to dominate the Muslim world would abate if Israel were to disappear tomorrow. He thanked me and said he had been hoping someone would bring up the issue of Israel.

I had asked this question because I had a vivid memory of the Israel-loathing columnist Robert Fisk asserting on

11 September 2001 that the World Trade Center attacks were about the Saudi Royal family, not Israel. To my astonishment, Professor Avery did not take this view but launched into a discourse on the ill-begotten Jewish state, and the deleterious effect its creation and continued existence had had on the region and on the Muslim world. In the context of his paper, in which he emphasized the hatred Muslims had for western troops desecrating their sacred soil, I could, to a limited extent, understand his point that, as far back as Lawrence of Arabia, the idea of a Jewish homeland had enraged the indigenous population. He also reminded the audience that he had for decades been a staunch admirer of Israel as an oasis of culture and scientific achievement in a less-than-advanced region.

What I was not prepared for was an impassioned assertion by Professor Avery that the Zionist lobby in the United States drove American foreign policy and that 'the Jews' control the media. He was adamant that this aspect of world affairs was lamentable. The implication was that the American public could not be expected to appreciate the influence the Israel lobby has on their national destiny if Jews control the flow of news.

I went back to my lodgings and decided to do some research on 'Jewish control' of the American media. What I found was sobering.

If one accepts that the Sulzbergers are Episcopalian, they can be eliminated as 'Jewish' controllers of the *New York Times*. The Knight Ridder group controls many newspapers. Betty Scripps, who is a stalwart of my local Washington National Opera company, is not exactly a Hadassah lady. The mighty Scripps Howard empire, which rose to prominence a century ago alongside the Cowles dynasty, still controls numerous publications. Names like Gannett, Robinson and McClatchey dominate other media empires, along with Boisfueillet Jones of the *Washington Post*. Then there is the Southern Tennant Bryan empire. Add to this mix Ted Turner, Murdoch, Dow Jones, Luce and Hearst, and I do not see any Jewish conspiracy.

Katie Couric, Brian Williams and Charles Gibson are the three heavyweight network news anchors, and I do not recall any Jews ever sitting in these chairs in my lifetime. Peter Jennings was a fierce critic of Israeli policies and made this known in his ABC News reports. Israel is covered infinitely less on American television than in the British media, but when it is it is often portrayed with a critical eye, most particularly on CNN.

The opinion-formers in the United States in primetime are non-Jews: Gwyn Ifyl, Stephen Colbert, Lou Dobbs, Chris Matthews, Bill Moyers, Bill O'Reilly and Keith Olbermann, who is of German Lutheran extraction. In fact, except for the occasional appearance by Bill Kristol, the vast array of television and radio punditry is the exclusive realm of Christian commentators.

In Hollywood, there are some prominent Jews, but except for *Schindler's List*, when did Spielberg or any other Hollywood mogul produce Zionist or Jewish-dominated material? Woody Allen's humour is New York Jewish, but except for *Crimes and Misdemeanors* he has never produced a rant on Zionist or Jewish themes.

Professor Avery may be an esteemed expert on Iran, but his perception of America as a cesspit of rampant Jewish and Zionist campaigning and media domination is ill-founded. It is a pernicious act to perpetuate the idea that Jews have some sort of gargantuan – and therefore negative – power over American thought and destiny. It is regrettable that such a consummate scholar could make such remarks to an audience that included many young and impressionable Cambridge students.

CHAPTER THIRTEEN

'IS GOOD THE JEW AND HINDU KILLED!'

Hello? Is anyone paying attention in Washington?

Well, in August 2006 it was admirable that the British police foiled a spectacular terror attack and equally noble that the United States was so supportive of Britain at that trying time. I have to confess to having been terrified to fly back to London.

Then again, in summer 2007, the British police and an intrepid Scottish baggage handler foiled three potentially catastrophic bombings in London's Haymarket and Cockspur Street, and at Glasgow Airport. That same summer, the 21 July 2005 bombers were given long sentences, and showed not an ounce of remorse. It was not just hatred of America and Jews that had inspired them, but an equal hatred of Britain.

But what is of concern to me is the hour-by-hour, obsessive rhetoric about al-Qaeda, al-Qaeda and al-Qaeda on the American media.

I have spent many a week with colleagues in Washington telling them of the appalling situation in Great Britain, where the BBC and BAFTA-winning filmmakers like Adam Curtis use Dr Azzam Tamimi, an avowed enemy of Israel, as a 'spokesman' on television programmes. I have told my colleagues about the proliferation of Muslim 'spokespeople' who pepper the airwaves from dawn until dusk, pontificating about every subject under the sun. These experts, including Faisal 'Israel Has No Right to Exist' Bodi, Yasmin Alibhai-Brown, Sir Iqbal Sacranie, Mohammed Abdul Bari, Ghada Karmi, Ahdaf Soueif, Abdul Bari Atwan and many others, have been particularly ubiquitous since 7 July 2005. This is because those in authority in Britain felt that 'reaching out to the Muslim community' would prevent further terror attacks.

To add to this, various liberal and left-wing activists have enjoyed unprecedented access to the media in their campaigns to blame George Bush and his Zionist neoconservative cabal for the 'Muslim rage' rampaging across Great Britain, from Glasgow to Cardiff to Luton to London. The new head of the Muslim Council, Dr Mohammed Abdul Bari, would like to see a limited degree of sharia law introduced into Britain and will not entirely condemn stoning.

Yet even when I spoke at a beautiful synagogue in Washington, at the invitation of Michael and Barbara Ledeen (who do understand the threat), several congregants confronted me afterwards, suggesting that my worries – mainly about anti-Jewish terror in Britain – were overblown. One suggested that this was a 'phase' that young men outgrow as their testosterone levels decrease. And some credence is given to this theory: Yasmin Alibhai-Brown wrote in the *Evening Standard* after the July 2007 thwarted horrors that young Muslim men are filled with anger and frustration as a result of being forced into arranged marriages. She said this was a grim factor in the channelling of aggression amongst young men in communities in Britain and around the world. However, I know plenty of Jewish men and women who have suffered in arranged marriages and yet have never harmed a fly.

I attended the Islam Channel's 'Global Peace and Unity Conference' at the ExCeL Centre in London in December 2005 (described in detail in the next chapter), thinking it would be a celebration of Islamic/Arab/Asian culture, food and literature. Behind a large grey curtain that separated the innocent-looking food and drink stalls from the rest of the enormous hall was a crowd of 25,000 angry young Muslim men and women being whipped up into a Jihadist frenzy all day by a succession of viscerally hostile white British agitators that included the *keffiyah*-clad lawyer, Michael Mansfield QC, and Yvonne Ridley. Ridley described Israel as 'that vile little nation' and the British police as 'jackboot Britain'. George Galloway MP exhorted the crowd to express its hatred of Israel by taking to the streets. The former cricketer and avowed opponent of General Musharraf, Imran Khan, gave a bizarre speech about the poor Germans between the world wars being like the Muslim world today, humiliated by the western powers.

Not once in the entire day did anyone mention al-Qaeda or Osama bin Laden. The hours and hours of rabble-rousing, mostly by British-born Muslims, concentrated on three basic enemies: the United States, Israel and Zionists, wherever they may be. The hatred and aggression of this group is something I will never forget. I felt I was in the midst of a Nuremberg-style rally, and was terrified that someone would kill me if they discovered I was American-born and a staunch supporter of Israel.

I was the only non-Muslim writer and filmmaker to attend the event, and this in itself is an indication of how badly the British media monitor this aspect of British life, though they devote endless column inches in their newsrooms to condemnations of the USA and Israel.

Al-Qaeda-obsessed reporting on all American networks is once again ignoring the point Melanie Phillips and I have been trying to drive home for years: that Osama bin Laden does not need to open his mouth for British Muslims to be inspired to plan and stage horrifying atrocities.

The 'Global Peace and Unity' event at the ExCeL Centre left no doubt in my mind that a massive number of British Muslims, mostly young, have been inculcated with utter hatred of Americans and Jews, and that Osama's goading is not necessary to lead them to the ultimate martyrdom. I look at Michael Chertoff and appreciate his vigilance, but he is not surrounded every day, as many of us in London are, by angry young men and women who have been born and educated in their country of domicile and who want to destroy as much as they can in the name of America-hatred and Jew-loathing.

The small community of Anglo-Jewry has been on the receiving end of what Chief Rabbi Sir Jonathan Sacks calls 'a tsunami of anti-Semitism'. This is a double-edged sword: the *Guardian*-reading Hampstead chattering ones can be as vicious as the tattooed hooligans yelling 'Turn on the gassssss' at Chelsea football club's Israeli coach, compounded by the general hatred from Muslim groups. I have met pinstripe-suited Englishmen who have told me they wish more Jews were killed when suicide bombers attack Israel.

I have met otherwise sensible Britons who become embarrassingly loud and abusive about everything under the sun in America, be it our food, our theatre, our baseball or our clothes. This quickly accelerates into a tirade about the Zionists bullying Bush, Rumsfeld, Cheney and Blair into 'crusades' to destroy the Middle East. If sober, educated Britons can rail about Israel and the USA from one end of the British Isles to the other, this creates a lethal mix for the angry young Muslims. 'If the local population hates the bloody Yanks and Jews as we do,' they deduce, 'then it is open season for our dream of martyrdom in our quiet houses in Hertfordshire, Norfolk and Hampshire.' If the eminent historian and novelist A. N. Wilson could rail against Israel and the USA in his weekly columns, does this not give reassurance to radicals? (One blessing is that Wilson was dropped by the *Evening Standard* in 2007.)

When the art critic Brian Sewell mouths off about the 'greedy Jews' of Manchester wanting to build a Holocaust memorial, and Tam Dalyell laments the 'cabal of Jews' that drives Anglo-American policy, do British Muslims not feel comforted? When the *New Statesman* prints a cover showing the British Union Flag being impaled by a Jewish star, is this not a partnership with terrorists? When streams of British commentators flood television, radio and the print media, denouncing the USA and Israel, do the potential airline liquid-bombers of August 2006 not feel reassured that they are in heaven on earth?

In 2006, a protracted illness left me with a lot of free time. One day I was in my local *halal* (this is not meant as a barb – it is now a *halal*-geared bank) branch of the HSBC bank in Edgware Road when two young men became embroiled in a very public shouting match with one of the managers. She firmly told them that their account had been closed because of 'large amounts of money going in and going out'. They argued that they had '£20,000 and will just open a new account', but she suggested they go elsewhere. It was indeed odd that the manager had been so indiscreet as to chastise these young men in public, but one had the impression that such scenes occurred every day. I have watched young men withdraw massive amounts of cash and stuff it into their jackets or into black bags. Should I go to the anti-terror police? Maybe so. But if I do, I worry that I will be regarded as a paranoid Islamophobe. It is this very fear amongst the general population that also contributes to the environment of free-range terror planning.

At my local corner shop in London, run for 40 years by cockney Jack, the new owners from Bangladesh have emptied the shelves of bacon, sausages and even tinned ham. They will no longer carry any of these goods, which the majority local population had been buying for generations. When the Columbia Shuttle exploded, the young man who runs the shop told me he was rejoicing about the 'Jew and Hindu killed' because his imam had told him it was a blessed event. On 9/11, cars with men and women playing loud Middle Eastern music paraded up and down Edgware Road in London. I saw it.

Building societies think twice about displaying piggy banks and giving them away to children. Sir Iqbal Sacranie, the recent head of the Muslim Council of Britain, boycotts Holocaust Memorial Day, and Muslim spokesman Inayat Bunglawala writes to the *Jewish Chronicle* that the creation of the state of Israel was the greatest disaster of the last century. One wonders how the Muslim community of Britain would react if a Jewish dignitary proclaimed the creation of Pakistan to be the 'disaster of the century'. The Muslim Public Affairs Council UK (MPACUK) allows shocking rhetoric, way beyond sensible criticism of the United States and Israel, on its 'moderated' (*sic*) website, and is opening new branches across the UK. Its so-called 'moderator' allows bloggers to post vile comments about 'Zionazis', but bars me from writing on the website. Again, I have tried again and again to explain to the Washington elite the proliferation of a massive culture of extremism in Britain and have got the glazed-over look. I recall attending a gala at the Kennedy Center and trying to engage the columnist Cal Thomas and his wife about the problems in Britain. Believe it or not, he, too, glazed over, said 'Why don't you just do some celebrity-watching?', walked off and left me with his wife.

The Anglo-Muslim 'leaders' should be bringing their people together with other religious groups in Britain, but what I have seen in the past year has confirmed my worst fears: that the British Muslim community is moving farther and farther away from the tranquil assimilation that every other ethnic and religious group has enjoyed in the United Kingdom. Eliza Manningham-Buller, and now Jonathan Evans, head of MI5, have warned that some 4,000 terrorists are working inside the United Kingdom.

It is not Osama who is driving the spectacular rise of terror in Britain. Rather, it is the support from the white population, the Israel- and America-bashing from public figures (London Mayor Ken Livingstone being a prime agitator) and the support the radicals feel they enjoy from a large swath of Britain that is creating this happy breeding ground. The Church has obsessed about boycotting Israel, the media fixate on 'Zionist conspiracies' and the imams, many of whom do not speak English, exhort their young worshippers to anything but ballet lessons, football sessions or outings to the Natural History Museum.

The American authorities need to get real about the threat from Britain and Europe and stop concentrating all their attention on the madrassahs of Pakistan. The white Englishman and war hero who drove me to my holiday hotel spent the entire trip berating me about the evils the Jews, Yanks and Zionists have inflicted on the world. If he is so full of rage, what is the Muslim population feeling, when they know his ilk will give them succour?

What happened in Britain in summer 2007 did not surprise me. Those of us who live there, in the 'coming Caliphate', know that the threat is huge, is massively supported and may never be extinguished. I am not hopeful.

CHAPTER FOURTEEN

THE HATE-AMERICA/HATE-ISRAEL FESTS IN LONDON, SPONSORED BY THE POLICE AND WESTERN UNION

What follows is my account of the Islamic Rally held less than six months after the 7 July London bombings.

One Sunday in December 2005 that will forever be etched in my memory, I attended the 'Global Peace and Unity Conference' at London's ExCeL Centre, presented by the new Islam Channel and sponsored by Emirates Airlines, Western Union (yes, that old American establishment!) and the Metropolitan Police.

It was advertised as a diverse event to which non-Muslims were invited, and the impression one got from the website was of a celebration of Middle Eastern culture, food, music and children's activities in a London milieu.

To my utter horror – my physical and emotional shock rendered me nearly inert for several days afterwards and culminated in an attack of shingles – it was a seven-hour call to Jihad by a succession of ranting and shouting rabble-rousers.

The eminent barrister Michael Mansfield QC, wearing a black-and-white *keffiyah* scarf, shouted into the mike about the heinous crimes of the United States and western coalition countries. The crowd chanted and thundered its appreciation.

The menacing demagogue George Galloway ascended the podium and exhorted the crowd to stand up for the redemption of the oppressed Muslim world, or else the nation had better get ready for 'rioting in every street in Britain'. The 'slaughter in Palestine and Iraq' being only part of the equation, Chechnya, Bosnia and Kashmir were also mentioned all day by every speaker, including Yvonne Ridley, a crazed, *chador*-clad Muslim activist of the 'Respect' party, whom I expected to self-immolate at any moment, such was her fury at the Zionists, the Americans and her fellow Britons. To my utter disbelief, she condemned the British police force as some form of fascist brigade in 'jackboot Britain'.

To all of these exhortations came cries of 'Allahu Akhbar' from the enormous, simmering crowd of what looked to me like the angriest gathering of young men and women I had ever had the misfortune to be near.

For the benefit of non-British and non-Commonwealth readers, it should be noted that the arrival from Pakistan of cricketer Imran Khan to give a speech would be the equivalent of having Muhammad Ali or Magic Johnson turn up in an American arena. The crowd of some 20,000 adoring, mostly young, British Muslims went mad with joy when he ascended the stage and took to the dais. What followed was a stream of invective about his own leader, Pervez Musharraf, Egypt's leader Hosni Mubarak, and, of course, the 'axis of evil' Bush, Blair and allies. (It must be noted here that in May, when the controversy arose about the American soldiers allegedly flushing a Koran down a lavatory, Khan's power over world Islam was such that he gave one short speech and riots ensued across Pakistan and around the globe, including the horrifying flag burnings in London's Grosvenor Square.)*

Khan actually said that we should feel the degradation of modern Muslims in the context of Hitler and the Germans after Versailles. He used this example to accentuate the reason for 'Muslim rage' – there was poor Germany, belittled and humiliated, like the Muslim world today. He recounted a story of having been confronted by a fellow Pakistani after 9/11 who asked: 'Do you not feel ashamed?' And he told the adoring crowd that he did not see what there was to be

* *Weekly Standard*, 31 May 2005, from article by James Forsyth and Jai Singh: 'People are looking for someone to blame for the riots that flowed from *Newsweek*'s "Koran" story [of members of the American military flushing a Koran down a lavatory]...the real villain is Pakistani politician Imran Khan...on Friday May 6 Khan catapulted the 300-word *Newsweek* story...into headline news across the Muslim world by brandishing the article at a press conference.'

ashamed of – and anyway, 9/11 was an excuse for the criminal Washington neocons to start a New Crusade against Islam. To illustrate the extreme to which this event had degenerated, one of the organizers actually took the mike and said the event team wished to distance themselves from Khan's 9/11 views.

I had thought that the various artists present would offer a variety of musical numbers, but instead they gave loud, piercing renditions of what seemed the same chant about Allah. OK, that's fine, but where are the Muslim Placido Domingos, Joan Sutherlands, Isaac Sterns and George Balanchines? Why were there no Muslim educators present at this 'cultural festival' asking this vast multitude of young people to sign up for music, theatre and art programmes?

An elderly sheikh in Pakistan was beamed in live to tell this excited crowd that he could barely articulate the word 'Israel', as this is not a country that even exists. His English was barely comprehensible, but he appeared to imply that Jews from '80 nations' were brought to Palestine to drive the Arabs away and to commit murder, torture, imprisonment and theft of land and homes over 50-odd years. The young and impressionable crowd seemed ready for a collective Jihad at this point.

What was interesting was the theme, repeated by a string of sheikhs from around the globe, that the leaders of Arab nations were a weak, spineless bunch of puppets of the Americans, and did not have the guts to stand up to Israel and the United States. This theme caused tremendous excitement in the crowd, as if a global Intifadah might just start in this London arena.

After the event, I went to get some fresh air upstairs and, as I looked out at a quaint old mill on the quay, a young English Muslim in a long robe and head-covering asked me about this place where we stood, Canary Wharf. I told him that it had been decimated and nearly obliterated by the Luftwaffe in the Blitz and that the conflagration could be seen as far away as Hertfordshire. He looked at me and said: 'Who did you say did the bombing?' I replied: 'The Luftwaffe.' He said: 'Who are they?' I said: 'The Germans.' He said: 'Really? Well, I've learned something today.'

Like the Muslim cab driver who asked me what St Paul's Cathedral was, this young Englishman had no sense of British history or identity.

Shame on the Muslim community of Great Britain for organizing an event that could serve only to further agitate an already radicalized segment of the British population!

The anger, aggression and totally obsessive nature of the day left me feeling shocked and personally assaulted. How far would a white Christian group get holding such a rally? Cries of racial incitement would ring far and wide, and the police would be summoned. In this instance the police were actually sponsoring the event! These are the moments when I think: 'Has Britain gone completely mad?'

When the Muslim community of Great Britain, with its multitude of organizations, mosques and even its own parliament, can organize an enlightened and civilized event that makes Jews, Christians, Hindus and all nationalities – including Israelis and Americans – feel welcome, then Great Britain will have achieved true multiculturalism.

Until then, I am not ashamed to say that I am scared out of my wits and would suggest that Americans, Jews, Israelis and Hindus get out of here as soon as possible. British Christians? A good many have expended boundless energy on condemnation of Israel and the USA, but the anger I saw one Sunday in December will also decimate them. Wake up, dear, tolerant Britons, before it is too late.

CHAPTER FIFTEEN

THE ISRAEL FACTOR – 'YOU PEOPLE INVENTED TERRORISM, AND ISRAEL IS AN ABOMINATION SUPPORTED BY THE OTHER TERRORIST STATE, THE USA!'

It is important to note that the following appeared in October 2003. Has time stood still? In 2007, British Chief Rabbi, Dr Jonathan Sacks, said that Britain and Europe were gripped by a 'tsunami of anti-Semitism'. After the 2003 account comes my October 2007 assessment of the increasing hatred of Israel, which relates to hatred of the United States.

DIARY: FRIDAY 10 OCTOBER 2003

On Thursday evening, I went to the Marks & Spencer department store. On the way, the bus conductor wanted the passengers to know that he was Moroccan. He went from seat to seat, making a point of greeting passengers in Arabic, and animatedly chatting with women in traditional Muslim clothes. He did make a point of grunting to those of us who were, shall we say, 'traditional locals'. I did not feel slighted, but, as we approached Oxford Street, he went to the front of the bus and told those of us seated at that end that 'Marks & Spencer sell things and then send the money to the Jewish'. He then said something – one assumes a similar piece of useful information – to a Muslim woman and both became rather agitated. The bus driver, a white-haired London Buses old timer of decades standing, leaned out of his cab and, with considerable irritation, lectured the conductor on the history of the Holocaust and of the 'Jewish'. As I was leaving the bus, I could hear the driver and conductor arguing; the latter reminding the Englishman that all Marks & Spencer money goes to the 'Zionist murderers'.

I then found myself in Oxford Street. Outside M&S, as it is affectionately known, was a contingent of policemen and women who were protecting a small group of young Jewish men who had set up a table with an Israeli flag. The men were further protected by a substantial metal barrier, to separate them from what can only be described as a hysterical crowd of hate-filled people of every shape and size. What was so depressing was that non-Arabs in the noisy crowd outnumbered those from the Middle East.

I have noticed that for years, Palestinian groups have had a stall outside Marks & Spencer to protest about the history of the Sieff family and to discourage people from shopping at a store that stocks Israeli goods. The Palestinian young people are never attacked, and when Jews approach them the most that happens is a lively discussion. To a lesser extent, its neighbour store, Selfridges, has had leafleters outside for years, protesting about the presence of Israeli wines on its shelves. One day, I went into Selfridges and accosted the first couple I saw. They said they agreed with the Palestinian leafleters and thought no 'Zionist apartheid' goods should be sold anywhere in the UK. When I asked this otherwise charming English couple where they had learned the word 'apartheid' in relation to Israel, they said they had read about it in the *Independent* and had seen 'atrocities on the BBC'.

Anyway, I began to pick up snippets of shouts from this viscerally angry crowd. One woman in religious Muslim attire standing next to me – actually jumping up and down – screamed at the top of her voice at the Israel supporters: 'You Jews destroyed my country, Iraq.' Someone asked her what Israel had to do with Iraq, and she screeched: 'You killed 60 of my family in Iraq.' She was asked how 60 Iraqis were killed by Israelis, and she said: 'Israel – USA! Same thing! And now you will take over Iran!' She became so agitated that she had to be led away by the police.

Then came the chorus of really quite terrifyingly angry English people, with their shouted mantras of: 'You people invented terrorism in Palestine'; 'Israel is expanding every day and will soon own the whole Middle East!!' (doh???); 'Israel is slaughtering thousands of Palestinians every day' (again, doh?).

But the crowning glory was an elegantly dressed businessman next to me who seemed normal – except for the fury in his eyes. He said: 'I love and revere the suicide bombers. Every time I hear of a suicide bomb going off, I wish it had been 80 or 90 Jews instead of a pitiful handful.' He then went on to shout every time anyone opened their mouth and had reached a point of hysteria – 'You people have been trying to acquire land across the entire globe and will soon own every nation if you are not stopped!' – when, thankfully, a policewoman came over. I can think of a few people I know who, had they been armed, would be in prison tonight, because his suggestion that not enough Jews are killed each time a bomb goes off would have 'made them go crazy', as the saying goes, but I was pleased to see that the policewoman was making every effort to book him.

Imagine how far he would have got had he said such things in New York or Washington about Americans.

What does this tell us about British society? Pim Fortuyn was assassinated because he expressed what were considered to be extremist views about the rise of Islam across Europe and in his native Holland. What alarms me is the sheer, visceral hatred shown by the crowd on Thursday towards a mild-looking group of young Jewish men and towards the Jewish bystanders.

Does this mean, as Melanie Phillips has said so often in the British press this year, that Britain is no longer a place where Jews may live without fear? Yes, I think it does. My liberal friends will say that the actions of the Sharon government are making life hell for Diaspora Jews.

Here is a crucial point: when Yitzhak Rabin was making peace and Israel was booming – and the Palestinian territories were beginning to flourish – terror bombs were exploding as often as during the dark days, and my British hosts were saying unspeakable things about 'you people invented terrorism in Palestine'.

Sadly, I believe anti-Semitism is endemic in the world at large. The young men on the Israel stall on Thursday should make *aliyah*. NOW.

MY VIEW IN OCTOBER 2007

There is now a disturbing spectrum of trade union boycotts of Israel proliferating across Great Britain. Never have I known the small (260,000) Jewish community of the UK to be in such crisis and so besieged. Impassioned journalism by Howard Jacobson, Chief Rabbi Sir Jonathan Sacks and Melanie Phillips, embellished with the expressions 'Jew-hatred' and 'witch hunt', reflect the rising anguish in both secular and religious Anglo-Jewry.

I am in the unusual position of being one of a tiny handful of British-based Zionist-American members of one of the institutions demanding a boycott, the National Union of Journalists (NUJ). It is perhaps because I can bear witness to the sheer hatred displayed towards me at a recent NUJ meeting that I am best suited to explain and chronicle the British boycott saga.

This is not a sudden phenomenon. Following Israeli military actions in the occupied Palestinian territories, Professor Steven Rose and his wife, Hilary, advocated a boycott of Israeli academics in a widely disseminated letter to the *Guardian* newspaper back on 6 April 2002. This caused a national stir, and soon the boycott gained momentum and widespread support in British academia and beyond. In the intervening years since the Rose letter, they have become 'regulars' in the British media.

British newspapers have, from time to time, published articles calling for the demise of Israel ('Israel Simply Has No Right to Exist' by Faisal Bodi, *Guardian*, 3 January 2001), and editorials by numerous British Muslims have been joined in the Zionist-hating chorus by the historian A. N. Wilson, London Mayor Ken Livingstone ('I would not have created an Israel') and art critic Brian Sewell, who, in the London *Evening Standard*, have all griped about Zionist and Jewish aspirations. 'It is time for the world community to consider dismantling Israel' is not an uncommon phrase in the current social discourse. At the 'Enough!' rally in London on Saturday 9 June 2007, members of Parliament, actors and religious leaders called for a siege on Israel through boycotts.

As the anniversary of the Six Day War passed, the British University and College Union voted at its May 2007 conference in Bournemouth to formulate a nationwide boycott policy of their Israeli counterparts. Their campaign would 'consider the moral implications of existing and proposed links with Israeli academic institutions'. It would also host tours of British universities by Palestinian academics and trade unionists. At the conference, the *Jewish Chronicle* reporter heard delegates referring to Israel as an apartheid state, guilty of ethnic cleansing and barbarism. Having seen at first hand the profound hatred of Israel amongst my union colleagues, I can well imagine the fury of the college lecturers ranting about Israeli barbarism.

In the summer of 2007, a group of some 150 British doctors and consultants signed a letter, published on various Muslim websites, condemning Israeli policies towards the Palestinians and demanding an end to cooperation with Israeli medical associations. In addition, the Royal Institute of British Architects (RIBA) is discussing rekindling its 2006 attempt to boycott ties with Israel. The architects, including RIBA President Jack Pringle and President Elect Sunand Prasad, have signed a petition organized by the group Architects and Planners for Justice in Palestine (APJP).

'APJP asserts that the actions of our fellow professionals working with these enterprises are clearly unethical, immoral and contravene universally recognised professional codes of conduct', a spokesman told the *Guardian* on 26 May 2007. The idea that Jewish architects in Israel are somehow complicit in immoral activity is reminiscent of the German Nazi cartoons linking Jews to every grievance known to mankind. The British union UNISON also tabled a comprehensive motion that called for boycotts of Israel that would have affected everything from pension funds to British supermarket produce, but this move did not bear fruit (no pun intended).

It is vital for Americans to appreciate that the BBC, major network broadcaster Channel 4 and newspapers in Britain, which weekly, if not daily, give air time and space to innumerable angry Palestinians and British Israel-bashers, have added to a climate of universal condemnation. Sudan, Zimbabwe, Venezuela and Myanmar escape the attention of the British media and trade unions. I doubt your average Briton knows who Hugo Chavez is, but even a beauty therapist will lecture me about the brutality of the Jewish state and the 'genocide of the Palestinians'.

A recent two-hour documentary about Jerusalem by former MP and Bosnia negotiator Paddy Ashdown was a relentless, claustrophobic indictment of Israel, with factual errors in the script. His show was followed by two more documentaries about the evil Israelis; not once did we see Zubin Mehta and the Israel Philharmonic, the Habima or Cameri Theatres, the Technion, the Weizmann Institute or the selfless work of the Hadassah and other Israeli hospitals. Another documentary about 'Palestine' made no mention of the Holocaust or of Theodor Herzl's worthy Zionist movement; he and non-Jewish writer Emile Zola witnessed the Dreyfus trial, a watershed in Jewish history and aspirations that resulted in the screed '*J'Accuse!*', but the British programme never touched on this – only the theft of land from the indigenous Arabs of Palestine.

It is therefore little wonder that so many sectors of British society are filled with boycott mania.

This loathing of Israel and America was brought home to me in June 2007, at a meeting of the London chapter, or 'chapel', of the NUJ, which had called a special May gathering to discuss the Israel boycott motion that had been passed on 15 April at its national delegates' meeting.

I went along, armed with a book by Hillel Halkin, *Letters to an American Friend: a Zionist's Polemic*, written after the Yom Kippur War and chronicling the agony of daily life as a reservist in Israel – a man who is also husband, father, son and brother. I never had a chance to read from the book because the meeting degenerated into a series of furious diatribes by NUJ members.

I heard about the brutality of Israel and every other imaginable crime against humanity. Each member who spoke made sure to tell the group that they had 'been boycotting absolutely anything and everything from Israel for years and years', and the editor of the union's *Journalist* magazine spat out the comment I hear almost every day in London about 'rich American Jews' funding and driving Israel's disgraceful policies. I was refused the floor when I wanted to correct the calumnies being hurled at Israel. Later I escaped to a nearby pub, but the angry members piled in to continue their assault on me.

I really felt under siege. One said Jews needed to 'get the Holocaust out of their system and get that chip off your shoulder because slavery was a much worse genocide', while another said: 'Israel is plain thievery – you nicked their land in '48 and Zionism is out-and-out racism.' All of the members were incensed that I had dared come to the meeting to defend Israel's right to exist, and their barely contained anger was something I do not recall ever having witnessed in any situation.

In the *Daily Express* newspaper of 31 May 2007, one of the tiny handful of non-Jewish voices in support of Israel, Leo McKinstry, noted that an NUJ member, Pamela Hardyment, had written a letter to an Anglo-Jewish communal organization stating that Israel is 'a wonderful Nazi-like killing machine backed by the world's richest Jews', whilst referring to the 'so-called Holocaust' and adding: 'Shame on all Jews, may your lives be cursed.'

Notwithstanding the efforts of non-Jewish journalists Richard Littlejohn, Charles Moore and the above-mentioned Leo McKinstry to stop these boycotts, in the coming weeks it is highly likely that Britain will see a massive labour-movement campaign against everything Israeli. In the *Jerusalem Post*, a comment page reminded the world that England had expelled its Jews in 1290 after the brutal York, Lincoln and Norwich blood libels and massacres, and had not readmitted them until the time of Cromwell.

The generosity of Britons to Jewish *Kindertransporte* children and to refugees from Nazi Germany was considerable; but my experience over 32 years has, sadly, been one of perpetual astonishment at the blatant anti-Semitism and Israel-hatred I have witnessed on the 'polite (*sic*) dinner-party circuit'. At a London tea party I attended after the assassination of Yitzhak Rabin, a frail 90-year-old lashed out at me when I said I had been to Rabin's grave at Mount Herzl, snarling: 'That Rabin and all of those Jewish terrorists should have been executed in 1947.'

As so many Israel boycotters shrilly proclaim, criticism of Israel is not anti-Semitism. They use as their protective shield the fact that many prominent Anglo-Jews, including the playwright Harold Pinter, deplore every breath Israel takes. The puce-faced British journalists who lambasted me could barely contain their hatred of everything I am. If that is not anti-Semitism, I do not know what is. And don't tread on me.

CHAPTER SIXTEEN

WHEN ALL ELSE FAILS, BLAME THE JEWISH LOBBY!

Anti-Americanism always has a Jewish–Israel quotient. Sitting in the Green Room of a Soho television studio before going on the air, I was verbally assaulted by a young man also waiting to be on the broadcast. As soon as he saw my American flag pin, he was in overdrive, launching a tirade about the Jewish lobby forcing President Bush to go to war against Iraq. This and the following chapter provide in some detail the panorama of views in Britain about the Israeli–American policy connection.

DIARY: 30 JUNE 2007

If one blinked on Thursday night, 28 June 2007, one would have missed a comment by Sir Menzies Campbell, leader of the British Liberal Democrat party, on the BBC television programme *Question Time*. Panellist Michael Howard MP, a Tory, was discussing with considerable dignity the benefits of Tony Blair being appointed Middle East envoy by the 'Quartet' nations. Sir Menzies interrupted, stating: 'You ignore the extent to which the pro-Israeli lobby has an enormous influence in Washington.'

What is laughable about the British fixation on the 'Jewish' or 'Zionist' lobby is that the – heavily Democrat – Jewish contingent in the House of Representatives and the Senate is overwhelmingly liberal. In 2007, they would be more inclined to seek the impeachment of George Bush than to be hammering away at the White House to bolster Israel.

Although the 'Jewish vote' might be important in New York and California, it seems inconceivable that a 'cabal of Jews' (in the words of British MP Tam Dalyell in *Vanity Fair*) would command such immense influence over American policy. Tom Lantos of California is not exactly a Zionist neoconservative in the pocket of the Christian Right; he accompanied House Speaker Nancy Pelosi on her trip to the Middle East, where she had talks with President Assad. The only Jewish member of the Senate who could be construed as a staunch Bush supporter is Norm Colman.

And then there is Bernie Sanders! Notwithstanding the image projected in the British media of a fierce Zionist neocon conspiracy driving American policy, the socialist senator from Vermont is about as non-right-wing as one could find; after his decades in Congress, we can safely assume that he is not planning to be hopping on and off airplanes to and from Tel Aviv. Frankly, it is astonishing to hear the fictions generated by British politicians and highly paid media pundits about the 'Jewish lobby' and the 'Zionist cabal' ruling America; one might expect them to have done even some rudimentary homework about these Jewish congressional Zio-demons.

George Bush has never had a close Jewish cabinet secretary, and his confidante is Condoleezza Rice, not a Zionist agitator. Although Jewish Joshua Bolten is chief of staff, listening to the BBC one would think the White House is overrun with zealous and aggressive Zionists bullying the administration night and day.

Just as *Guardian* readers love to refer to the 'religious fundamentalism' of Israel (for those who are not in the know, 85 per cent of Israelis would rather watch paint dry than attend synagogue), they harbour an obsessive fantasy, aired at every opportunity on television and radio, that Jews basically control every move America makes. It is galling beyond belief to a majority of Britons that America supports Israel, which is viewed as a pariah state committing genocide against the Palestinians and extending the 'apartheid wall'. This is not an exaggeration: whenever I socialize, I am bombarded with these standard mantras about Israel and the Jews – they control world affairs through their undue influence in Washington and Downing Street, and they are a cruel, fanatically religious, expansionist state. (I always love the faces on said angry folks when I remind them that expansionist Israel is so small that soon there will not be enough space to bury their dead.)

No matter how hard one may try, it is an impossibility to convince the dinner-party set that Israel and Jews have very little influence on the daily workings of the Bush administration. Jewish influence is regarded as a negative factor in government by an increasing number of high-profile British commentators and politicians.

Putting aside political influence and Washington lobbying (of which, no doubt, there is a considerable amount), one of the truly remarkable influences Jews have had on American life is their omnipresence in science, the arts and entertainment. They have had a tremendous impact on American life in every way, but frankly the anger and hostility I see on the faces of many people when Jews are discussed is something I find disturbing.

As we hear about terrorist car bomb incidents in the United Kingdom in July 2007, I cannot help being amused by a thought: Israel being approached for help in tracking down the would-be perpetrators of what MI5 predicts will be a 'sustained series of attacks on mainland Britain'.

Eric McDonald, the Birmingham branch secretary of the latest British trade union to vote for a boycott of Israel, the 800,000-member Transport and General Workers' Union, has told the *Jewish Chronicle* (29 June 2007 issue) that he has never been to Israel but considers its actions Nazi-like and typical of a 'fundamentalist religious state'.

Inasmuch as every trade union in the British Isles seems to be boycotting Israel, should said workers need advice and aid from the pariah state on new terror threats to their businesses, will Israel help?

Perhaps the Jewish state will turn around and say 'no', and suggest that Britain seek help from Robert Mugabe on how to clamp down on internal troublemakers.

After all, there are no boycotts against his benighted country from any British trade unions.

But then again, there aren't a lot of Jews in Zimbabwe.

CHAPTER SEVENTEEN

THE *INDEPENDENT*'S SHAMEFUL 'JEWISH AMERICAN FLAG'

DIARY: 4 MAY 2006

Following on from the theme of the 'Jewish lobby' spoiling things for the whole world, the relentless animosity shown by the British print media towards Israel goes hand in hand with America-hatred.

Robert Fisk (*Independent*, 27 April 2006) has written a long and passionate defence of the Harvard academics John Mearsheimer and Stephen Walt, whose major paper about the influence of the 'Israel lobby' on American policy has angered both Jewish and non-Jewish recipients worldwide. The paper has caused a storm of controversy. Many learned academics and policy thinkers have, in turn, written responses to Walt and Mearsheimer, inspiring the two scholars and their defenders to suggest that any criticism of Israel is regarded as anti-Semitism. Even Noam Chomsky, no fan of Israel, has pointed out that the world of corporate business drives American policy, not necessarily Zionist lobbyists.

It must be noted here that the *Independent* newspaper has accompanied Robert Fisk's article with a painting of the Stars and Stripes with fifty Jewish stars instead of the traditional ones. This is a pernicious image, but the *Independent* seems unconcerned, despite a thundering complaint from the British Board of Deputies, that such imagery is reminiscent of the literature of neo-Nazis and of other bigoted hate groups. At the end of the piece, the *Independent* also attaches an outrageously distorted 'time-line' of supposed Jewish history.

Inasmuch as Benny Morris has written a long treatise in response to Walt and Mearsheimer, refuting many of the accusations made in the Harvard monograph, I will not attempt to pick it apart. I will, however, point out that Fisk makes the usual accusations that pepper the British press on an almost daily basis: if you dare criticize Israel, you are labelled an anti-Semite. Well, Mr Fisk, if your article is illustrated with a symbol used by Nazis, is that any wonder? Fisk says the *Wall Street Journal* is 'ever Israel's friend'. Really? I read it every day and see no such favouritism. Fisk says that the American media are gutless and biased. I watch the NBC, ABC and CBS news every night and rarely hear Israel mentioned by the 100 per cent Christian anchormen and women.

If, as Fisk, Walt and Mearsheimer suggest, Israeli and Jewish lobbyists get away with anything, why are the Jewish Larry Franklin and Jack Abramoff going to jail? If Jews have such a stranglehold on the Bush administration, why is Scooter Libby the only one indicted in the Valerie Plame affair and why has Bush never had a senior Jewish cabinet member? Fisk also asserts, in defence of the Harvard paper, that neoconservatives are gaining strength in the USA. Since when? Perle, Feith and Wolfowitz are out of the Defense Department. The Bush administration has a 32 per cent approval rating. Neocons like Fukuyama are running around like mice deserting the ship.

Fisk is infuriated about the British play *The Death of Rachel Corrie* being pulled from the New York stage. I would be happy to see the play run its course in the USA when a British theatre company also devises a play about the innumerable Jewish Rachels and Avis who have died in endless, endless wars and terror attacks since 1948.

What I would like to do is approach the 'Israel lobby drives American policy' theme from an entirely different perspective. I have no idea how much exposure Messrs Walt and Mearsheimer had to ordinary Jews in their growing-up years in the USA, but their distorted idea of the influence of Zionist lobbyists indicates they have a worrying attitude of suspicion towards what is a tiny percentage of the true number of lobbyists populating K Street. I would wager that Israel lobbyists make up a small percentage of the masses of pharmaceutical, oil, insurance, retail, underwriting, manufacturing and agricultural lobbying that goes on every day of the Congressional year.

As for Robert Fisk's experience of Jewish culture, hospitality, philanthropic generosity and achievement in every field of endeavour – that is unknown; what one does know about him is that he has spent most of his life in places like Beirut and Damascus, where he is not going to discover what it is that makes Jews so popular and so much a part of US national cultural life.

What does this have to do with accusations of the 'Israel lobby driving American foreign policy'? I do not believe Jews and Zionists drive American policy. If they did, Joe Lieberman would have taken Al Gore to a landslide win in 2000. Conversely, if Israel is admired by a majority of Americans, and if Jewish lobbyists do get a favourable reception in Washington, it is because Jews have made such a staggeringly positive contribution to the American national story since the days of the very first colonists.

Jewish people have mixed well and integrated in every aspect of American society. They are liked. When I was a teenager, the course of study in the Philadelphia school system required all young people to see the shattering *Night and Fog* Holocaust film by Alain Resnais. I have never met an American Jew who wants Palestinians to suffer. But the difference between the way the Jewish story is told in the United States and the way it is told elsewhere is that in the USA, Jews are never, ever accused of 'using the Holocaust to take Palestinian lands because of Nazi crimes committed a continent away'.

I have no Holocaust victims in my immediate family, but when I hear the British media accusing those tortured, starving survivors of Hitler's extermination camps of 'brutally stealing Arab lands' and 'committing genocide and apartheid in Palestine', I am speechless with hurt and rage. This is the flip side of 'don't tread on me'.

If Jews are so violent and will steal land and commit genocide, why are they not doing so in the many other countries where they live? When I visited a prison in the north-east of England holding just under a thousand men, one of my interfaith group asked one of the three chaplains why there was no resident rabbi. He replied that there was no need, as there were no Jewish prisoners. One of our group, a Christian, said 'Jews don't commit violent crime'. The way the birth of Israel is taught outside the USA suggests that huge brigades of angry, robust Jews arrived in Palestine and set about murdering willy-nilly. What is never taught is the relentless aggression and hatred that emanated from the Arab nations – nations that could have welcomed the Jews with open arms and to this day resolutely refuse to accept a non-Muslim presence in their giant territory.

And if we look at it another way, what the dickens is wrong with supporting a thriving, workaholic, culturally magical Israel? When relief money comes into Israel from the many Jewish charities, it goes to hospitals and libraries and ballet companies. Jewish charities have also helped countless non-Jews across the globe. Where have the billions sent to the Palestinians gone in recent decades? How do the thousands of marching, armed Palestinians afford those glamorous green bandanas, leather jackets and combat trousers and boots if they are starving? Somewhere they have a 'lobby', too. Where is the condemnation of that lobby?

In Woody Allen's *Radio Days*, the lead character is seen holding up a Blue Box to raise pennies for a Jewish national homeland in Palestine. How many Jewish children held these little tin boxes in the hope of a homeland being established with no malice intended towards the Arabs? Why is it that this cherished hope is such anathema to the non-Jewish British media? Yes, Israel has fought bloody wars and is no more an angel than any other nation; but what is it about Jewish aspirations that so angers British writers when there are other countries in the world requiring media attention?

Only when I came to Britain as a very young woman did I ever hear anyone refer to Israel as a terrorist state. If ever a young woman with immense pride in her heritage felt trodden on, that was the moment. (You may ask, 'So why did you not now go home?' Good question. I think I felt I had a mission to enlighten hostile Britons to the fact that people with Jewish blood are not all 'terrorists'.) It is unacceptable that British people continue to use the incidents of the tragic lynching of two of their soldiers and the bombing of the King David Hotel 60 years ago to totally repudiate the miracle of the Jewish state. It diminishes one's opinion of Britons that they can obsess about a tiny minority of Israeli Jews in the Stern Gang and Irgun, who were a small part of the birth of Israel.

Had the Palestinians larger-than-life leaders like Theodor Herzl, Chaim Weizmann, David ben-Gurion, Golda Meir or Yitzhak Rabin – or for that matter Menachem Begin, who went from right-winger to peacemaker embracing the president of Egypt – they might develop a state as awesome as Israel.

It is time for Great Britain and its many media pundits to understand what Israel means to Jews born after the Holocaust; to the dwindling number of survivors still walking about with a Nazi tattoo on their withered arms; to every thoughtful person across the globe who keeps in the back of their mind that another *Shoah* could unfold; and that the Jewish state would be the only haven in the world for the remainder of world Jewry.

It is time for those – including Professors Mearsheimer and Walt and Jimmy Carter – who have never experienced being abused and ridiculed from childhood for adhering to one of the oldest and most civilized faiths humankind has ever generated to stop writing hurtful diatribes about 'Jewish terrorism' and instead pay heed to the grave dangers the world faces from the medieval, violent and turbulent regimes that degrade women, that cut off tongues and hands for minor misdemeanours, and that threaten the demise of all of us.

CHAPTER EIGHTEEN

'THAT VILE EXPANSIONIST LITTLE NATION' AND 'THAT VILE IMPERIALIST SUPERPOWER'!

MY NEW YEAR GREETING TO MARGARET DRABBLE, 2005

The eminent British novelist Margaret Drabble wrote an article in the *Daily Telegraph* entitled 'I Loathe America and What it Has Done to the Rest of the World' (8 May 2003). If you think the title is scary enough, the text of her piece is even worse.

Now, let me explain a few things. Technically, Margaret is a fellow Brit and fellow novelist. I, too, am a published hardback fiction writer and I am also a British citizen. I have lived most of my life in England and feel culturally close to the island race and to our national traditions, such as the Glorious Twelfth, the appearance of the new Beaujolais, the onset of the cricket season, Wimbledon and Bonfire Night.

So it may seem odd to the reader that Margaret's article provided the impetus for my alarm at the direction in which British society was going, and for the vague feeling that I might wish to live elsewhere. After all, in two world wars Americans sacrificed their lives to rescue Europe from its seemingly interminable internecine wars. However, a distinguished writer felt no compunction about describing the Yanks as loathsome. I was reacting more as an affronted Brit than as an insulted American; although I spent my formative years in the USA, my psyche is deeply embedded with the sensibilities of a Briton.

What so enraged me about the article was the novelist's condemnation of things American: she detests 'Disneyfication ...Coca Cola...burgers...sentimental and violent Hollywood movies that tell lies about history'. Not only does she hate these things, but 'my anti-Americanism has become almost uncontrollable...it has possessed me like a disease...rises up in my throat like acid reflux, that fashionable American sickness...I now loathe the United States.'

You may ask, what does it matter what an angry British lady thinks about the USA? The trouble is that people like me, who are proud citizens of Great Britain but who still have American accents, are on the receiving end of this vitriol to such an extent these days that it has made business and social life almost impossible to conduct. This anti-American venom started before Bush the younger. I remember being at the receiving end of a stream of abuse about 'American genocides and cultural destruction of the world' from a crowd of people at a human rights conference in St John's Wood when Bill Clinton was still in office.

The irony of it all is that Drabble's article was written long before the revelations of the Abu Ghraib prison abuses. She goes into a paroxysm of rage about the custom of putting a cartoon character and nickname on the side of fighter and bomber aircraft, as if this is an atrocity curious to Americans. Having written about the women transport pilots of the Second World War, but being too young to have lived in that era, I was astonished that Drabble, who is considerably senior to me, did not know that pilots have put such images on their aircraft since the very first men took to the air in the First World War. She refers to an unfortunate report on CNN suggesting that the people of Vietnam are speaking 'the language of Shakespeare' as 'this squalid piece of revisionism'. I would like to remind Margaret Drabble that the two most reviled revisionists of the past 50 years – the Dowager Lady Birdwood and David Irving – were not Americans but our fellow Britons.

Drabble goes through the usual laundry list of atrocities committed in the name of American democracy, as if Great Britain has exercised model behaviour through our many centuries of bloody history – as chronicled by the aforementioned Mr Shakespeare. Does she remember the atrocious massacre at Amritsar, overseen by our very own British General Dyer?

Does she know that the very first blood libel against the Jews occurred in England? That the first expulsion of Jews in European history (shamefully, they were not let back in until the time of Cromwell) and the York massacre happened in gentle Merrie Olde?

Drabble brings up the issues of Guantanamo and of capital punishment in the United States. She adds that the British army is better trained than the Yanks. (This is another mantra we US-born expatriates are sick of hearing: the words 'yellow', 'cowards' and 'incompetent' are used by countless friends on the London dinner-party circuit to describe American GIs. If these fighting men are so useless, why are Brits not speaking Japanese or German?)

If one blinks, one will miss a throwaway line in her long list of grievances: that the world has stopped noticing when suicide bombers are referred to as 'cowards'. What would you like to call them, Miss Drabble? Heroic Jew-and-Yank-killers? Brave martyrs confronting the worldwide Zionist scourge?

At the end of her 2003 diatribe, Drabble is generous enough to acknowledge that there is 'another America' – not the one she says is consumed by 'American imperialism, American infantilism, and American triumphalism about victories it didn't even win'. It is nice of her to do this.

Now that I have spent some time in the United States – after a pause of nearly 11 years – I can say to Margaret Drabble that wherever I went, from remote Vermont villages to rural Virginia to central Washington or Manhattan, I met only thoughtful and articulate people with generous hearts and an extraordinary amount of unconditional love for the Mother Country.

That is where I take issue with Margaret Drabble and with the long stream of people who, for the past few years, have felt it necessary to rant at me about the horrible country that spawned me: what the hell right do Brits have to spew forth endless streams of bile about the United States of America? Where did most of our original settlers spring from? Where did instruments of torture and the stocks – not to mention the gallows – enjoy widespread use as recently as the 19th century? Where did slavery flourish? Except for Winston Churchill, when in recent European history have men as remarkable as Thomas Jefferson, the genius Ben Franklin, John Adams or Alexander Hamilton emerged and come together to inspire the rest of the world, as they did at the 1776 Miracle in Philadelphia, my home town? When has the United States spawned a Hitler, Stalin or Pol Pot?

Drabble concludes that she 'hates feeling this hatred'. What on earth would make anyone feel hatred towards the charming, generous and gentle 'folks' I met across the 11 states I visited? Yes, there are millions who hate the Bush administration. But I have a serious problem with my fellow Britons who, over the past few years, have been filling newspaper columns and my own private breathing space with voluminous lists of 'hatreds' towards the USA.

Drabble refers to the Orwellian imagery of 'a boot stamping on a human face'. Yes, this happened at Abu Ghraib and it is shameful. But to have 'almost uncontrollable' loathing of Americans is uncharitable and frankly insulting to Britain's greatest and most energetic ally.

If there is one virtue in Margaret Drabble's 'I Loathe America' article, it is that she inspired me to make the effort to journey across the ocean to find loathsome, beer-guzzling, violent and vulgar Americans baying for the blood of the rest of the world's peoples. What I found were immaculate cities and hard-working people of all races and creeds, who rise with the sun and uncomplainingly get just two weeks' holiday the whole year. These are people who stay cheerful from dawn to dusk and will man a call centre in the wee hours with enthusiasm and immense ability. (Incidentally, whilst in the USA, I did not have to spell my name and address four times running when contacting a call centre, as I have got so used to doing when ringing a British call centre.)

Where are these dumb Yanks, then? Wherever I ventured in Washington, Philadelphia and New York, I encountered staggeringly forthcoming citizens who, seeing me hobbling on a stick, even at the height of the rush hour, would bend over backwards to help me out. These are people who love family, who gather for prayer on Sundays (Jews on Saturdays), and who celebrate Thanksgiving whatever their ethnic heritage. In the USA I had to get used again to being called 'Ma'am' and to addressing men in authority as 'Sir'. 'Thank you' and 'I apologize' are *de rigueur*, and I was never mown down by a car driver (the pedestrian has right of way and drivers observe this); nor was I on the receiving end of the obscene road rage and abuse to which I have become resigned in central London.

I was once informed at a very posh dinner party in London, by no less than an Oxford Don, that it is 'such a pity America has achieved so little in devising anything original and enduring'. To this man, I rattled off my standard list yet again: Mark Twain, Edgar Allen Poe, Eugene O'Neill, Tennessee Williams, Arthur Miller, Margaret Mead, Ernest Hemingway, Norman Mailer, Leonard Bernstein, Jackson Pollock, Aaron Copland, jazz, ragtime, the Blues, Soul and on and on until he turned rather pale. Whenever I am in the United States, I cry every night that I am unable to find the time to attend the stunning plethora of cultural events in the wastelands he seems to believe are Washington, Philadelphia, Chicago, Boston, Los Angeles and New York. If one regards the Mayo Clinic, NASA, Microsoft, Apple, Boeing, the Centers for Disease Control, and even Ben Franklin's bifocals and Jonas Salk's polio vaccine as 'original' achievements that 'endure', then I think I win the argument.

Shortly after I returned from the USA, an elderly neighbour in London stopped me on our road in St John's Wood to inform me that 'your country' (he meant the USA, even though people in my street know I am a British citizen) 'is by far the most appalling influence on every aspect of the world'. I told him that I had just been to the United States for the first time in nearly 11 years and that I would give a black eye to anyone who criticized the Americans. He turned puce and said: 'I am terribly sorry, but there isn't anything about the United States that is to be admired. Wherever we go we are swamped by it and it is a horrifying thing to witness.' I could not change his view, but I refrained from giving him a black eye.

It is time anti-Americanism came to an end. Bush and his colleagues should not be a part of the equation when 'America' is being assessed. It is not loathsome, Miss Drabble. It is a great and awesome place. It is filled with fine and worthy people, whose ancestors and recently arrived families have built a magnificent and bustling universe that envelops visitors with its warmth and bounty.

When loathsome Americans buy your books, Miss Drabble, do you send the royalties back? I doubt it.

God Bless America. And, in the words of the colonial flag: 'Don't tread on me.'

CHAPTER NINETEEN

SIR DAVID HARE AND RUMSFELD

In September 2004, I attended the first preview of Sir David Hare's new play, *Stuff Happens*, directed by Nicholas Hytner at the Olivier Theatre in London's National Theatre complex.

Because I had been glued to Rumsfeld's utterly compelling and supremely witty press briefings for the past three years, I was expecting a play that possessed, at the very least, some of Rummy's humour. Alas, this was about as funny as a wake. Hare's one-man show, *Via Dolorosa*, about the Israeli-Palestinian conflict, was filled with rich irony and humour at the expense of both sides and was so compelling that I saw it twice.

Not so with *Stuff Happens*. Aside from my dismay that a writing and directing team as eminent as Hare and Hytner could get wrong some basic facts, like Rumsfeld's *alma mater* (according to the script, he attended the University of Chicago, when, in fact, he attended Princeton with distinction), the play unfolds like an evening around a dinner table, with angry and irrational left-wingers fixating on the evils of the Project for a New American Century (PNAC). (I happen to believe that PNAC was astonishingly prescient in 1998, when its leadership warned Bill Clinton of the threat of international terrorism emanating from the dictatorships of the Middle East. In that same year the US embassies in Kenya and Tanzania were blown up by al-Qaeda.) One of the traits of the Left is an irrational hatred of people like Cheney, Rumsfeld and Rice. In fact, these people (as reactionary as they may be in the eyes of many) have been students of world affairs and terrorism for decades and are – at least in the eyes of others – not the personification of evil the Left makes them out to be. How many large terror attacks have there been on the US mainland since 2001?

What disappointed me about *Stuff Happens* was that I had expected better from a man as sophisticated as David Hare, whose perception of human nature should have risen above the usual 'they are all baddies!' rhetoric from the *Independent* and *Guardian*. There were far too many long transcripts of meetings amongst Powell, Tenet, Rumsfeld, Bush and Rice, some of which are actually rather dated. The ultimate irony was that the energetic – even thoughtful – figure of Bush (portrayed by Alex Jennings) and the fiery figure of Colin Powell (Joe Morton) are so appealing that one wondered why anyone would have wanted Kerry as a replacement!

Aside from the fact that Dermot Crowley's interpretation was not at all vintage Rummy, it seemed unlikely that the defence secretary would speak like a Christian evangelist. In fact, Rumsfeld was a better entertainer than Crowley if one ever bothered to watch one of his vintage briefings. Emphasis was laid on his love for defence contractors; but in reality, Rumsfeld made a shrewd point of working only in pharma (low-cost AIDS drug development when he was head of Gilead Sciences) and fibre optics/broadband in the event that he was ever appointed defence secretary again (after having served under Gerry Ford). Incidentally, Rummy, unlike Dubya, did not say 'Eye rack' or 'Eye ran'. Notwithstanding all of this, the iconic picture of Rumsfeld shaking hands with Saddam in 1983 will, like the photograph of Lynndie England holding an Iraqi prisoner on a leash, speak for themselves for eternity in the eyes of his critics.

As an American, I worry about the line: 'After 9/11 America changed. It just became stupider.' Lest we forget, the USA has given the world a few small things – like NASA, Microsoft and Boeing, not to mention Jonas Salk and Albert Sabin, etc., etc. Sir David, the USA is not a stupid country. And even if there are a few nincompoops, no one asked the 9,370 GIs who died at Omaha Beach, the 10,000 slain in the Hertgen Forest or the 9,000 buried or listed as missing at Madingley Cemetery in Cambridge what their IQs were.

Had I been a 'swing voter' Republican veering towards John Kerry in 2004, *Stuff Happens* would not have changed my viewpoint. The occasional swipes at Ariel Sharon were tiresome. The polemic about 'the Zionists' by an angry and humourless Palestinian woman at the opening of Act Two, to an audience already indoctrinated by the BBC, *Independent* and *Guardian* about the 100 per cent virtuous Islamic 'warriors' and the 100 per cent appalling 'Zionist imperialists', rolled off me without effect, as news of hundreds of children murdered by Islamic 'warriors' in Russia reached me that evening.

What was so bitterly disappointing about this much-hyped play was that Hare had an opportunity to bring to life the much-hated figures of the Iraq War, but instead reinforced the stereotypes generated in the world of Michael Moore. For example, a portly Caucasian actor walks onstage as 'Yo-Yo Ma' (one of the weirder bits of casting I have seen in recent years) and had a totally inscrutable discussion with Dr Rice. Unless one is a Washington insider, one would not know that Yo-Yo Ma was accompanied on the cello by the classical pianist Condi Rice at a Kennedy Center recital. Had anyone involved in this production bothered to learn something about these people, they would have discovered that they have complex personal and intellectual lives. (Is it not fascinating that Paul Wolfowitz's lady is reputedly a Muslim?) That would have made some real theatre. If British network television can air a film about the 'human side' of the 9/11 hijackers, why can't we also see the human side of the Bushies?

CHAPTER TWENTY

HAROLD PINTER AND HIS 'AMERICA OBSESSION'

'Israel has these weapons and has used them.'

'The USA is intent on controlling the world and the world's resources.'

'Bush is on a par with Saddam.'

'Israel's injustice to the Palestinians is an outrage.'

Oh, here we go again. Is this a string of quotes from an Arab newspaper? No, you guessed: it is the litany of an otherwise rational and brilliant man – but, of course, he is British and left-wing. Readers may think I spend an inordinate amount of time complaining about the British – that they (left-wing or right-wing) hate Israel and that they (left-wing) hate the USA. However, when one watches prominent Americans – be they in the arts or politics – for the most part, even if they are critical of their own country and of Israel, they do not lash out against their European allies, whose collective, blood-curdling history far outstrips that of the USA.

In July 2001, in New York, a large number of people turned out for a Harold Pinter Festival. He was feted and wined and dined, and enormous amounts of money were raised to pay for a vast re-staging of his plays. The generosity of those Americans, who had spent years planning this event, was rewarded by Harold Pinter in his rhetoric on his return to Britain. His criticism of the United States has been a long-term affair.

On 26 October 2002, on BBC television's *Newsnight*, Pinter was charm itself until the interviewer, Jeremy Paxman, brought the conversation around to politics. The playwright said that he was ashamed to be British, because the present Labour government seemed to be a kind of clone of the Conservatives – something with which many of us would not disagree – but then he added that his real shame and disgust came from Britain's subservience to the United States.

Because I reject the concept of 'subservience' as it relates to the US–British alliance, I will not ask: 'Would Mr Pinter like Britain to be subservient to Rwanda or to Libya instead?' However, I will ask Mr Pinter if he would like the British government to form an alliance with, say, Burundi or Colombia?

Pinter took off like a 747, describing President George W. Bush as the world's worst leader with weapons of mass destruction (well, some might agree), but he then said that Bush was on a par with Saddam Hussein. Jeremy Paxman, who is not known for defending the honour of George W. Bush, was nonetheless incredulous. His face contorted, Paxman retorted: 'George Bush doesn't torture people and kill his own family!' To which Pinter responded: 'Look, there is a vast Gulag going on in America.' (If Mr Pinter is so concerned about human rights in the United States, why did he accept the hospitality of scores of Americans, who spent a fortune on feting him in 2001?)

Pinter elaborated: he claimed that there are 2 million people in jails across America, kept in this giant Gulag, characterized by brutal, ruthless and horrific imprisonments, for what in many cases are minor offences. Paxman, again not known as a defender of the American prison system, countered that at least the prisoners of whom Pinter spoke had received due process of law.

Pinter went on to assert that the one situation that outraged him above all else was the Israeli 'injustice to the Palestinians', which is an issue that exercises many. But he then said, in the context of George W. Bush's pursuit of Saddam and his weapons of mass destruction, that Israel possesses these weapons 'and has used them'.

If anyone reading this can provide me with proof that Israel has used chemical, biological or nuclear weapons against anyone, I would be interested to know about it.

Harold Pinter, who at this stage in the Paxman interview had gone into orbit, literally shook with rage as he thundered that 'the United States of America is intent on controlling the world and the world's resources'. This is another mantra I, as an American, find mystifying, even after some 30 years of living in Europe.

The Pinter interview ended with his telling Paxman that we 'must understand' terrorism. He regards the present American administration as 'hysterical' and arrogant, and this is a great danger to the rest of us. (I would be hysterical, too, if 19 Arab guests in my country had taken hundreds of innocent air passengers hostage and then flown them to their deaths, taking with them more innocent people at their places of work.)

Frankly, I am sick to death of hearing Europeans berating the USA as if it were a rogue state intent on annihilating the rest of humanity. This viewpoint is a sick one, and represents a paucity of spirit as we try to form an alliance amongst enlightened western cultures to combat the repressive, homophobic and misogynist regimes of so many Third World countries.

On only one point did I agree with Harold Pinter: he complained that (now former) Prime Minister Tony Blair never discussed anything with Parliament or with the people. In many columns I have praised the excellent weekly press conferences by the Pentagon and White House. Some of us are old enough to remember the superb press conferences held by President John Kennedy and, more recently, by President Clinton. It is lamentable that British leaders do not conduct these enlightening and frequent briefings, and on this point Pinter was correct.

It is of note that BBC's *Arena* programme broadcast a three-hour special on 27 October 2002 on the life and work of Harold Pinter. I am prepared to register here that it is of great pride to the Jewish people that such a remarkable, indeed legendary, playwright has made so profound an impact on several generations of theatregoers and students of drama, and in 2006 won the Nobel Prize for Literature. What a pity he is so filled with verbal bile against two cultured democracies that present his work year in and year out.

In 2003, Pinter, still recovering from the ravages of cancer, granted an interview to Fiona Maddocks of the *Evening Standard* ('Pinter's War Against Bush', 5 June 2003). She noted that he had appeared in Turin in November 2002 to receive an honorary degree, but had departed from his prepared notes to launch into a discourse about the United States. Please note that this was pre-Iraq War. He decried the '...nightmare of American hysteria, ignorance, arrogance, stupidity and belligerence: the most powerful nation the world has ever known effectively waging war against the rest of the world'. (Interestingly enough, in the last week of November 2007, Archbishop of Canterbury Rowan Williams levelled virtually the exact string of accusations against the United States.) Pinter then provided the Italian crowd with an inventory of atrocities in Latin America, Cambodia and Vietnam, and said any action in Iraq would be premeditated murder. Maddocks described the crowd: a standing ovation from academics and students, and, she suggests, mortar boards thrown into the air in exultation.

Maddocks illustrates Pinter's long-held hatred of America with his definition of US policy on the Balkans intervention: 'Kiss my arse or I'll kick your head in.' Pinter tells her: 'Some people would say I have an unnatural obsession [against America]...Murder is murder. Poor old God is tarnished with blood.' Maddocks suggests that he has been a victim of repression because of the problems publishing his fiercely anti-American works, but in a post-9/11 world one somehow feels a work castigating the USA might not sell magazines. His post-1991 Gulf War poem 'American Football', which Maddocks says he calls his 'obscene poem about obscene facts', was rejected, she reports, by the *London Review of Books*, the *Guardian*, the *Observer* and the *Independent* – but it did appear in the *Socialist*.

In Europe, his screed *War* has been accepted with glee by Italy, France, Portugal, Greece and Spain, and he says he walks around Paris shouting '*Vive la France!*' The rampant anti-Americanism in Europe fits in with his mindset, and he says the French despise Britain's 'lick-spittling subservience [to America]' and find it criminal. Maddocks ends her interview with the great man by sharing a joke with him about George Bush's decision to stop reading Proust as a personal boycott of the French, and he laughs long and hard.

Now, as I write this in 2007, what I find deplorable is Pinter's continued public loathing of the United States: a country that has provided him with millions of dollars in theatre takings and that has honoured him with recognition – indeed adoration – that ties in with the traditional Anglophilia of America. His suggestion that the United States wishes to dominate the world is absurd. (Only more absurd was the accusation hurled at me by a former work associate the day after the Bali bombing – that the CIA had masterminded the atrocity to draw the world into the war on terror.) Pinter's assertion that Americans wish to control the world's resources is also absurd: had they wished to do so they could have 'got there' a long time ago.

On the same day that the Pinter interview was aired on the BBC, CNN International/Europe aired a major special about American Defense Secretary Donald Rumsfeld. He was challenged with the same accusation by an interviewer – isn't America trying to rule the world? To which he replied:

> I am an American; I live here and I know the American people...The United States isn't interested in the rest of the world in terms of taking anyone's real estate or changing anyone's views on their religion. That is utter nonsense. The United States was not a colonial power – WE didn't go in and occupy Africa and other parts of the globe. We are a nation that recognizes how closely linked we are with the rest of the world from an economic standpoint. We recognize that in Western Europe in particular our views and our values and our political values are very similar.

How refreshing it would have been to have heard Harold Pinter, whose plays are a breathtaking revelation, show a degree of *seychel* about America and Israel, two nations that adore his work and that are havens of free expression and vigorous cultural activity.

How far would Harold Pinter have got had he been a Jew born in Syria or Libya? And how far did the Jewish writer Daniel Pearl get venturing into the streets of Pakistan?

Other theatrical notables have verbally demolished the United States when given an opportunity; an American friend who lived in London for 28 years and eventually got tired of being told 'you still have your accent!' recalls an evening with actor Edward Petherbridge, who, according to her, spent a considerable amount of time criticizing the USA, even though his audience was full of well-meaning, adoring American tourists.

In the *Evening Standard* of 4 October 2006, the British actor Alan Cumming, who has made his home in the United States since 1998 and who has reaped many riches from adoring audiences there – not to mention being given the right to work – rips into the president. He describes Bush as a fascist. He observes: 'In America, hatred is being used as a political tool again.' He actually compares the world of *Bent*, the play in which he is appearing, and which deals with the Nazi incarceration of homosexuals in concentration camps, to America. It is a land of 'tyranny', and he thinks he is living under tyranny 'of various kinds'. He asserts that everybody is scared and that Bush fits all the tenets of fascism, having 'whipped up hatred over gay marriage and abortion. There was a huge hike in gay-bashings.'

Perhaps Alan Cumming, who has benefited from American adulation and even a line in cosmetics, might like to trade in his Green Card and move to gay-friendly Iran?

CHAPTER TWENTY-ONE

'HOW CAN 57 MILLION PEOPLE BE SO STUPID?'

One memorable tabloid headline appeared on the front page of the *Daily Mirror* the day after George Bush was re-elected in November 2004 (some might say the *Guardian*'s interference in the Ohio election had helped him):

'HOW CAN 57 MILLION PEOPLE BE SO STUPID?'

Well, two years later, the Congress and Senate changed hands. Those dumb Yanks are not so dumb after all. In May 2005, the fiercely anti-war British electorate had a chance to oust Tony Blair but re-elected him. Did any American papers have headlines asking why the Brits are so stupid?

When I returned to the USA for further visits in 2005 and 2006, I found a populace, especially amongst American Jewry, more concerned with Evangelical Christians than with the rise of worldwide Islamic extremism. It was very hard trying to convince even those Republican friends who were vowing to vote Democrat in November 2006 that George Bush was less of a threat to world stability (despite his unfortunate friendship with the Saudi Royals) than the radicals assembling all over England in large rallies to re-establish the Caliphate. When I merely attempted to explain to Americans that Dick Cheney, Donald Rumsfeld and Bat Ye'or had got it right with their public warnings about the re-establishment of the Caliphate, I was shouted down – even by Republicans.

When this shouting starts, there is no reasoning with people who have come to believe that America is now a 'police state' and that the USA is a 'disgrace across most of the world'. My suspicion is that the World Wide Web has enabled Americans to read the mountains of liberal introspective navel-gazing in the *Independent* and the *Guardian*, and be brainwashed into believing that the huge amount of US taxpayer money ploughed into Israel is actually making the world a more dangerous place. Again, I was sternly rebuked when, on these trips, I tried to convince even Jewish Americans that the radicals in the Middle East, funded by billions from the EU and the Arab League (money that is meant for humanitarian aid but ends up clothing and arming the 100,000-plus young men regularly marching down the Gaza streets, chanting and carrying machine guns and wearing expensive leather jackets and boots), are more of a threat to stability in the region than is Israel.

I have therefore compiled an extensive collection of newspaper articles and headlines that, I believe, have contributed to the mood of America-hatred in Europe and the UK, and that have poisoned the minds of what is becoming a legion of self-hating Americans at home and abroad.

It is a wonder I can walk around my flat in London for the boxes of clippings reflecting the years of America- and Israel-bashing in the British media. Amongst those I culled for this book is an editorial by Alexander Chancellor in the *Guardian* of 28 June 2003, in which he lists the misdemeanours committed by America, the 'Big Bully' as he calls it: he says America wants to put the world to rights and therefore can't admit error and can't apologize when American soldiers kill Iraqi children or British servicemen in friendly fire accidents. (Did anyone ever ask the British Empire or Europe to apologize for centuries of countless bloody conflicts?) Chancellor concludes: 'America's perception of itself as morally superior to everyone else is a frightening reality with which we all have to come to terms.' What is he talking about? It is June, and most Americans are wondering what to do for 4 July or who will be playing in the All-Star Game. Still other Americans are attending the graduation ceremonies of their children, while the thousands of summer music, dance and theatre festivals are opening their doors.

I have yet to meet an American who wants to take over another country or who wants to dominate the world. In fact, in chapter five I have come to the conclusion that leaders trying to bring American values to far-flung regions really believe these societies want to live as they do. They don't. That is their loss. Let them stew in their 11th-century juice, I am inclined to say when I see Iraqis slaughtering each other with drills in hospital wards that they have turned into charnel houses. Does this make me a Patrick Buchanan isolationist? Maybe.

My absolute prize winner for vicious, tasteless and ill-timed anti-Americanism in the British press comes from 4 July 2002, when the *Daily Mirror* published an image of George W. Bush standing in a room filled with American flags. It had the banner headline 'MOURN ON THE FOURTH OF JULY' and was accompanied in slightly smaller text by the statement that Bush had been responsible for the deaths of more people than were killed on 9/11: 'THE USA IS NOW THE WORLD'S LEADING ROGUE STATE: John Pilger's Damning Independence Day Verdict.' Perhaps this United States is believed by some to be a rogue nation, but was this tableau necessary on the first Independence Day holiday since 9/11? If it had been the other way around, and had the United Kingdom of Great Britain and Northern Ireland been attacked, I cannot imagine even the most left-wing of American newspapers, tabloid or broadsheet, running such a front page.

Inside, John Pilger provided a double-page spread about 'America's bid to control the world' and compared President Bush's description of the Afghanistan operation as a triumph over evil with 'lauding the superiority of the German war machine in 1940 as a vindication of Nazism'. In essence, Pilger was saying that America's servicemen and women were Nazis, serving a regime akin to the Third Reich. He went on to enumerate the evils of America, from intimidating Europe to blocking the UN investigation of the Israeli attack on Jenin (no British journalist ever, ever explains that 'Jenin' happened after a Palestinian terrorist, later traced to Jenin, walked into a hotel in Israel on the First *Seder* Night and blew up a room full of Holocaust survivors about to welcome in the Passover). Pilger said that Americans were afraid to speak out as the media were censored and heavily controlled. Yes, John, and the frightened

'Third Reich' Americans then went and freely elected a Democrat Congress in November 2006 and nobody died and nobody got put into death camps by the 'Führer' George Bush.

John Pilger pretty much condemns anything and everything about America and Americans, concluding that Uncle Sam has 'blocked genuine aid, such as clean water and electricity, to the most deprived people on earth'. When Pilger tells us that the USA is increasing food subsidies by 80 per cent, he makes sure we know that this is being done to 'secure American domination of the world food grains market'.

My thoughts for John Pilger go something like this: until the early 1950s, the world was crippled by the scourge of polio. An American scientist, Jonas Salk, developed the polio vaccine. Salk personally arranged for thousands of free vaccines to be distributed around the world. Next time an American discovers a cure for MS or cancer or motor neurone disease, is John Pilger going to warn the rest of us that America seeks world domination by distributing the vaccine worldwide?

It was reported in the press after the 'rogue' front page that a major American shareholder in the Mirror Group had complained to the newspaper about its 4 July edition. I was glad to know that other Americans felt as I did. We are still raw inside and, like the British after the Blitz, know what our empire's faults are; but we would like our critics to give us time to heal. I must confess to glee when Piers Morgan was marched off the premises of the *Daily Mirror* after the debacle of his paper publishing what appeared to be dubious images of British soldiers abusing Iraqi captives.

One thing I am grateful for: when I saw that horrifying and deeply hurtful front page on 4 July 2002, it moved me to think about visiting my homeland. Thanks to John Pilger, that was the beginning of my long journey home.

* * * * *

For me, one of the most memorable magazine covers of recent years appeared on the *New Statesman*, in its 9 June 2003 issue, entitled (wait for it) 'How to Stop America'. It had a picture of George W. Bush looking at a globe, dressed in the

Hitleresque costume of the *Great Dictator* motion picture. Inside, George Monbiot chronicled the good intentions of a series of American presidents in the global arena of social and economic responsibility, but concluded that the men who govern the United States are greedy and have no interest in granting concessions to anyone. Monbiot wrote that America wanted 'unmitigated global power' and was 'prepared to destroy the institutions whose purpose it was to sustain their dominion'. He claimed the Iraq War had 'crippled the UN'. Considering that, as Donald Rumsfeld pointed out about the United Nations on 17 November 2007 in a speech to the Claremont Institute (I still think he has guts), 'Sudan is elected to the Human Rights Commission; Iran is elected vice president of the Disarmament Commission; Syria is elected vice president of the IAEA Committee and Zimbabwe is elected to the Sustainable Development Commission', the 'crippling' of the UN is a subjective concept!

Monbiot's article has a go at poor little Tuvalu (population 10,000) because it has the same number of representatives in the UN General Assembly as does India (with its 1 billion-plus population) and then bemoans the injustice of Wyoming (population 500,000) having the same number of senators as California (population 35 million). It is tough trying to get to the bottom of his theories in this long, tedious piece, but his main premise is his ideal world, in which a new world assembly would put the USA in its place. In his brave new world, a citizen of Ouagadougou would have the same say as a resident of Washington (actually, a Ouagadougan would have more, because Washingtonians, at the time of writing, still suffer taxation without representation).* His

* Washington DC does not elect senators or congressmen, though Eleanor Holmes Norton is its 'Representative at Large'. This is because it is not a State, but a District – not quite part of Virginia and not quite part of Maryland. Hundreds of thousands of Washingtonians have 'Taxation without representation' emblazoned on their car licence plates because they feel they deserve senate and congressional representation. The original saying 'Taxation without representation is tyranny' was one of the mottoes of the American War of Independence.

world parliament would recruit global public opinion in its 'struggle' with the US government and would bring to a halt the 'war-mongering, wealth-concentrating, planet-consuming world order' (translation: the mean old 'merkins) with a new world order. I wish him all the best. Perhaps Robert Mugabe could be the first secretary-general.

Next to the Monbiot article is an advertisement for a writing competition entitled 'Is the US a Rogue State?', sponsored by the Webb Memorial Trust and Foreign Policy Centre. That proposition has already become a 2003 book, *Rogue Nation* by Vernon Coleman, in which every conceivable evil any nation, people or individual could manifest is attributed to America and Americans. One of my favourite little rants of his goes like this: 'The Americans always like to claim that they have invented everything. In fact they have invented relatively little – preferring instead to steal from other countries.' Another gem from this British physician, turned maven on Americana, is that two-thirds of American graduates do not speak a second language. Can he find us a substantial clutch of British graduates that is bilingual?

Finally, Coleman comes out with a mantra I have heard at countless dinners and teas to which I have been invited over the decades: 'Modern Americans celebrate the theft of their [Native American] nation with the annual feast of Thanksgiving...they also seem incapable of understanding just how their support of Israel offends the Arabs from whom Israel seems intent to continue stealing land.'

If you can't spend lengths of time in the UK but want to learn about everything horrible, loathsome, destructive, malevolent and despicable in the world, you will learn that it all emanates from the USA. So read this Briton's book, and just begin to experience the tip of the iceberg that is anti-Americanism.

* * * * *

Headline in the *Guardian* on 3 January 2001: 'Israel Simply Has No Right to Exist' by Faisal Bodi. For good measure, here is one of his observations to greet the New Year of 2001: 'the sympathy evoked by the Holocaust was a very handy cover for Israeli atrocities'. Bodi continues to appear frequently in the British press.

* * * * *

In the *Independent* of 6 February 2001, Robert Fisk, who has always been totally obsessed with Israel, gets a huge, emblazoned large-print full-page spread, reading in capital letters as follows:

> THIS IS A PLACE OF FILTH AND BLOOD WHICH WILL FOREVER BE ASSOCIATED WITH ARIEL SHARON. IN ISRAEL TODAY, HE MAY WELL BE ELECTED PRIME MINISTER. THEN HE WILL BE MASTER OF THE MOST POWERFUL NATION IN THE MIDDLE EAST; HE WILL TRAVEL TO AMERICA, HE WILL VISIT THE WHITE HOUSE AND SHAKE HANDS WITH PRESIDENT GEORGE W BUSH. BUT FOR EVERYONE WHO STOOD IN THE SABRA AND CHATILA REFUGEE CAMPS IN BEIRUT ON 18 SEPTEMBER 1982, HIS NAME WILL BE SYNONYMOUS WITH BUTCHERY; WITH BLOATED CORPSES AND DISEMBOWELLED WOMEN AND DEAD BABIES, WITH RAPE AND PILLAGE AND MURDER...

Yes, Israel is not without blood on its hands. No, I do not believe Israel can do no wrong. But the rest of the long article is a classic Fisk diatribe about one day in the history of the Middle East that was indeed ugly and awful, but that does not by any stretch of the imagination define Israel and world Jewry, any more than My Lai or Abu Ghraib define the United States and Americans wherever they may dwell. Throughout my 32 years in Britain, I have never ceased to marvel at the seemingly endless supply of permutations Robert Fisk can conjure up to demonize Israel. Indeed, he had receptive audiences when he spoke in the United States, but my complaint about his disturbing, perpetual loathing of the tiny Jewish state is that a similar obsession about a Muslim country spread in capital letters across whole broadsheets would evoke cries of 'Islamophobia!'

* * * * *

On to another lover of Israel and America, Ken Livingstone, who wrote in the same newspaper, the *Independent*, on 21 February 2001: 'Let's not help the US in its mission to become an insatiable world power.' Right, Ken, would you like America to sink without trace?

What is so riotous about this particular article (I am so glad I am a magpie and that I save everything in boxes so voluminous that I can no longer invite anyone to dinner) is that Livingstone's topic is the absurdity of the United States thinking it will ever be attacked (he calls the concept 'eccentric') and the arrogance of American leaders who think they should have a missile shield.

In his diatribe, Ken writes about 'the hypocrisy of successive US administrations towards the Middle East' and observes: 'When Israel invaded the West Bank, the Golan Heights and East Jerusalem in 1967, the reaction of the US was to do nothing.' Excuse me, Ken, but where were you when Nasser was calling for the annihilation of Israel, and the United Nations Security Council, led by the dashing Dane, Hans Tabor, was deliberating day and night over the looming crisis that threatened the very existence of Israel? Or maybe you did not care, Ken, since in 2007 you stated that you 'would not have created an Israel...'? Ken continues: 'The United States is quite happy to stand by as Palestinians – including children – are massacred by Israeli soldiers...'

Livingstone then goes on at great length to tell the world that the United States has absolutely no right to 'tear up the international agreements on nuclear defence' and create a national missile defence system. He says: 'The US rationalisation for attempting to develop a missile shield to protect itself from attack is absurd...' Claiming that the United States is attempting to obtain absolute military superiority under the pretext that 'rogue' states could attack the mainland, Livingstone calls this possibility just plain eccentric. Yes, well, the people of New York, Washington and Shanksville, not to mention the loved ones of the dead in the buildings and on the airplanes used as human missiles on 9/11, did not see much eccentricity in the event.

Ken voices his fury that Britain is thinking of allowing the Great Satan to use its land for a missile defence facility. Heaven forbid that the USA might be allowed to protect the free world. He concludes with an impassioned plea to the British government not to conspire in the 'special relationship' and 'allow the United States to become the unassailably dominant military power on the face of the planet'.

Yes, Ken, and next time you are faced with a Hitler, the USA should keep its military might to itself, I guess.

Throughout his tenure as mayor of London, Ken has come out with some priceless comments targeting Zionists and Americans, but none can compare with his calling Robert Tuttle, Ambassador of the United States to the Court of St James, a 'chiselling little crook' (an episode that was briefly mentioned in an earlier chapter). This quite specifically refers to the refusal of the American legation, and many other embassies, to pay the congestion charge since July 2005 (*Evening Standard*, 18 October 2006). It is viewed as a municipal tax, from which some overseas representatives consider themselves exempt. As of October 2006, the USA owed over a million pounds. It was followed by the Third Worlders Angola, Nigeria, Sudan, Tanzania, South Africa, Kenya, Sierra Leone, Zimbabwe and Algeria. Frankly, if I had had anything to do with this issue, I would have said: 'We'll pay the charges we owe.' In a 21 September 2006 article in the *Evening Standard*, Ross Lydall noted that Livingstone had said he would like to crush Ambassador Tuttle's official car 'with the envoy inside'.

The mayor's outbursts about the ambassador were ugly and unnecessary and did nothing to promote Anglo-American relations. In August 2007, at the end of the horrible, wet, cold summer (is this global warming?), when the pound's inexorable rise against the US dollar stopped American tourism in its tracks, the head of English Heritage appeared on British television lamenting the atmosphere that had developed in Britain and that had put Americans off. She said it was not just the weather and the pound: a nationality had to be made to feel welcome, and she asserted that, in her view, this had not exactly been the case in recent years.

* * * * *

Even though this book is about anti-Americanism, I cannot resist including some priceless gems from the anti-Semites who abound in the pages of the *Evening Standard*. (My contention from the outset has been that anti-Americanism is inextricably linked to anti-Semitism, as the USA is seen by many in Europe as a giant Jewish-Zionist enclave, influenced at every turn by the nasty, pushy Hebrew tribe, and that British lads are dying in Iraq to keep Israel safe.) One of my all-time favourites is the rant by art critic Brian Sewell about the greedy Jews wanting another Holocaust museum.

In the 27 April 1999 *Evening Standard*, in an editorial entitled 'Why Manchester Shouldn't Have a Holocaust Museum', Sewell provides this priceless piece of revisionist history:

> Why should Manchester build a Holocaust Museum? Why should any city in Britain think itself obliged to do so? In our medieval day, we persecuted our small population of Jews, but they were not always the put-upon minority that they picture themselves to have been, for in the 19th century Jewish families entered the highest ranks of society...The Holocaust has no particular relevance here.

Yes, Dear Brian, in your medieval day of a 'small persecution' you expelled the Jews after burning them alive in York, where, to this day, Jews are not inclined to dwell. The Holocaust has no particular relevance here? Have you met any of the thousands of now-distinguished camp survivors, *Kindertransporte* and refugees who have made such a profound impact on British culture in every field of endeavour?

I recall Dr Jonathan Miller commenting in a television documentary that he had chosen to attend University College because of Jeremy Bentham's insistence that Jews be allowed to study there in the 19th century, at a time when they were spurned. (Needless to say, my ancestors were thriving in the USA and had been for several generations, unhindered by the anti-Semitic walls of prohibition here in Europe and the UK.) Some of us on this side of the ocean, Dear Brian, who have been on the receiving end of some mighty anti-Semitic verbal garbage from Europeans, would say that medieval inclinations still thrive and that the Holocaust has had no impact on Jew-hatred. It is very relevant here, and every child in Manchester and Leeds should be taken to the proposed museum.

Sewell continues: 'For how long must we remember the horror of man's inhumanity? Is it possible to recall with any genuine feeling an event that is outside both our experience and our time?' This is a telling comment. Throughout my life outside the United States, I have at times been rendered speechless with shock and hurt when thoughtless comments have been made to me about the Holocaust. When I worked for the Dutch conglomerate JE Entertainment, one of the senior executives said to me: 'I have lived in Amsterdam all my life and have no desire ever to see the house of Anne Frank.'

My fellow union members in London have demanded: 'Carol, get the Holocaust out of your system.' And when I have said it is impossible for many souls born of Jewish ancestry after 1945 to just throw off the genocide of a portion of their peoplehood, I am then told by another non-Jewish union member: 'You lot walk around with a chip on your shoulder.' The Hollywood film *Gentleman's Agreement*, in which Gregory Peck masquerades as a Jew to see how he is treated in various situations, would be worthwhile viewing for Brian

Sewell and my many charming acquaintances of the past 30 years.

Finally, Sewell delivers the clincher: 'can we not say to the Jews of Manchester that enough has been made of their Holocaust and they are too greedy for our memories?'

For those of you interested to know what happened to Brian Sewell after this nasty outburst: he continues to write every week for the *Evening Standard*.

* * * * *

A good decade ago, on 25 July 1997, the historian A. N. Wilson, who from time immemorial has had a serious problem with anything that Israel does, fulminated in the *Evening Standard* about the Swiss money revealed to have been stolen from Jewish Holocaust victims. He says the money should not be given to the descendants of these people, nor to survivors, but to the villages of the Palestinian people 'despoiled by the Israelis'. He says that, though it is customary for unclaimed money of this nature to be given to 'Jewish charities' (his quotation marks, not mine), 'surely that is just what shouldn't happen'.

Finally, Wilson provides his clincher, which is, I am afraid, an ugly mantra thrown at me so many times that I finally had to start my journey away from Blighty: '...would it not be a helpful reminder that one of the evil consequences of the Second World War was to encourage Jews themselves to behave in an aggressive and racialistic way in the Middle East?'

* * * * *

On 27 May 2002, Wilson wrote a piece entitled 'Israel's Crimes against Cultural Heritage', in which he accused the authorities in the Jewish state of causing mayhem and pillage on the West Bank. He quotes Jean-Francois Lasnier in *Art Magazine* as providing evidence of extensive damage done by Israeli forces to stone paving, mosques and Roman cisterns. What he fails to explain is that Israel had been in a violent war with the al-Aqsa Intifadah since September 2000, that many Israeli places of importance had been damaged or destroyed, and that many, many Jewish civilians had been killed in bombings and shootings. What is so loathsome about Wilson's rhetoric ('killing hundreds of innocent Palestinians and destroying their homes and workplaces, the present Israeli government was also deliberately destroying monuments and artefacts...') is that he never once mentions the miracle of preservation that has unfolded in the Holy Land since Jordan ceased holding the West Bank and since the Jews took responsibility for antiquities. Neither side is innocent in the conflict, but my assertion is that A. N. Wilson represents a mindset in Britain – one that has finally driven me to flee – that sees Jews as the eternal villains, the ones who let Jesus be crucified, who became moneylenders, who became Shylocks, and who became the monumental thieves and wreckers of society in the Goebbels–Streicher lexicon.

A. N. Wilson continued to write for the *Standard* for another 10 years, until one day in the spring of 2007 he made a sudden departure. There was a notice in the newspaper on 5 April that he had written an article on 1 September 2006, suggesting that Cherie Blair had been 'offensive and disrespectful of the Queen' and that this had not in fact been true, the matter had now been settled and damages and her legal costs met by the newspaper. It was never made clear whether A. N. Wilson left the paper in 2007 because of this incident, but I was one wounded reader who was glad to see him go.

Anti-Semitism has often gone hand in hand with anti-Americanism, as if there is a seamless interconnect between the ills of the world and these two groups. In the *Jewish Chronicle* of 8 March 2002, a good few years before I embarked on this book, it was noted that the philosopher George Steiner had concluded that Jew-hatred had reached 'unprecedented levels' in the Diaspora, and that one should always have one's bags packed. In a discussion with British Chief Rabbi Jonathan Sacks, who felt it was his duty to stay and fight rather than run away, Steiner said: 'All history is against you. The moment things change, you will be chased from here like a dog.'

Five years later, in 2007, Jews are leaving Britain in increasing numbers, and the previously decorous Chief Rabbi Sacks has said with passion that this side of the ocean is being 'consumed by a tsunami of anti-Semitism'. Interesting, too, that a member of an American expatriate group in St John's Wood said to me as far back as 2001: 'Sometimes I feel as if Americans over here are like the Jews of Germany in 1938.' On 16 April 2006 the BBC's website published a long blog item inspired by American expatriate Christian Cox, who had written in to say that the level of America-hatred in Britain felt to her like racism; she even suffered a black eye when her group was set upon in a pub. After that she went back to the USA.

George Galloway MP, whose obsession with Israel outdoes that of any British public official, met his match when the American actor John Malkovich said at a Cambridge Union Society debate in May 2002 that he would like to fight the parliamentarian to the death. I was heartened when I read this, because Malkovich is not Jewish; but he does live in France, reads the British papers and, according to the *Scotsman* newspaper (4 May 2002) deplores, as I do in this book, the biased and 'dangerous, very dangerous' ranting of Robert Fisk and Galloway in the British press about the Palestinian–Israeli conflict. Malkovich pointed out to the Cambridge students that one cannot summarize thousands of years of history in a few paragraphs because one is angry at something. What is interesting is that Galloway's response to Malkovich was the same as his to me when I wrote a piece about Jew-baiting: he threatened the actor with a writ. Arrogantly, the editor of the *Independent*, renowned for its breathtakingly biased reporting about Israel, responded to the actor's comments 'with the contempt they deserve'. Well, contempt can be a two-way street.

* * * * *

Here are some choice one-liners that do so much to boost my self-esteem in Britain:

In *ES Magazine*, 16 February 2007, Charles Finch, son of the late actor Peter and CEO of Finch and Partners, is given the lead feature space. He writes: 'Parties in Hollywood end at ten tops because Americans have nothing to say.' He 'survived' Los Angeles and New York for 13 years (poor baby), but is now back in London attending parties. I would like to suggest to Charles that the reason why parties end at 10 in places like LA and Washington is because Americans get up so damned early, work hard, take an hour for lunch, get pitifully short vacations and also discipline themselves to stay away from booze.

Having attended many boring 'dos' in London, where alcohol flows for hours and nothing is eaten (whilst I get a hypoglycaemic attack), I am used to such scintillating conversation as:

'You still have your accent!'
'What brought you here?'
'Why would you stay in England for 32 years?'
'You still have your accent!'
'What brought you here?'
'We have something here called GLYNDE-BOURNE.'
'We have something here called the GRAND NA-TIO-NAL' (as if I am deaf as well as stupid).
'You still have your accent!'
'We have something here called THE NA-TION-AL HEALTH SER-VICE!'
Finished off by:
'Oh my God, you aren't some sort of ZIONIST, are you?'

Dear Charles Finch, parties end for me at 10 in London because so many Brits have nothing to say.

* * * * *

In the *Evening Standard* of 24 September 2007, the father of a victim of the terrible 7 July London bombings got my unmitigated sympathy until he said: 'Closure might be an awful American word, but you don't get to that point.'

Why, oh why can't anyone in Britain say anything about America without it being awful, ghastly, or worse?

* * * * *

After the dreadful mass-shooting at Virginia Tech University, *The Times* runs a headline: 'America, a Nation that Believes in Violence' (20 April 2007). Joan Smith pens a long and anguished piece about the cult of the Man in the United States and the insurmountable goal these images engender in the fantasy world of inadequate young men. What she does not understand is that Cho Seung-Hui, the mass-murderer at the university, is atypical. As I explained on the BBC *Any Questions?* programme in a November 2006 broadcast, one of the saving graces of the high-school and college world of North America (I include Canada in this) is the proliferation of organized and well-funded sporting activities. No, a high-school football placing or college baseball scholarship might not stop a Columbine atrocity, but these calamities are few and far-between. As this book is being written, crime in the United Kingdom amongst children is reaching unprecedented proportions; I call it 'Lord of the Flies Now'. Millions of American children go through school without a shred of violence entering their young lives, and hundreds of thousands go on to productive careers, having been in the magnificently run sporting teams, in bands, or in cheerleading groups (or not).

Joan Smith asserts in her editorial that young male violence is not an exclusively American scourge, but her contention that knives are less dangerous than guns is a dubious one. A string of brutal murders in Britain have been knife related, and the tragic death of young charity worker Alan Senitt in Washington DC saw him die with his throat slashed. The irony there is, as I blurted out on that terrible 9 July 2006, that, had handguns not been banned in the District of Columbia, Alan might have fended off his attacker, and the attempted rape of his female companion, with a gunshot.

Smith contends: 'it is clear that a tragically mistaken belief in the efficacy of violence is embedded in the American psyche'. And she goes on to say that this mindset may be found in all echelons of society, white or blue collar. She makes the usual noises that about 90 per cent of Britain makes to me every day about the United States going in violently to every corner of the world, guns blazing and asking questions later. She then makes the assertion – one I also hear at least thrice a week – that 'American popular culture goes on repeating the same old message about...solving every type of conflict...through violent means'. She says bestselling US authors create a world in which 'the good guys can survive only if they wage a remorseless war on a population largely composed of freaks, perverts and serial killers'. I do not know what books she is reading, but there are a lot of other genres to choose from. A country that has given the world Mark Twain, Ernest Hemingway, John Steinbeck, Pearl Buck, James Michener, Sinclair Lewis, Norman Mailer, Willa Cather, William Styron and Lillian Hellman amongst others cannot be all that perverse and freak ridden. Joan Smith concludes that Cho's world was the world of American popular culture. Were this so, there would be dead bodies strewn across campuses 365 days a year. I suggest she watch NASN on cable television for a few days to see the hundreds of thousands of high-school and college athletes, band musicians, cheerleaders, families and fans filling stadia across the country to capacity. Their behaviour is impeccable, and police are only required at low levels. That is the America I know. It is the real one. Joan, as bad as Cho was, please don't tread on it.

* * * * *

Were every extraordinary British and European headline – not to mention the mountain of anti-Bush front covers of *Der Spiegel* since 9/11 – to be included in this book, it would be as large as an encyclopaedia. But here are some more of the top gems I have culled from my mountain of clipping-boxes:

On 18 November 2003, the *Evening Standard* has a huge headline emblazoned across its front page: 'SO THEN MR BUSH, WHERE IS SADDAM?' It quotes various British military pundits who refer to American 'incompetence' and prints comments from anti-war campaigners who warn that the president will have a rough ride when he visits London. The paper provides a long list of protests planned for the presidential tour, including a 'Resist Bush' mock tea party outside Buckingham Palace, schoolchildren holding their own protest in Parliament Square, and the Muslim Association of Britain, most famous for its annual boycott of Holocaust Memorial Day, urging all Britons to join the Ramadan Fast. A hail of 'Where is Saddam?' criticism rains down on the USA in this feature.

Saddam was captured by American troops a month later.

* * * * *

And so on.

* * * * *

When the visit by President Bush to Britain unfolded in November 2003, unprecedented bile and hatred poured from every corner of the media and in public discourse.

My favourite headline could once again be found in the *Evening Standard*: 'BUSH SECURITY ROBS PUPILS OF HOT DINNERS.' Omigod! Children will starve here in London if Bush visits. The story, alongside a cartoon of President Bush behaving like a dim-witted cowboy at a Royal banquet, reveals that security surrounding the state visit will prevent the delivery of meals to hundreds of schoolchildren in Westminster. As an emergency measure, the schools tell the newspaper that they will be preparing sandwiches. The report continues with the ominous suggestion that had the schools, including the 'cash-strapped' St Peter's Eaton Square Church of England Primary, not decided on the sandwich arrangement, the pupils would have gone without anything at all. The story even says: 'Some fear the move may prompt a fresh wave of anti-Americanism amongst the younger generation.' Dr Digby Anderson, however, gets the last word: 'If they are making a sandwich it is more likely they will succeed in producing something edible than attempting a three-course meal.'

My sentiments exactly.

* * * * *

The weeks before, during and after the presidential visit to London engendered a wealth of hatelines in the press. In a piece by former Labour cabinet minister Roy Hattersley in the *Guardian* ('Bush is Not Welcome in Britain', 27 October 2003), it is posited that the occasion was planned to help the Republican party in the 2004 election. Hattersley also suggests that the president is 'being elevated to put the uppity French and Germans in their place'. Bush, he observes, is 'simultaneously sinister and ridiculous', a man who is 'despised by most of the British public' and whose itinerary has had to be truncated because of the strength of feeling against him. Many will agree with this view, but the ceaseless paragraphs of Lord Hattersley's bile about the head of state of an ally visiting his country border on the childish. Throughout my many years in Britain, I have never ceased to be floored by the length and breadth of dislike and disdain shown by Britons for their American cousins, when the opposite would not likely happen in the United States – even if a deeply disliked British prime minister visited Washington.

The British newspapers provided a feast of anti-Americanism in the wake of the 2003 presidential visit. Amongst the general public, I witnessed a crowd burning and stomping on American flags in Trafalgar Square. Most of the offenders were older, hunting-jacketed Middle Englanders. I felt intimidated and even physically threatened by their fury. Yes, the Iraq War made millions indignant. Yes, Bush's malapropisms cause worldwide mirth. But I do not think I could ever imagine a circumstance in which Americans would burn the Union Jack in Times Square.

A prize headline was 'BUSH OFF' in the *Daily Mirror* of 14 November 2003. The article stressed that the newspaper's poll had found 75 per cent of Britons to be furious that the presidential visit was costing $7.5 million. Inside the paper, the lead editorial shouted 'State Visit is an Insult to Our Country' and said it was outrageous for a president viewed with such contempt by so many Britons to be afforded a state visit. It boldly asserted: 'Britain still performs great ceremonies better than any country in the world. Let's not waste one on George W. Bush.'

The columnist Paul Routledge claims ('We'll Suffer for Bush's Liberty', *Daily Mirror*, 14 November 2003) that Londoners would not be able to walk the streets of our city for three days because of lockdown. This is nonsense; I live in central London and could get out and about without hindrance during the visit of President Bush, whom Routledge calls 'the cross-eyed thief of democracy'. Yes, I can hear all of you Bush-haters laughing, but if you were in London during his visit you would have feared for your life in the company of many citizens. I sampled the mood of many taxi drivers during the Bush visit, and one would have thought Adolf Hitler or Osama bin-Laden had come to town, but their dislike of the man went beyond sensible criticism. I had the tirades about Americans still supporting the IRA, oppressing the blacks and Native Americans and committing other collective crimes. One driver could barely contain himself, his hatred was so intense; he was angry at me and at all Americans, and I did not like it.

A. N. Wilson added his two cents' worth about the presidential visit ('I Despise Dubya, but not America', *Evening Standard*, 21 November 2003) by suggesting that the terrible bombings in Istanbul the day after the Buckingham Palace dinner were a message to the war-mongering leader. He also adds in the terrorists of Gaza, who need a 'legitimate political voice'. Wilson should know that huge bombs went off in Africa when Clinton was president. He expressed his sorrow over the massive security in London, which he felt American and British war veterans would find disturbing. The fact is that hatred of the president and of America was so intense that the authorities had no choice: when Tony Blair and Her Majesty the Queen came to Washington and Virginia, even at the height of anti-Iraq War sentiment in the USA, they would have been in no danger, and indeed travelled about with ease.

George Monbiot, in the *Evening Standard* of 13 November 2003 ('Why We Are Right to March'), says something unprecedented is about to happen in Britain: an American president will arrive and be greeted not by cheering crowds but by cries of disgust. I am certain many reading this will say 'Good on the Brits!', but it has to be explained here that the sheer hatred of the American visitors was to me repugnant and scary. In fact, I was reasonably sure that Bush and Powell would be assassinated. Again, my sense of graciousness stepped in: unless a head of state is a Hitler, such a massive expression of loathing leaves me feeling not impressed but uncomfortable. Monbiot delivers a priceless evaluation of the situation, stating that it is time British patriots stopped fretting over the European Union and started recognizing the grave danger posed by Britain's subservience to the United States.

In the *Guardian* of 17 November 2003 ('US and UK Officials Dread Presidential Trip'), it is noted that Woodrow Wilson was the last president to be afforded a state visit, in 1918, and that his path was strewn with roses from a nation grateful for his support in the Great War; the *Guardian* points out that this trip will be characterized by protestors dogging Bush's steps until the moment he leaves.

In the *Independent* of 14 November 2003, a letter writer, Dave Mate, an expatriate American working in Oxfordshire, writes: 'Americans seeing large crowds demonstrating against the president won't be shocked and turn against Mr Bush. Americans will turn against England and no longer consider you an ally. You really do not know us at all.'

It should be noted here that, in 2004, when a British newspaper meddled in the Ohio election process, Bush won and some felt this was an 'inversion reaction': swing voters who might have gone for John Kerry were revolted by the puerile 'how could you people be so dumb?' campaign and voted for Bush as a gesture against the British intrusion into their election. Ohio was crucial to the Democrats. In 2005, I was in Washington and saw a sheepish British journalist admitting on C-SPAN that the Ohio letter-writing campaign had needled the voters, backfired and resulted in a Republican victory.

In the *Evening Standard* of 14 November 2003 ('Whaddaya Mean, Tony Hasn't Got a Ranch?'), a full-page A to Z satire provides a guide to the tour, with 'Z' being 'zzzzz', or the sleep the visitor will not get due to the incessant noise in Green Park being perpetrated by anti-war protestors. And so passed the visit of Dubya to a warm and welcoming London.

The *Daily Telegraph* of 19 November and 21 November provides a detailed story and stirring photographs reflecting the ire of residents of Tony Blair's Sedgefield constituency, one of whom had put 'Stop Bush' signs on his house. There is keen resentment of the near-$2 million cost of the presidential visit to Blair's home and to the Dun Cow pub and the village, with anti-war protestors not allowing the president to enjoy a quiet pint. In the 19 November edition of the *Telegraph* ('Why This Protest is Deeply Shameful'), David Frum, former White House speechwriter, gets the last word: 'Many thousands of British people intend to converge on central London to protest against the overthrow of one of the most cruel and murderous dictators of the 20th century – and to wave placards calling the American president... "the world's number one terrorist".' Frum calls this a deeply shameful context. He extols the elderly taxi driver displaying a poppy and calling the demonstrators traitors. He concludes, as I did at the time, that the protestors can make fools of themselves and burn American flags because of western leaders who have regularly rid the world of dictators and given these citizens the freedom to screech their heads off in Grosvenor Square.

* * * * *

Another prize headline and front-page tableau turns up in the *Independent* of 11 October 2006 – 'SUPERSIZE NATION', with the Stars and Stripes interwoven with the lettering. The headline continues: 'As its population reaches 300m, how America is eating the world.'

Oh, golly, so now those ugly Americans are sitting down to Sunday lunch after church, and not realizing that the rest of the world is about to disappear from starvation and deprivation because of the churchgoers' unforgivable gluttony? The *Indy* then tells us that life expectancy in the United States is 75, whilst in the developing world it is just 63. The same paper is likely, on other occasions, to be telling us how violent 'merkins are. So, if enough of them shoot each other dead, the life expectancy will drop and the British media will be happy.

The *Indy* informs us that 678 pounds of paper are consumed by each American per year, whilst only 44 pounds are consumed in the developing world. I bet those folks-in-development are a lot happier! In fact, they are so happy without a paper trail that they will probably outlive the poor American sod suffocating in the 678 pounds of paper.

According to the *Indy*, 37 per cent of the world's vehicles are on America's roads. Inasmuch as one cannot breathe in Beijing, according to my colleague Sue Kaye, who visited China in November 2007, I suggest China, India and the former Soviet Union deserve a 'rogue's gallery' front page, too. The inventory of crimes committed by the American people continues with the statistic that they eat 58 billion burgers each year. Isn't this better than the gallons of liver-destroying alcohol consumed by Britons at younger and younger ages? In my decades in Britain, I have watched colleagues destroy their lives with alcohol addiction. Now their children are ending up in hospitals with alcohol poisoning. I'd rather eat a hamburger. And anyway, in the USA you won't get BSE or have to worry about foot and mouth. Hot dogs, as mentioned in another chapter, are often Hebrew National because so many 'folks' (not all Christian Zionists, by the way) love kosher food. The *Indy* mentions the 300,000 deaths per year from obesity, but again I urge the same paper to devote equal time to the calamity of drinking that has made Britain number one in Europe (and likely the world) for alcohol-related health problems and fatalities.

Finally, the *Indy* reminds us that the USA, representing just 5 per cent of the world's population, uses 23 per cent of its energy, 15 per cent of its meat and 28 per cent of its paper. In 1918, Spanish flu wiped out masses of people around the world. Some say it started in Europe and was

German bio-warfare against American and British troops. The Americans arrived back in massive ships at the port of Philadelphia. The City of Brotherly Love was hit hard. Considering the fury with which the energy-consumption statistics are regularly hurled at me even by my seething beautician, the America-haters seem ready to unleash bio-warfare and end it all for those infernal, world-destroying Yanks. I am reminded of the angry white-haired Scotsman who was in the audience of a Jonathan Dimbleby television special I attended after 9/11. He got up and said America had got it in the neck and that next time it would be 3 million dead, not 3,000. His inexplicable hatred of Americans was terrifying. The *Indy*'s hamburger report was equally hostile.

I plan to eat a hamburger as soon as I arrive at Dulles Airport – and to eat many, many more in the comfort of my SUV.

* * * * *

A one-liner I had to put into this section on the media came on 3 May 2007 from General Sir Michael Rose, who commanded British forces in Bosnia in the 1990s. Quoted in the *Evening Standard* by reporter Pippa Crerar, he says the insurgents are 'right' to attack American troops. She explains that in a book he has written he compares the Iraqi insurgency to the men serving under George Washington in the American War of Independence. General Rose claimed frontline soldiers had lamented to him the futility of the occupation, and he said on BBC *Newsnight* that the Iraqi militias were within their rights in trying to drive American forces out of Iraq.

Some found President Bush's 'Bring 'em on' highly provocative and offensive. General Rose's view is equally deplorable.

* * * * *

In the *Evening Standard* of 30 July 2007 ('The Day Edgware Rd Became Baghdad'), writing about the Iraqi soccer team's victory in the final of the Asian Cup in Jakarta, Amar Singh reports on the heavily Muslim Edgware Road in London, where crowds of Sunnis, Shias and Kurds joined together to celebrate the win against Saudi Arabia. Roads around Hyde Park were closed as huge crowds of men, women and children poured out to *shish* bars and restaurants through the night. Ammar Khalid, a 22-year-old student, is quoted as saying: 'Today we can show the world we are strong. Iraq is strong.' (Go tell the BBC that good news!) The article does mention that Islamists have now made it impossible for the team to practise inside Iraq, and that even small children kicking a ball around are targets for militias. Indeed, more than 50 football fans were killed in Mosul by a suicide bomb during the semi-final.

The uplifting report is then spoilt by a quote from the Iraqi team captain, Younis Mahmoud, who says he will be killed if he goes back to Iraq and declares: 'I want America to go out. Today, tomorrow, or the day after tomorrow, but out. I wish the American people didn't invade Iraq and hopefully it will be over soon.'

Yes, Younis, and had you lost and Saddam still been in power, his sons would have done some unspeakable things to you and your team mates.

Living in the Edgware Road area of London as I do, I have tired of the constant whingeing of local Iraqis about the state of Iraq since the liberation from Saddam. Did Germans or Japanese kill each other in the hundreds of thousands with power drills after the fall of their respective dictatorships? Japan and Germany were rebuilt by the United States, and one assumes this could have been done in Iraq had the various factions not decided to slaughter one another into eternity. Archbishop of Canterbury Dr Rowan Williams blames American 'in and out' invasions for the turmoil in the world; but had the USA left in 2003, would Iraq be any better off?

* * * * *

Independent, 7 February 2007: 'The relationship with America is what opens doors everywhere' – quote attributed to Tony Blair.

Then come images of 100 grave markers of British soldiers killed in Iraq. Inside is yet another article about the US friendly fire death of British serviceman Matty Hull in Iraq.

I cover the Matty Hull story in a separate chapter, but here I would like to illustrate the obsessive attitude taken by the British press and television – even the Murdoch media on Sky News – towards this one incident. What is so astonishing is that the tragic death of Lance Corporal of Horse Hull occurred in 2003, but only in 2007 did the British authorities set about investigating it. Headlines in British papers like 'Friendly Fire Pilot Now Flies Boeings' abounded in early 2007, when the inquest was unfolding: an angry *Evening Standard* of 8 February wrote with indignation that the American pilot, Gus Kohntopp, who had killed Hull in error, 'took part in more than 25 combat missions during Operation Iraq Freedom, was awarded the Bronze Star and now works as a commercial pilot'. The amount of space devoted to this story was mind-boggling.

On the front page of the *Evening Standard* of 16 March 2007, this headline is emblazoned: 'MY MERCY FOR MATTY KILLERS' – and the accompanying article provides further thoughts from Matty Hull's young widow, who says she hopes the Americans who killed her husband feel some remorse. Coroner Andrew Walker even suggested the incident was not a mistake, stating: 'There is no evidence the pilots were acting in self-defence...in that respect it was criminal.'

What is so jarring about the extensive, loud and raucous coverage of this incident is the vitriolic attitude towards the supposed ally across the Atlantic. My feelings of resentment were further exacerbated by a dinner host who took the opportunity to tell me how 'yellow' American servicemen have always been. To add insult to injury, a British friend who invited me to stay for the weekend (I left a day early) brow-beat me about the cowardice of American soldiers in the First World War, reported to her by her great-uncle, who had watched them 'run off' when asked to take a hill. Yes, I am sure all those men buried at Omaha Beach 'ran off'.

Interestingly enough, in the *Evening Standard* of 20 November 2006, there was a tiny item about British Royal Marine Chris Maddison, of 539 Assault Squadron, who was killed by friendly fire along the Khawr Az Zubayr River in Iraq in March 2003. The British troops who killed him in error were described at the inquest as 'tired and tense', and the unfortunate tragedy was said to be the result of a 'breakdown in communications'. The story was never mentioned again.

Independent, 12 July 2007: 'For the First Time, American Soldiers Tell the Truth About How They Fought the War in Iraq', then (in huge typeface) 'A dead Iraqi is just another dead Iraqi' (Specialist Jeff Englehart, 26, 3rd Brigade, 1st Infantry Division).

Inside (just one page, with one-liner quotes): 14 American servicemen offer brief sound bites: 'I just brought terror to someone under the American flag', or 'A lot of guys really supported that whole concept that if they don't speak English and they have darker skin, they're not as human as us, so we can do what we want.'

On the front page of the *Evening Standard* of 24 August 2007 is emblazoned the headline: 'US KILLS THREE OF OUR TROOPS.' Once again, it appears a friendly fire tragedy has resulted in the deaths of British servicemen. As the culprits appear to be American, the tone is that of hysteria, veering on lynch mob. Jason Beattie, the correspondent covering the story, reports that three servicemen trying to repair the Kajaki Dam were killed during a fierce battle in Helmand Province, Afghanistan. Though the spokesman for the Ministry of Defence points out that no battle is without risks, the paper goes on to remind the world that the British government has had ongoing problems with Washington, principally the withholding of information about friendly fire investigations. These deaths are tragic, but it is the way the incidents are portrayed in the press that causes me concern, as if the Americans are the Taliban.

Then there is the issue of British ITN journalist Terry Lloyd. Like Matty Hull, he died under friendly fire in Iraq in the early days of the war. The completely out-of-proportion fury in the British media about this event was, again, intimidating to me as an expatriate American trying to live day to day in an increasingly hostile culture.

* * * * *

On we go to the *Financial Times* of 6 July 2007:

Letter to the editor from Lynn Forester de Rothschild, chief executive of E. L. Rothschild, London SW3, responding to a 4 July *FT* caricature of America by advertising executive Maurice Saatchi, 'Wake Up, Sleeping Beauty, America' (keeping in mind that British papers have been known to pick on the USA on Independence Day): 'It is quite unfair, and indeed untrue to say that the nation is "too stingy, giving away less of its wealth than other countries".'

De Rothschild continues: 'The fact is that in 2006 Americans gave away $295 billion. Charitable giving is a broad-based and long-standing American characteristic...the character and generosity of the American people have never wavered.'

If I were to write to the British papers every time a columnist or reporter misrepresents the United States or Americans, I would be in a permanent, unpaid occupation.

* * * * *

In the sports pages of the *Evening Standard* of 26 March 2007, Matthew Norman comments on the bid by American tycoon Stan Kroenke for a stake in Arsenal football club: 'If Mr Kroenke does end up owning Arsenal – and after selling its soul to have its stadium named after the Emirates, selling its shares to an American jew [*sic*] shouldn't be a huge moral dilemma – one must assume that [team manager] Wenger will resign immediately.' Aside from the fact that Stan Kroenke is not Jewish, such commentary would likely land an American sports writer in as hot water as that being suffered by Don Imus.*

* A legendary American radio talk show host who lost his slot because of comments he made about female and black basketball players.

Please note that the Arsenal chairman was quoted in the same newspaper on 20 April saying about the American: 'We don't want your sort here.' I wish some of the Brits who of late have been hurling abuse at me about my vile country and religious background had been in your face and said that to me 30 years ago. I would have left there and then.

* * * * *

In the *Evening Standard* of 26 March 2007, the ubiquitous Andrew Gilligan, whose famous interview with Dr David Kelly at the Thistle Charing Cross Hotel ended with Kelly's bloody suicide, writes: 'Do we really want a New York accent?' He then spends a well-paid column making various cracks about 'American hype'. Gilligan suggests that *New York Magazine*'s recent branding of London as 'the new New York' is actually an honour Britain does not need or want. He also compares London's stagnating public transport system to that of the USA, but as Mr Gilligan spends 95 per cent of his year in London, how does he know how stagnant the Washington Metro is? And despite the endless *kvetching* of my American friends about the New York, Philadelphia and other transit systems, how long would they tolerate the 76 per cent of London tube stations that have no elevators, no escalators and no air conditioning – not to mention the hellish 'new' buses that overheat and catch fire?

But then Gilligan writes the cherry on the sundae: he accuses Londoners and Britain of being obsessed with all things American, but that this is never reciprocated. Never reciprocated? Hello? Has Andrew never met a gushing Yank the minute he or she hears a British accent? Has he never watched the Emmys and Tonys, when gushing American presenters practically bow and kiss the feet of the endless stream of Brits receiving most of the awards? Gilligan must be one of the most highly paid journalists in London, but like so many who rise to the top he fails in the most basic of childhood tasks: doing his homework.

* * * * *

In the *Evening Standard* of 5 April 2007, 'Another pounding for the US in Iraq' describes a play by Jonathan Holmes presented at the Old Truman Brewery in London. In it, a long string of testimonies is heard from suffering Iraqis, mercilessly beaten into submission by brutal GIs. I saw this play and can only say 'Hats off' to critic Kieron Quirke. Here are some choice clips from his review:

> If you don't like the US, you might like *Fallujah*. Sometimes, this piece of documentary theatre seems more interested in fomenting anti-Americanism than in informing its audience... As Harriet Walter's journalist Sasha tears around the place and into the US generals, you hope she'll stop for a moment and get the basics of the conflict straight... [You] can't help but notice that all the American soldiers are idiots, and the few Arabs lovely and reasonable... US claims that insurgents were using civilians as human shields go uninvestigated.

* * * * *

In a previous chapter, I wrote at length about faith and leadership. Living in a fiercely secular country (Great Britain) has actually made me more aware of my religious roots and more of a believer.

In the *Evening Standard* of 25 May 2007 ('Kaka Display was God-Awful'), Matthew Norman writes with considerable fury about the young Brazilian football star Milan Kaka, who revealed an 'I Belong to Jesus' vest under his shirt at a Champions League match. Unbelievably, Norman says: 'You certainly do not, you Brazilian twerp, I heard a drunken voice scream in rage (mine, alas).' He rants incoherently about Kaka belonging not to Jesus but to Sergio Berlusconi, whom Norman describes as a 'right wing media billionaire who allegedly bribes judges and gropes every passing female bum'. Norman says Kaka should be 'made to wear a crown of thorns and join Opus Dei'.

Norman goes on to lament the 'voluble' piety of some sports figures, and says the mention of Christ by Evander Holyfield when he beat Mike Tyson 'ruined' the event. He says Sean Murphy's 2005 snooker win at the Crucible was besmirched by the player's evangelical Christianity, which he describes as 'an abomination'. Norman says it is bad enough that the world's three major leaders, Blair, Bush and bin Laden, are what he calls 'religious maniacs', and he finishes off by suggesting the football authorities impose a six-match ban on players who display religious piety.

Well, Matthew, that kind of piety is what Stalin hated, too.

CHAPTER TWENTY-TWO

FROM GREENHAM COMMON TO TRIDENT – THE SMALL MATTER OF LONDON MAYOR 'RED KEN' LIVINGSTONE

I had vowed not to waste the reader's valuable time ruminating over the bizarre and obnoxious antics of London Mayor 'Red Ken' Livingstone (other than in my account of his January 2007 conference in the next chapter). However, a comment from a Canadian friend who is a neutral observer has made me break my vow of silence. Please note that the 'Red' tag does not connote ginger hair, but a past career cultivating the extreme Left that so enraged Margaret Thatcher that in 1986 she abolished the Greater London Council just to be rid of him (or so it is commonly thought).

So, it will have gone virtually unreported that, on 18 March 2006, the London mayor got up at an anti-Iraq War, anti-'Apartheid Israel' rally in Trafalgar Square to announce that the Hugo Chavez government of Venezuela had agreed to participate in an upcoming summer 'people's rally'. Mayor Livingstone said we would celebrate the revolution sweeping South America – and most particularly Venezuela, which was aiming to cut off the oil supply to the USA. Livingstone then said he hoped this would be an inspiration to 'the Arab peoples of the world' to turn off the oil taps to George Bush.

There I stood, next to a demonstrator with an upside-down US flag, on which he had daubed 'F*** Bush', thinking of my large family in the United States which, if one were to take the London mayor literally – and if his vision became reality – would starve and freeze to death sometime soon, along with the rest of America. When I told my Canadian friend about this, she, with no axe to grind, made an astute observation: 'If Mayor Bloomberg of New York got up in

Times Square and said he hoped the oil supply to Britain would be cut off, he would cause such an outcry that he would have to resign.' Indeed, he would be taken away in a straitjacket.

During my early years in Britain, I was puzzled by the antics of the 'Greenham Common Women', a Wales-based contingent of aggressive protestors who wanted American cruise missiles removed from the RAF base in Berkshire. They also staged loud protests in the early 1980s at RAF Lakenheath and High Wycombe, where there was an American presence. At the time, I was in shock at the rhetoric of the women: their hatred of the United States went beyond the fears of the public that missile bases in Britain could provoke a Soviet attack. I simply could not understand how Britons, saved from Nazi tyranny in their darkest hour by America entering the Second World War, could have such visceral hatred of the United States. Would a group of American women, even in liberal California or New York, be so ugly about Britain if an advanced missile protection system had been installed in vulnerable American locations? I doubt it. The missiles were removed from Britain in the 1990s and that upset me: anti-Americanism had resulted in an unwise bowing to the radical Left by a hand-wringing government – a Tory one, no less! – and this is one example of anti-Americanism damaging the security of Britain.

Now, moving forward 20 years, we have a new wave of 'anti-everything' madness that has emanated from 'Red Ken' Livingstone – the male version of a Greenham Common agitator, whose hatred of George W. Bush is matched only by his obsessive bile directed at Israel and, inexplicably, seemingly harmless Jewish reporters and property developers. (Inasmuch as George W. Bush's approval rating at home is almost as low as any president's has been in living memory, many will say the mayor has good taste in his pet hates. His city, however, still hosts major American business and tourism interests, and, with a booming pound crippling 'US dollar tourism', cannot afford to project a puerile loathing of the US head of state.)

One has to go all the way back to 2003 to find the best of Red Ken's Bush-hatred on display. In a large headline 'Zip the Lip, Mr Mayor' (*Evening Standard*, 9 May 2003), Paul Barker, senior research fellow at the Institute of Community Studies, asserts: 'Ken Livingstone must remember his role is to represent London – not to attack America.' On another two-page spread is the headline: 'Why Did You Have to Attack America Now, Mr Livingstone?' This condemnatory rhetoric, which was reported to emanate from 'politicians and London business leaders' venting their fury, relates to an appearance by the mayor at City Hall in front of 200 schoolchildren in which, according to the *Evening Standard*, he referred to the American president as a 'coward' and the illegally elected head of a 'venal and corrupt administration'. This being the week of the launch of the $7 million 'Totally London Month', tourist chiefs were sickened by the outburst. The report says the mayor pressed on with his tirade and quoted him as saying: 'I look forward to it [the US government] being overthrown as much as I looked forward to Saddam Hussein being overthrown.'

Even the mayor's own deputy, Nicky Gavron, is quoted as saying: 'I don't think it was in the interests of London to make these comments.'

Livingstone, who also described the American administration as 'a completely insupportable government', was condemned by the head of a Wall Street bank, whom the *Evening Standard* quoted as saying that Americans were already worried about investing in the UK. He went on: 'We've already seen the damage France and Germany's stances have had on US investment.' (The Greater London Authority was reported to be putting at least £15 million into the Visit London Campaign.) Simon Milton, of the central London Westminster Council was quoted as saying: 'I seriously think he may be going mad.'

The Tory mayoral candidate, Steve Norris, observed that this did nothing to help the major drop in visitors from the United States. (As of December 2007, the figures were abysmal.) According to the *Standard*, when asked to comment, the White House said: 'Ken who?'

But Paul Barker in the *Evening Standard* takes the *faux pas* more seriously: he asserts in his editorial piece that 'the old Livingstone', who invited 'IRA supporters to release black balloons from the roof of County Hall' during the height of the Troubles, and who once said 'capitalism has killed more people than Hitler', bubbles up from time to time like a 'sudden upsurge of pollution'. Barker notes that one of the wonderful things about the United States is that it gets on with daily life, regardless of who sits in the White House. At the same time, he reminds the mayor that most Americans revere the office of the president, regardless of the shortcomings of its occupant, and that the reporting of the tirade will proliferate across the USA. Despite Livingstone's 'pick and mix' attitude towards America (he admired Rudy Giuliani for a long time after 9/11), it would be inconceivable for any American mayor, in front of a gaggle of schoolchildren, to launch a broadside against the sitting British prime minister. Barker concludes that it would be useful for Ken Livingstone to do as Professor Harold Laski of the London School of Economics did, when admonished by then Prime Minister Clement Attlee: 'A period of silence on your part would be welcome.'

Moving along all the way to April 2006, I noticed a tiny item in the *Evening Standard* about Livingstone's appearance in March 2006 in Cannes, at an Olympic 2012 planning junket. The article said Livingstone had got up at the Riviera event and made a verbal assault on property tycoons Simon and David Reuben that others in the planning group had found startling and out of place. This is the mayor who was suspended so recently for insulting a Jewish reporter with a 'concentration camp guard' slur. I said to myself: 'No, no, no, it isn't anti-Semitism again!'

Lo and behold, a week later came his outburst in London, in which he said the Reuben Brothers could 'go back to Iran and live under the ayatollahs'. 'Go back!' – an expression that strikes a chill in every immigrant. But for our champion of multiculturalism, Ken Livingstone, to utter this epithet was an egregious act, only made worse by his next jibe. When asked by reporters about his outburst, Livingstone said he was not aware that the Indian-born Jewish Reubens were not, after all, Iranians, and that he apologized unreservedly to all the Iranian people for suggesting he would have inflicted the Reuben Brothers on them. Then, to top it all, the mayor said he thought the Reubens might perhaps be Muslims.

But, as the expression goes, it isn't over until it's over. So in the same month, March 2006, we also had the mayor of London, the international goodwill envoy for our ancient city, calling United States Ambassador Robert Tuttle a 'chiselling little crook' on nationwide television (as mentioned several times before). Americans making British boys die in Iraq but not paying the London congestion charge, over which some 55 embassies are reported to be similarly in arrears, is the cause of his ire. The *Evening Standard* has pointed out that Mayor Ken did not go after the communists at the Cuban embassy, who it reports also owe back charges.

Many American expatriates in England have never forgotten that Ken Livingstone boycotted the November 2003 State Dinner in London for President and Mrs Bush. No doubt thousands reading this book will say: 'But how wonderful! Good on him, boycotting the loathsome George W.!' But equally, millions of others, including me, will never forgive him for insulting Her Majesty the Queen by this petulant act that violated all manner of protocol.

In subsequent weeks, Holocaust survivors told me how deeply hurt they had been by his 'concentration camp guard' slur. Liberals rushed to Livingstone's defence, most notably the *Guardian* newspaper, which was filled with even more hurtful articles by non-Jewish writers, suggesting that the small Anglo-Jewish community was engaging in some form of intellectual blackmail. Having seen how devastated my elderly Holocaust-era friends had been since Livingstone berated the Jewish reporter and then refused to apologize (this resulted in his suspension), my inclination was for Livingstone to be removed for the Nazi slur. Now, to defame an ambassador to the Court of St James in a public forum was a further act worthy of removal from office.

Many argue that Livingstone's trusted deputy mayor is Nicky Gavron, who is Jewish, and that his top-level transport executives, Bob Kiley and Tim O'Toole, are Americans. Perhaps his regular attacks on Jews and Americans can be attributed to a mental quirk, or what British journalist Melanie Phillips calls 'London's Tourette attraction'.

Notwithstanding the fact that Livingstone has Jewish and American co-workers, those of us old enough to have put up with his warped humour and hurtful ultra-Leftist verbal barrages know just how much his recent slurs have damaged community relations.

The poet Roger McGough pulled out of a Liverpool Philharmonic concert because Condoleezza Rice was to be in attendance. This was churlish behaviour, but he is not the mayor of one of the world's most important and economically influential cities. Ken Livingstone is an embarrassment; his refusal to apologize to a Jewish reporter is hideous and, in light of his slur against the American ambassador, he should have been removed from office. What is so scary is that I write this book in fear of the worst: that in 2008, Livingstone remains in power and may one day rise to even greater heights in Britain.

When that happens, I think I would rather be in – well, Camden, New Jersey.

CHAPTER TWENTY-THREE

KEN LIVINGSTONE AND DANIEL PIPES IN A CLASH OF CIVILIZATIONS

In January 2007 I attended a conference hosted by Mayor Ken Livingstone, entitled 'World Civilization – Clash of Civilizations', to which the eminent American scholar Dr Daniel Pipes had been invited. During the previous year, as I read, with mind boggled, websites and blogs that referred to Dr Pipes as a 'Zionist pervert' and other delightful monikers, I had wondered what would happen to this brave man, based in my home town of Philadelphia, were he to cross the ocean. When I learned of the mayor's event, I have to confess I was deeply worried that harm would come to Daniel Pipes in England.

Livingstone pontificated on the Cold War, in which he said 22 million lives had been lost. In 1943, he said, the pre-CIA American Office of Strategic Services had reported: 'we are a nation of nations and our way of thinking should be spread around and dominate the world'. And in 1945, he said, 45 per cent of world productivity came from the USA. This was meant to be greeted by hisses and boos – and a few did break out near me (I was seated in the midst of a large contingent from the many Muslim organizations of Britain).

It might be worth noting here in passing that there are still some who feel that the United States promoting its values and aspirations to the rest of the world is an admirable goal.

Livingstone then went on to mention that, for 500 years, Europe and the USA (500 years, Ken?) have 'dominated the world' and that there is no 'nexus' around the White House, Washington and Wall Street as they try to impose their culture on the world. He concluded by saying that the

'Islamophobic' media in the UK are trying to show that a 'lower culture is taking over'.

If the media are Islamophobic, how is it that Abdul Bari Atwan, Sir Iqbal Sacranie, Dr Muhammed Abdul Bari, Dr Azzam '*I want to be a suicide bomber in Israel*' Tamimi, Yasmin Alibhai-Brown, Ghada Karmi, Inayat Bunglawala, Rageh Omaar, Asghar Bukhari, the aforementioned Salma Yaqoub, Sarah Joseph, Halima Hussain, Faisal Bodi, Ahdaf Soueif, Tariq Ali, Tariq Ramadan and many others are an integral part of our daily media broadcasts and newsprint in Great Britain?

After Mayor Livingstone came the Philadelphia-based Middle East scholar Dr Daniel Pipes. His dignity and aplomb were breathtaking. One could hear a pin drop.

Pipes reminded us that we are in a clash of civilizations and barbarism, and that Samuel Huntington said the dominant clash will be cultural. The Khomenei–Salman Rushdie *fatwa*, he said, was complex – Muslims supported one or the other of the protagonists. The 'Clash' of the title of the conference, Pipes added, is between the civilized, ethical cultures and ideological barbarism. Multiculturalism, he said, is breeding radical Islam – and Britain is becoming a danger to the world: British terrorists have committed acts in 15 countries. The biggest threat, from the Pipes perspective, is not from Iraq or Afghanistan but from London. (I have been saying this for years, and even my neocon friends do not grasp it. Pipes does.) What we are talking about is Islamic-flavoured totalitarianism.

To illustrate his point about London being the centre of Jihad, he observed that, on 16 February 2003 in Hyde Park, there was a rally to promote radical ideas. Pipes quoted the composer Karlheinz Stockhausen, who said that 9/11 was the greatest work of art in the whole cosmos.

Daniel Pipes concluded by asserting: 'We must defeat Islamic radicalism as we defeated Nazism and Fascism in 1945.' There was considerable applause, but when he listed Islamic moderates who deserve support, many laughed. (Later in the day, this was wheeled out time and again to show that

Pipes was promoting 'mouthpieces of the Republicans and neoconservatives who had received payoffs'.)

Salma Yaqoub, of George Galloway's 'Respect' party, got off to a roaring start by announcing that terror attacks are actually 'reprisal events'; it is not, she stressed, Muslims but the American neocons who 'present a problem as a culture clash'. It is western foreign policy that has caused millions of lives to be destroyed in the Middle East – or better still, 'western state terrorism' (millions, Miss Yaqoub?). A truly acid moment came when Yaqoub said: 'there is no minute of silence for the Muslim dead because of western state terrorism'. I found this distasteful and cruel; without doubt, had she said this in the USA, there would have been serious audience anger. Did she mean the silence on Remembrance Day? On 9/11? On the recent one-year anniversary of 7/7 in London?

Holocaust historian Sir Martin Gilbert was given the floor. He stood up and said: 'Miss Yaqoub, my son was caught up in King's Cross on the day of the London bombings. What "reprisal" did people like my son merit?' She was flustered. Yaqoub, who is very young and obviously knows little in the way of world history, said that 'pre-9/11, the Muslims had no quarrel with the West'. Really?

I wanted to ask if she had heard of the Munich Olympics massacre of Israeli athletes, of the countless PLO hijackings, of the *Achille Lauro* hijacking and hideous murder of wheelchair-bound Leon Klinghoffer, of Lockerbie and the 241 dead marines in Lebanon and the Khobar Towers and Bali and Madrid and the 1998 African embassy bombs.

Yaqoub said the American plan to re-map the Middle East is a 'weapon of mass destruction' and that the neoconservatives 'pose the biggest threat to civilization'. If this anti-American and thinly veiled anti-Jewish rhetoric was not so scary, it would be laughable.

Douglas Murray, then of the Social Affairs Unit and now director of the conservative think-tank Centre for Social Cohesion, who had been selected by Daniel Pipes to support his side of the panel, set about demolishing the many assertions of Yaqoub – and demolish her he did. He said: 'Far too many Muslims are being elevated from the wrong end of Islam.' For readers not familiar with the internecine strife in Britain amongst the scores of well-funded Muslim groups now operating throughout the United Kingdom, this referred to the power the Muslim Council of Britain has over national policy. (The MCB's most recent chair, Sir Iqbal Sacranie, has expressed his loathing of homosexuals and his sympathy with the *fatwa* against Salman Rushdie, and has boycotted Holocaust Memorial Day four years running. One hears of the power of the 'Zionist lobby' at least once a day in the British media and even from ordinary people on phone-in programmes, but the plethora of Muslim pressure groups in Britain is nothing short of staggering.)

A delicious moment unfolded when Murray asked: 'How is multiculturalism going in Saudi Arabia?' And this was greeted with laughter and applause. 'Are there any synagogues or churches there?' More applause and laughter.

It should be noted that, just before the morning session got off to its start, I asked Inayat Bunglawala, a Muslim who gets huge, year-round British media exposure, what he thought about my having been threatened with death at the London Central Mosque when I was making a documentary about the Abrahamic faiths almost 10 years before – long before Bush, Guantanamo and Iraq. Bunglawala's reaction astonished me. He produced a rather chilling smile and was dismissive. He said: 'People film at the mosque all the time!' Then he turned his back on me. Fine. Maybe I'll pop over next Friday wearing my Star of David and American flag pin.

* * * * *

Unbelievably, Mayor Livingstone asserted in the question and answer session that radical sheikh and suicide-bombing sympathizer Yusuf al-Qaradawi was the 'strongest force for modernization of Islam – he is the future of Islam'. This is like saying a drug dealer is the best candidate to run a pharmaceuticals empire. (Look at the way the Left has evolved in my lifetime: Tom Wolfe wrote about the 'Radical Chic' hosting the Black Panthers in Leonard and Felicia Bernstein's Manhattan apartment, and now we have a much more terrifying threat to social cohesion – the radical sheikh.)

Then came Mayor Livingstone's moment of the day, when an audience member who had confronted him in a London suburb quoted him as saying: 'Israel should never have been created in the first place.' Livingstone calmly replied to this with: 'I would not have created an Israel; it was a travesty, the creation of Israel. The UK and USA should have opened their doors to Jewish refugees and not displaced Arabs for 60 years.' Had I not had a Press badge I would have shouted: 'And would you not have created Pakistan, either, in 1948?'

Immediately following this, an audience member sitting near me shouted: 'Mr Pipes and his supporters have blood on their hands!' And there were shouts of 'shame' when Pipes answered. A member of the audience bellowed: '600,000 Iraqis have been killed by the US and UK'. This was followed by an Afro-Caribbean woman chanting: 'God Bless America! God Bless America!' At this point, the magnanimous Ms Yaqoub agreed to bless the USA, the UK, Arabs and Palestinians, but not Israel. People near me shouted: 'Bless Israel!' Again she refused, but said: 'I bless the Jews.'

If this was not a clash of civilizations, I do not know what is. After the opening session, an absolutely furious Palestinian woman came down to the front and, for a fleeting moment, I thought Dr Pipes would be in mortal danger. But he was surrounded by well-wishers and I took her on. Her rage was frightening, and even when I took her arm she was impossible to deal with. No matter how I tried to reason with her, she raged at me. There I was, a well-meaning theatre and film artist and great-granddaughter of rabbis, and there she was, telling me how murderous all Jews are. Again, a clash of civilizations.

* * * * *

The one bright moment of the day was the appearance by Daniel Pipes, who was a shining example of American scholarship and aplomb, and the eloquent Briton, Douglas Murray. These two brave and gritty men gave me hope that Israel and the United States will never, ever be trodden on.

CHAPTER TWENTY-FOUR

FRIENDLY FIRE – THOSE CRIMINAL AMERICAN GIS!

As I described in my chapter on newspapers, the British media began to obsess in 2006 about the deaths by friendly fire of ITN journalist Terry Lloyd and soldier Matty Hull. Tragic events without a doubt, but the media have been running these stories as if it is a chase to find Osama bin Laden. Blood-curdling descriptions of 'criminal' American pilots and servicemen proliferate across tabloid and broadsheet papers, and furious Britons ring up radio stations to denounce Americans. One of the American pilots has gone into hiding. Carol feels she may soon have to go into hiding, too, or get the last boat to America.

* * * * *

THE US MILITARY'S 'CULT OF CRUELTY'

Diary: 28 October 2006

It is not a popular occupation to be an American in Britain. The war in Iraq has degenerated into a sectarian bloodbath, with 93 Americans killed and coalition troops caught in the middle, no longer sure of their mission. British General Sir Richard Dannatt suggests that the presence of troops is exacerbating the situation and worries that he will not have a fit and healthy army for future needs if the conflict continues.

America is blamed for everything, and some even think Madonna has suffered unprecedented media condemnation in her bid to adopt a baby from Malawi because of overwhelming British hostility to all things American.

In recent weeks, the Coroner's report on the death of British ITN journalist Terry Lloyd has inspired a stream of invective about the brutality of American troops. Lloyd, a veteran newsman known across the nation, had chosen to cover Iraq in his own way, without being embedded with American or British troops. He was killed during a fierce battle, and the Coroner has determined that he was alive and being rescued by an Iraqi civilian when American troops filled him with bullets as he was being evacuated in a makeshift ambulance.

Lloyd's daughter and the lawyer representing the family were shown on British television over and over again, making fierce pronouncements about the cruel and reckless behaviour of the trigger-happy American 'cowboys'.

As a journalist, my complaint is that Lloyd did not take advantage of the embedding facilities that might have kept him from danger, and that ITN seems to have underestimated the peril in which he was placing himself on their behalf.

This story generated the expected clamour about the appalling battle etiquette (is there such a thing?) of Americans, but the ultimate insult came when John Simpson, the BBC's world affairs editor, wrote an editorial for the *Independent* (15 October 2006), in which he said:

> Since the First World War, every war in which the Americans have fought has been marked by unnecessary civilian deaths and wholly avoidable 'friendly fire' incidents. Now, it seems, there may be a new distinguishing feature of American wars: the killing of journalists.

His comment brought to mind a cavalcade of images: the firestorms of Coventry and London; the devastation of Dresden, an RAF raid masterminded by Bomber Harris; and the millions killed by Nazi Germany in concentration camps and Eastern European killing fields. Though not in wartime, Stalin's purges ended the lives of countless civilians. In 1919, British General Dyer ordered the execution of crowds of civilians in Amritsar.

The thrust of Simpson's charge against American servicemen and women is the audacity of his accusation. Yes, all armies cause carnage during wartime, but the idea that the presence of Americans means extra civilian deaths is an unfortunate slur. One wonders if the Crusades worried about civilian casualties. The First and Second World Wars were perpetrated by Europeans. The United States was at peace and was a booming and flourishing nation led by a man of integrity, Woodrow Wilson. He would have given anything to have been able to engineer a bloodless solution to the tribal hatreds of the European protagonists. His vision of a League of Nations would inspire the establishment of the United Nations. America entered the Great War as a reluctant participant. Eventually, the Spanish flu contracted by troops coming back from Europe to the Philadelphia navy yard (Philadelphia eventually suffered more deaths than any other city in the 1918 pandemic) killed almost as many soldiers as perished in the trenches. The idea that Americans caused unnecessary civilian deaths in the First World War is a cruel slur against men who fought with courage to help their British and French friends.

Europe was in turmoil whilst Franklin Roosevelt was pulling America out of the Great Depression, and again it was a reluctant United States that joined the Second World War. It is difficult for Britons and Europeans to understand why Americans were reluctant to enter the war, but it has always been tough for Americans to understand the passionate and visceral hatreds that European cultures harbour against one another. (One might venture to say that they never understood the depth of the hatred between tribal factions in Iraq.) In any event, along came Pearl Harbor and America was in the war. A quarter of a million American men died in action, and more than a million came home maimed or mentally scarred for life. At Omaha Beach, the Americans suffered far more than the British or Canadians at the other beachheads because modern war historians generally accept that intelligence was betrayed at Omaha. The Americans lost thousands of men in the Normandy invasion. Some 600,000 brave Americans fought in the subsequent land battles, and one unit alone lost 91 per cent of its men. Americans fought with valour in the Pacific, all five of the Sullivan brothers dying on the *Juneau*, resulting in the rule – observed in many other countries now, as well – that siblings may not serve on the same vessel if there are no other children in the family.

John Simpson may have some obscure document showing civilian losses in battles fought by Americans, but his suggestion that Americans create unnecessary deaths is unfortunate, because the overwhelming number of United States service personnel, including First and Second World War veterans in my own family, served with valour and honour. Yes, Vietnam and the Gulf Wars have been bloody and ugly, but Britain has not been angelic in its wars either.

This brings us to Robert Fisk's article 'The US Military and its Cult of Cruelty' (*Independent*, 16 September 2006). He cites the American military's new 'Warrior Ethos':

> I am an American soldier.
> I am a warrior and a member of a team. I serve the people of the Unites States and live the Army values.
> I will always place the mission first.
> I will never accept defeat.
> I will never quit.
> I will never leave a fallen comrade.
> I am disciplined, physically and mentally tough, trained and proficient in my warrior tasks and drills. I always maintain my arms, my equipment and myself.
> I am an expert and I am a professional. I stand ready to deploy, engage and destroy the enemies of the United States of America in close combat. I am a guardian of freedom and the American way of life.
> I am an American soldier.

Fisk refers to this as 'ferocious' and says that it fits in with 'Bush's rantings'. Frankly, having sampled the American way of life, one can understand its citizens being willing to fight to the death to preserve it. The creed is a standard military oath and is very likely a lot less chilling than that of a Syrian or North Korean regiment. One wonders if Fisk ever served in a military unit and pledged to stand by his nation and his brave band of brothers.

Fisk's references to atrocities and sadistic torture perpetrated by American servicemen and women no doubt have basis in truth, the world having seen the images from Abu Ghraib and having heard snippets of testimony from Guantanamo Bay. He says his facts derive from letters and testimony from soldiers and parents of servicemen. What is troubling is his assertion that, when children or babies are thrown into the road by insurgents, the Pentagon has ordered its forces to 'drive over the children without stopping'. A serving soldier is given attribution for this evidence and it may well be true. If Fisk can show a Department of Defense document that rubber-stamped this, then it is indeed the lowest point in American military history; but if it is Fisk using his unlimited column space to defame the American serving man, that is unfortunate.

Hundreds of thousands of fine young men and women have served in Iraq and Afghanistan, and the overwhelming majority have no doubt behaved with decency and honour. These two journalists, however, seem to want to paint a picture of what Fisk describes as 'humiliation, beatings, rape, anal rape and murder' in a 'cult of cruelty'. Indeed, a group of US soldiers is on trial for murder, and it is admirable that the wheels of justice are dealing with this. What is the Fisk tableau? It is of an American military that has degenerated into a force for evil. It is possible that the hell that is Iraq has sunk many service people into depths of despair and loneliness. They are in a country where they cannot have a drink, cannot carouse with ladies on weekend leave and cannot make friends or comprehend the complexities of Iraqi culture. This can lead to aberrant behaviour, but it is simply inconceivable that the forces serving in Iraq are all barbarians.

The atrocities being committed at present by Iraqis against each other are beyond human comprehension. According to recent television reports, Sunni and Shia militias are using power drills to torture people to death and are using hospitals for these activities. Of the thousands who have died in Iraq, the huge majority have been killed not by Americans but by fellow Muslims, most heavily during Holy Ramadan. American Defense Secretary Donald Rumsfeld has been one of many lamenting the expected rise in violence during Ramadan. Perhaps Robert Fisk might like to investigate the atrocities committed by thousands of Iraqi militias, including those against children and teachers at schools.

Towards the end of the Second World War, Germans prayed that they would be captured by the Americans, because they knew the cruelty they would suffer in Soviet captivity. Fisk, in ending his article by comparing the American forces to al-Qaeda, enters the territory of the bizarre. He asserts that 'under the fists of US marines' cruelty abounds, and that the marines proclaim: 'We are warriors. We are Samurai. We draw the sword. We will destroy.' He then says this is the creed of Osama bin Laden.

Just what do journalists like Fisk, Simpson and the US-loathing John Pilger want? Had America remained isolationist in 1941, the Thousand Year Reich would have taken command of the world's destiny. When Eisenhower refused to be part of Suez, American tourists were refused service in British establishments and hatred of America lasted for years. The United States has chosen intervention in recent years, and most of these choices have had a bloody cost. But the vast majority of its forces have been men and women of decency.

The American media rarely, if ever, level venom at British forces or politicians. It would be good to see a small amount of civility in the discourse from Britain's newspapers as American forces suffer unspeakable sacrifices in service to their country. Some in the anti-war movement say this death and blood-letting was for oil and Halliburton, but whatever the reasons, the troops are doing something no one else in the world is doing, or wants to do right now, and some decency from the media would not go amiss.

Diary: 7 April 2007

I might not have written about the issue of American friendly fire incidents in Iraq and Afghanistan, but an entry in True Crime Blog UK provided the incentive to put pen to paper.

In the True Crime essay, decorated with a Union Jack, the writer provides a comprehensive report on the recent decision by the Oxfordshire Coroner to record the death of Lance Corporal of Horse Matty Hull as unlawful killing, the culprits being the 190th Squadron of the United States Air Force Air National Guard. The event was a tragedy, and on the tapes shown on American television one could hear the anguish, tears and remorse of the pilots, whose commander in the air was Gus Kohntopp, an A-10 Thunderbolt fighter pilot with the Idaho Air National Guard.

What bothers me, and what irks True Crime UK, is the excessive zeal with which the British media have been reporting this story and that of ITN reporter Terry Lloyd, also killed by American forces in the middle of a fierce firefight in Iraq in the opening days of the invasion.

Take, for example, the 29 March BBC weekly news review hosted by Andrew Neil. He allowed Charles Glass, a former hostage of Hezbollah, to get in a dig at the Americans, who, he claimed, had never been brought to justice by their own authorities for friendly fire killings against British servicemen. In fact, there had, as the British papers acknowledged, been a Pentagon inquiry long ago into the Hull killing.

What has struck observers of the coverage of the friendly fire death of both reporter Lloyd and soldier Hull has been the aggressive way the story has been reported to the British public, as if both men had been killed by the Taleban or by ruthless insurgents. In both the Lloyd and the Hull cases, the families and solicitors have sought the nearest microphones and cameras to condemn the 'trigger-happy' and 'cowboy' American troops and airmen. The Oxfordshire Coroner had complained about the lack of transparency from both the British Ministry of Defence and the Pentagon, but what was that video I kept seeing on television over and over again? Where would it have come from?

Friendly fire has been a sad, centuries-old by-product of war, ever since the days of the Battle of Barnet. In the heat of conflict mistakes are made. But the amount of coverage of these two incidents, and the hatred that the various players have shown towards the Americans at fault, have been disturbing. Whenever the lawyers have emerged from the courthouse they have talked about the American service personnel as if they were terrorists.

Kohntopp flew 27 combat missions in support of United States and United Kingdom military forces involved in Operation Iraqi Freedom. He called the deployment 'the epitome of my career'. He was awarded the Bronze Star for his performance during the operation and promoted to colonel.

On 28 March 2003, two 190th Squadron A-10 Thunderbolt aircraft flew a mission to destroy artillery and rocket launchers from Iraq's 6th Armoured Division 25 miles north of Basra. During the mission, the two A-10 aircraft mistakenly attacked a patrol of four FV-107 Scimitar armoured vehicles from D Squadron of the Blues and Royals of the Household Cavalry that were supporting the 16th Air Assault Brigade in Operation Telic. The air attack killed Matty Hull, and five of his squadron were injured.

The True Crime site says: 'There is an America-bashing slant to some of the press attention.' It adds: 'I once worked with someone who was passionate about fighting racism...but she thought nothing of claiming that all Americans were complete and utter idiots...she totally failed to see how prejudiced, how racist, her own anti-American views were.'

Carrying on, the True Crime blog discusses the most grotesque exploitation yet of the Matty Hull case by the British media: a visit by ITN to the home town of pilot Gus Kohntopp. The British film team camped out in the village and accosted a few locals, who seemed completely bewildered by the intrusion of an Outside Broadcast unit in the middle of rural America. One woman just burst into tears when the British reporter began pressing her about the wrongdoing of Colonel Kohntopp.

Then came the crowning moment: ITN wheeled in one Eldon Anderson, who scolded the British government for not pulling its finger out with terrorists and other rogues 'just like in World War Two'. I immediately knew what he meant: the wilderness years in which Winston Churchill tried and tried to warn Parliament and the government in power of the mortal danger of the rise of Hitler. Had he been heeded, millions upon millions of lives would have been saved.

Instead of understanding what he had said, the great British public bombarded ITN with complaints (the studio anchorman stood holding a huge sheaf of paper) because his comments had been interpreted as 'the British were cowards in the Second World War'.

Poor old Eldon had to be brought back on air the following night to apologize to the British people.

Meanwhile, Gus Kohntopp is reported to have gone into hiding. The widow of Matty Hull has offered, in a huge tabloid headline, 'My Mercy for Matty's Killers'. Mrs Hull says she does not want to punish the 'US Criminals' (another blazing headline) and says this should be a lesson to other pilots about the enormity of what they are doing in the sky and that this has consequences. (Tell that to a squadron in the heat of a massive land and air firefight.)

What is so disturbing about the coverage of this case is the fact that, had the boot been on the other foot, it is likely the American press would have shown all possible caution and restraint in dealing with its close ally. It is simply impossible to imagine any major television network – or for that matter the family of a loved one – hammering away at 'cowboy' and 'trigger-happy' Britons.

The British National Union of Journalists recently circulated to its membership a proposal that the killing of journalists be made a crime under international law. Throughout the coverage of the Terry Lloyd incident, the British media have been brutal. The latest news story is the 'outing' of the soldiers who killed Lloyd. Shadow Foreign Secretary William Hague wants to see the soldiers brought to justice. (The Tories used to be pro-American, but those days seem to be waning fast.) Yes, he was in a makeshift ambulance, but in the heat of what was a fierce confrontation, did Lloyd and his camera team, who had decided not to be embedded with the military, seriously think the platoons were going to stop and say: 'Oh, do pass and then we will resume the battle?'

Members of the National Union of Journalists, in the week of 7 April 2007, received a magazine in which an article entitled 'New Moves to Nail Killers of Terry Lloyd' tells us that the British television broadcaster ITN revealed the names of 16 soldiers in the Red Platoon of Delta Company of the US Marine Corps, but that the American authorities had refused to confirm the names. The feature further details the efforts being made by the Metropolitan Police's war crimes unit to visit the United States to interview the soldiers. The NUJ's broadcasting section organizer, Paul McLaughlin, was quoted as saying: '[We] seek to bring Terry Lloyd's killers to justice. The US has shown contempt for the British justice system.'

The article goes on to say that various international media freedom groups and unions, along with the International Federation of Journalists, supports the NUJ, whose ultimate goal is to have all 16 soldiers extradited to Britain for trial. What I find fascinating is that Daniel Demoustier, the surviving camera operator, told the Oxford inquiry that the van was 'a Kuwaiti-plated vehicle with TV signs on it'. Why was Lloyd in a Kuwaiti car? Had he been an embedded reporter, he might have lived to tell the story. The NUJ story includes a piece by former Central TV reporter John Mitchell, who says: 'I fear it will be a long road before we get full justice...for the families of the estimated 650,000 other beneficiaries of George Bush's "trigger-happy cowboy" diplomacy.'

There has been considerable derision in the press about the lack of experience of the American 'cowboy' reservist pilots who have been deployed to Iraq from places like Idaho and Wyoming. In recent years, unfortunate images of Prince Harry exiting night clubs in the wee hours have made their way into the newspapers. He was about to deploy to Iraq. He should have been with his regiment preparing for his mission. Will he be any more battle ready than Gus Kohntopp?

Anti-American feeling runs high in Britain every day. The hostility to the Americans responsible for the deaths of Matty Hull and Terry Lloyd brings a new dimension to America-hatred in the British Isles. That the journalists' union wants to see prosecutions for soldiers in the thick of battle and that the widows of both men can express such excessive malice towards the Americans who inadvertently committed these tragic acts puts Anglo-American relations at a new low.

* * * * *

America's serving men and women are reliable and professional. They are not murderers. Don't tread on them.

CHAPTER TWENTY-FIVE

CASINOS WILL BRING 'AMERICAN-STYLE' SPENT NEEDLES, THROWN-AWAY CONDOMS AND PROSTITUTION TO ALL OF BRITAIN

For some years there was talk of a super-casino being built in Britain, possibly in the Millennium Dome. The minute I heard about this I knew it was a non-starter. There is something so un-British about a Vegas-style casino city. Those of us who watched Atlantic City burgeon from a quaint seaside resort to a gambling mecca know that the presence of the underworld and organized crime had something to do with this event in 'Noo Joisey', but we all turned a blind eye to it because it meant East Coast folks could have the time of their lives without having to get on an airplane.

And that is the Golden Nugget: in the 32 years in which I have resided in Great Britain, I have come to realize that one of the many things that separate us from our British cousins is our concept of 'the time of your life'. If you have ever watched Americans gamble in casinos, they do it with an alacrity that can only be compared to the passion with which so many Britons and Europeans guzzle alcohol. (Even the Germans were amazed when British fans turned up at 8:30am at the 2006 World Cup to find that the bars had yet to open, so desperate were they to get an early start on imbibing.)

I am sure there is a culture of alcohol consumption in the United States, but the fact (mentioned elsewhere) that Americans are entitled to only two weeks' vacation a year, and have no universal healthcare or a welfare state to cushion extended hangovers, may be the reason why alcohol is the main source of joy and rapture in Britain and Northern Europe, rather than in America. The climate is not nice, the sports facilities are not wonderful and drink is a wonderful outlet. Lest we forget that the USA was the home of Prohibition! Imagine Prohibition taking hold in Germany or even Italy... So, Americans like to go to casinos during their pitifully short vacation leave, and in Europe 'folks' like to drink. Eventually their socialized medical systems will take care of them. Americans know that liver damage means a million-dollar medical bill.

In this context, let us turn to the general attitude towards casinos expressed across a wide spectrum of British opinion in recent years. I was seated with a middle-class couple in a restaurant in London in 2007, and they were, shall we say, being generous in their consumption of alcohol. They berated me about the 'ghastly' American 'casino culture' that they feared would be brought to Britain by Labour cabinet minister Tessa Jowell and her cohorts. They said they were delighted and relieved to learn that plans for a super-casino for Manchester and Leeds had been stopped in their tracks. They kept repeating the 'ghastly American' mantra in describing a horrible hub of drugs, prostitution and crime as innocent Brits fought their way past junkies, hookers and muggers in and out of the ghastly American-style casino.

What a far cry from the thoroughly enjoyable, eminently safe and relaxing times my family and I have had in the many casinos of Atlantic City! My late mother, a cultured, well-read and much esteemed educator, looked forward with glee to her bus trips to the casinos from her building in central Philadelphia, as did so many other dignified retired professionals. Americans are masters of organization for one another (I stress one another, because though Iraq is a disaster, I blame the Iraqis, not Americans, for the mess): the bus trips to Atlantic City for city dwellers are organized with skill, and give millions of Americans a wonderful day out at the seashore and the chance to visit the slot machines.

Perhaps Britons know themselves all too well to relish the advent of super-casinos. The addictive nature of gambling is not too far removed from addiction to alcohol, which is becoming a plague that is putting 10-year-olds into hospital in Britain. So, Britons do not see super-casinos as a wonderful day out or a weekend by the sea, but as a miserable, dark journey into a netherworld of ruin and disgrace – not unlike a horrible, destructive hangover.

When I appeared on BBC's *Any Questions?* in Blackpool in November 2006, the buzz in the town was that it might be chosen to host the super-casino. In the end, Manchester was chosen, and I could not help but feel a twinge of sorrow for poor Blackpool, a seaside location that would have lent itself so readily to an Atlantic City-style resort. But it was not meant to be, and now even Manchester is in doubt due to the fierce opposition in Britain from the clergy and from all sectors of society, dreading that 'ghastly American-style den of prostitution, drugs and crime'.*

The couple who had lectured me about the prospect of a super-casino culture in Britain also said it would cause local degeneration and poverty. 'Look at all those down and outs in Atlantic City', they exclaimed. (I asked them when they had last been and they thought hard. 'Ummmm, oh, it must have been 1973.' I guffawed. That was the era of the Burt Lancaster film!) I explained to them that my sister, an intellectual who would be the last to hang out in casino towns, had pointed out to me the marvellous regeneration that had taken place in Atlantic City in the past decade and how many jobs had been created by a new and quite magnificent shopping precinct.

Here is what happens when Philadelphians or Washingtonians go to Atlantic City. They meet at the designated local ticketing centre and buy a seat on a Casino Bus. On the luxurious bus I take from Union Station in the nation's capital I have my own private movie screen and laugh my way through *Meet the Fockers*. It is a pleasant ride to the seaside city, and we are deposited at our chosen casinos. A uniformed supervisor boards the bus and gives instructions on how to

* As this book was being readied for publication, the Manchester project was scrapped; could this be the Scottish Presbyterian pragmatism of Gordon Brown and Alistair Darling winning the day? A sad day for Manchester in my view.

use the tickets and vouchers. (Some casinos provide superb food deals, and indeed some people just do the day trip to enjoy the bounty of American-style culinary plenty.)

I would venture that the vast majority of Americans who go to casinos know their limits and quit while ahead. My late mother had remarkable luck with slot machines, and when she hit a jackpot she would cash in and spend the rest of the day people-watching on the splendid Atlantic City Boardwalk or in the gorgeous, clean and lively casino food concessions. Needless to say, the cheerful and welcoming staff one finds across the United States of America are not in short supply in Atlantic City; one of the pleasures of these bus trips is the graciousness of the well-trained staff and the atmosphere of safety. Casinos are regulated and the presence of uniformed patrols eliminates any concern about 'prostitutes, druggies and criminals' consuming the entire enterprise.

Atlantic City has retained its 19th-century charm, with the legendary James's Salt Water Taffy store and the usual seaside attractions for children and adults alike along the Boardwalk, not to mention the jitneys* and mini-train service. There are the other shore points – Cape May, Ventnor, Ocean City, Margate – that have also retained their old-world charm and that offer a warm and safe welcome to visitors. Does this sound like a travel column? Well, I am trying to describe the real-world version of the American casino experience, in order to counter the ignorant and defamatory prose that has proliferated in Britain, generated by people who, I would wager, have never spent a minute in Atlantic City or Las Vegas.

Americans know how to have a good time. My sister and I stayed at the Taj Mahal on the Boardwalk in 2006 and had the time of our lives. We got up at 4am to watch the high rollers on the huge and deserted casino floor, playing the tables in the wee hours as a lone cleaning woman polished the slot machines. We went for a walk in the sea mist and fog and never felt threatened. We ate well, had hours of good sea air

* Very small human-driven carriages, similar to those now so common in London and other British cities.

and watched hundreds of others from all walks of life doing the same.

Yes, gambling can ruin lives, wreck families and destroy marriages. But having been to the casino cities for years, and having watched countless others like me quitting while ahead and enjoying the other pleasures of the beautiful, user-friendly resorts, I totally reject the nonsense being bandied about in the British media about the evils of American casino towns.

The regeneration of Atlantic City has created thousands of jobs, while at the same time the unique character of the town has been retained. One does not have to stay at the Taj; there are still little bed and breakfasts and motels in which to sleep, and the fish and oyster bars are still thriving as they did 50 years ago. The Korean War Memorial, for example, is one of the sights of the Boardwalk. Needles? Tarts?? Criminal gangs???

In the many, many trips I have taken to my favourite casino city, I have never seen crowds of druggies, crooks, drunks and hookers besieging innocent tourists, and I resent the implication in the British media – and to my face – about the squalor that is the American shore resort.

Shut up, Britain, get sober and get a ticket to Atlantic City and learn the facts before pontificating about something about which you really and truly know nothing.

And instead of falling down in an expensive alcoholic stupor on the Boardwalk, save your money and buy some Salt Water Taffy.

CHAPTER TWENTY-SIX

'YOU PEOPLE KILLED MOUNTBATTEN!'

I decided to be a tourist for the day and to visit Westminster Abbey. It is a vast place. The experience proved exhausting, and I had to sit down halfway through the building.

Whilst resting, I asked a warder why there are American flags in the stained-glass windows. He explained that many generous American donors had sent significant funds to sustain the work of the Abbey. These windows were a way of recognizing their generosity. Amongst the donors have been the Annenberg and Walton families. My fellow Philadelphian Walter Annenberg had been US Ambassador to the Court of St James, and the Waltons founded Wal-Mart. One window has a Star of David alongside a cross, with the word 'Reconciliation' across the middle section. This was in honour of a gift from an Anglophile American heiress who comes over every year and leaves flowers in various sections of the Abbey.

The warder said he bristles whenever he hears anti-American rhetoric. I do dwell on anti-Americanism in Britain, so I must say his kindness was a refreshing change from the rebukes I get most days of the week.

Resuming my tour, I found a tiny café in an outdoor section of cloisters and was told that there were no lavatories, just those across the road. I had a good chuckle as I looked down at the gravestone of John Burgoyne, partially obscured by the busy feet of the serving staff in the café. Burgoyne was the villain of my childhood schooling – the 'Redcoat' general who failed to defeat the ragtag Colonial revolutionary fighters, and thus was born the United States of America.

Leaving the Abbey, I asked another warder why, with donations pouring in from the USA, there was no proper restaurant or lavatory for weary visitors. He snarled at me: 'Madam, they gotta pay our salaries, and don't think the staff like having no lavatory.' I decided to leave him in peace, as I had obviously struck a nerve.

My recent illness had left me with limited energy, so I hailed a taxi. I told the driver that I had lived in London for 30 years, but had just learned something new: the story of American generosity to the Abbey. I added that I lamented the lack of facilities for the public. Obviously I hit a nerve with him, too. He launched into a lecture about the amounts of money sent to the IRA by Americans. In my naivety I had thought he would be touched that Americans, some Jewish, had opened their cheque books to help maintain this icon of Christian worship.

He went on and on about Noraid and the IRA, dismissing the Abbey contributions as irrelevant when it was Americans who were still sending funds to the Irish terrorists.

I reminded him that it was a tiny minority of Americans who sent money to the IRA. I also explained that Irish Americans have an entirely different relationship with others in the USA because they generate affection amongst the general populace, unlike the derision they inspire in some British circles. My ancestors, I told him, had come from Lithuania in 1905 and had no Irish connection. He was of Lithuanian-Jewish extraction but did not get my point.

I wish Londoners would stop lecturing Americans about slavery, the Indians, the IRA and genocides we apparently commit.

Yes, getting through immigration in the USA is not a nice start; but, once you are in the country, Americans adore Britons and offer unconditional warmth from Seattle to Boston to Houston to San Diego. They do not lecture Britons. I wish London would reciprocate.

CHAPTER TWENTY-SEVEN

INTERLUDE – IN PRAISE OF MI5, THE NHS, BRITISH VETERANS AND SOME WONDERFUL JOURNALISTS

This book is not intended to be an indictment of Britain. Indeed, when I am in the USA I sorely miss rose and violet creams, fish and chips with vinegar, our immaculate black taxis and the best of London's incomparable Jewish cabbies, scones with clotted cream, Marmite, Bovril, the stunning ancient cathedrals, the British countryside, Peter Crouch's little 'goal dance', Glyndebourne, Christmas crackers, mulled wine, cricket at Lord's (yes, I adore it) and the magnificent people of the National Health Service, not to mention my core group of loyal, immensely tolerant and kind friends who have seen me through thick and thin with a staggering degree of generosity of spirit.

No, this book is a critique of the curious rise of extreme British and European anti-Americanism and anti-Semitism/anti-Zionism, and, in the case of the national press, its inordinate influence upon public opinion. At a late 2007 event presented by the Henry Jackson Society in London, a retired member of the intelligence community said we needn't worry about US–UK relations because the intelligence services of both countries enjoy a superb relationship. So I would like to turn to a side of Britain that is one of its most admirable institutions – the intelligence community. Then, even if my conservative American readers throw this book into the incinerator, I will turn to the magnificent universal healthcare system, the NHS.

In the first week of May 2007, a remarkable achievement was marked in the annals of MI5 and MI6 (British domestic and international intelligence).

Omar Khyam, Waheed Mahmoud, Anthony Garcia, Jawad Akbar and Salahuddin Amin were convicted of conspiring to perpetrate an atrocity on the British mainland that would have put 9/11 in the shade. All British citizens, the men plotted, over a stretch of time, a meticulously devised series of attacks on the Ministry of Sound nightclub, the Bluewater shopping mall in Kent and the House of Commons that would have resulted in mass casualties. They were to use fertilizer bombs, a nuclear device and an airliner to generate maximum death and destruction in their country, Great Britain. They sought out jobs in the power industry to establish the routes of the gas and electric grids.

The tracking of their plot, known as Operation Crevice, involved hundreds of intelligence and police operatives both here and abroad. Credit is due to the vigilant young woman at the self-storage depot in England who wondered why the suspects were storing one gigantic load of fertilizer in their unit. She alerted police; in turn the security services removed the fertilizer for tests and replaced it with an exact visual replica made of cat litter. The terror suspects returned to inspect their parcel and were caught on a secret camera. The rest is history.

Over 13 brilliant months, the intelligence services managed to track the five Operation Crevice terrorists undetected and to accumulate evidence with meticulous care and discretion. Furthermore, the man who gave evidence against the five, Mohammed Babar, was arrested in New York; his evidence was fundamental to the trial. It is to the credit of the security services in the United States and the United Kingdom that he was apprehended and, as it were, 'cultivated' into turning state's evidence – become a 'supergrass'. (In a bizarre inversion of logic about Babar, a reader of the London *Evening Standard*, John O'Brien of Woldingham, Surrey wrote in to the paper: 'The Crown Prosecution Service is now claiming a major success...over the use of an American citizen to give evidence on its behalf.' He goes on to say that it is 'regrettable that members of the US forces have not been brought to witness or to justice when they have been involved in the deaths of British soldiers'. American soldiers who commit a tragic friendly fire mistake in the same league as five mass-murderers with fertilizer bombs and dirty nukes?)

During the Second World War, the British intelligence services performed remarkable feats in the defeat of Hitler. The new enemies of the West, radical religious fanatics dressed as ordinary Joes in jeans and Nikes, are being tracked down with the same skill possessed by the geniuses at Bletchley. If thousands and even tens of thousands of deaths in the UK and abroad have been prevented through the incarceration of the five terror masterminds, MI5 and the police deserve plaudits and, most of all, gratitude from a nation and world redeemed from an unspeakable and unprecedented tragedy.

THE NHS

When I was in the USA, people from varied backgrounds and professions were exercised beyond any semblance of normality about the cost of health insurance, the 45 million uninsured Americans and the ruinous cost of prophylactic medications. I heard countless horror stories about spiralling insurance costs and prohibitive prescription drug prices.

During my recent visits to the USA, I was plagued by ill health and by a crippling condition in my right leg. Having heard endless stories of woe from the American people I encountered on my multi-city visit, I was wary of going to a hospital. Even though I had travel insurance with an old and trusted British underwriter, I had heard horror stories about people being hit for five-figure bills, even whilst insured.

I waited until my return to Britain to see a doctor. My bright and cheery surgery (medical practice) full of welcoming staff provided me with the much-needed check-up and a prescription refill for the pills I take every day. I was told I needed a repeat of the comprehensive blood tests completed a year ago. None of this involved any money. When I went to the chemist to have the large prescription filled, I was handed my bag of boxed medications and no money changed hands. Each prescription costs the equivalent of $12.00 in Great Britain, but those on lifetime drugs pay $180 a year for an unlimited supply of prescribed drugs. Having been a British taxpayer all my adult life, I am delighted that in some small way my contribution to the common good has made this wonderful system possible.

However, when I was telephoned in autumn by a 2004 Kerry campaign executive in Boston, he became apoplectic when I said I might like to talk to American audiences about socialized medicine. He might as well have been a reactionary McCarthyite for his fury at the word 'socialized'. I was told that I would not be welcome at any campaign event if I so much as whispered a word about the British medical system. When I suggested I could refer to the majestic British medical system as the National Health Service, I was warned again that this would be an inappropriate subject for a local crowd. When I went to hear Senator John McCain speak in Friendship Heights, Maryland, the audience of retirees clapped when I asked him about the spiralling cost of medical care, diagnostics and pharmaceuticals. But he, too, seemed distinctly uncomfortable about the topic. I am not so naive as to believe that the pharmaceutical and insurance companies are shrinking violets when it comes to lobbying in the corridors of government.

Let me explain, before my American readers go ballistic. In Great Britain, politicians of all viewpoints revere the National Health Service. It will never be damaged by any political party in my lifetime. The British economy is healthy, and we have nothing to compare to the huge American budget deficit. The NHS has never bankrupted this country. Some of my medications are manufactured in the Third World, and I am not dead yet. Our doctors and consultants are amongst the most erudite and sought-after on the globe.

No one in Britain goes uncared for; the provisions for the disabled and elderly are not the best in the world, but they are improving.

What a pity Harry Truman did not create an NHS in the same year that Clement Attlee and the post-war British government did. I heard Ted Kennedy speak at the National Press Club in Washington. Some 50 years ago, he said, he would meet constituents in Massachusetts who were terrified of losing their homes to medical bills; today he was encountering their grandchildren, and they had the same worries. He considered that an utterly shameful situation in the richest nation on earth. This is one aspect of life in the United States that needs change, and the NHS is a shining example from Britain.

I do believe Britain can also learn from America in certain areas, so 'here goes'.

RETURNING SERVICE PERSONNEL

A disturbing discourse erupted in Great Britain in late 2006 over the appalling manner in which British servicemen and women are treated when they return from Iraq and Afghanistan. The aftercare of veterans is an aspect of American government that is admirable and worth replicating in Britain. I receive lectures about the appalling situations in which American veterans find themselves after release. This is simply untrue. My mother was a Second World War veteran and my father worked for the US Army Corps of Engineers, so the welfare of men and women in uniform is an issue deeply embedded in my psyche.

In one report in early 2007, Lord Bramall, a former chief of staff, was dismayed by the news of a British paratrooper being verbally threatened by a Muslim visitor to a public ward in a Birmingham hospital. Many of these men fear for their lives as they lie helpless in their beds with serious wounds and illnesses.

The intruder, at Selly Oak Hospital in Birmingham, had been seen more than once harassing civilian and military personnel at the hospital. Various reports indicate that the problem arises from the lack of facilities in Britain for returning and long-term injured veterans. One soldier is quoted as saying that British troops pray they are sent to Ramstein, which they describe as the 'outstanding American facility' in Germany. If sent to Britain, they 'have a mental health patient on one side and an incontinent geriatric on the other'.

I have read British columnists making the bizarre observation that American troops also have a miserable time when they return home, because George W. Bush provides tax cuts to the wealthy. What on earth this has to do with the welfare of wounded soldiers is beyond me. These are the times when I do believe Americans and Brits have more than an ocean between them where the processing of information is concerned.

Notwithstanding the daily drubbing America gets here in the United Kingdom, one of the many areas in which the United States is head and shoulders above any other nation in the world is its care of veterans. Before readers in America start yelling 'But what about the aging VA* hospitals? What about Walter Reed? It needs to be thrown down!' I say: 'Be grateful America has these hospitals at all. Britain is in dire need of a VA, and of facilities and benefits that match the extraordinary sacrifices its serving men and women make, and have made, defending these little islands for decades.'

As far back as 1636, the pilgrims of Plymouth Colony passed a law providing assistance for soldiers from the colony's resources. The United States Congress has passed laws over the years providing for ample care for veterans. There are literally hundreds and hundreds of veterans' homes, rehabilitation centres and educational programmes available to service personnel and their families.

When the United States entered the First World War, programmes were put in place to provide disability compensation, insurance and vocational rehabilitation. Finally the VA came into being by an Act of Congress in 1930, and of course after the Second World War the GI Bill of Rights was established. After the Second World War over 600,000 veterans were able to learn new skills and get further education because of the GI Bill.

The fact that the GI Bill of Rights enabled hundreds of thousands of war veterans and their families to attend university helped turn the United States into the hugely successful nation it is today. After the Second World War, immigration was not high, and veterans were given preference for job

* Veterans Administration.

placement and housing. This would have been a wonderful scheme for Britain. It is believed the GI Bill had more impact on American life and destiny than any legislation had had since the Homestead Act of 1844. More recently, the scores of 'Fisher Houses' – financed by elderly millionaire philanthropist Zac Fisher – provide subsidized housing for the families of thousands of hospitalized veterans.

For a moment, I would like to digress about Zac Fisher. Over the past few years, Lord Levy, a Tony Blair confidant, has been vilified in the British media and called 'Lord Cashpoint'. He is a wealthy man who has given to charity and helped the Labour party. He was arrested twice and was pilloried in the press about possible 'cash for peerages'. His generosity to charity and the man-hours given to the country as an envoy are ignored by the media, except when they want to accuse him of paying no taxes (his sharp retort was that he had worked tirelessly for the Blair regime and had not drawn a penny for his efforts). By contrast, in the United States, the very Jewish Zac Fisher became a national hero through his wide-ranging philanthropy. Imagine if a man like Fisher had been encouraged to flourish in Britain, and had helped our veterans with his immense personal wealth. I suspect the media would have found some excuse to vilify him as a 'Zionist show-off' or something similar. Here is a rundown – from his Foundation's website – of the Zac Fisher generosity table, unblemished by media and political assassination:

> In 1994, Mr. Fisher, in partnership with David Rockefeller, established the Fisher Center for Alzheimer's Research Foundation, which funds Alzheimer's disease research with the goal of finding a cause and cure. The Foundation operates the nation's largest and most modern Alzheimer's research laboratory, housed at The Rockefeller University in New York City.
>
> He was a major supporter of the Metropolitan Opera, Temple Israel, the Jewish Institute of National Security Affairs, the George C. Marshall Foundation, the

> Margaret Thatcher Foundation, the Reagan Presidential Library, the United Jewish Appeal and many other organizations. Mr. Fisher also served on the boards of Carnegie Hall... In 1998, Mr. Fisher received the Presidential Medal of Freedom from President Bill Clinton in honor of his wide-ranging contributions on behalf of the young men and women in the US Armed Forces...

It is a disgrace that Britain's brave fighting men and women are treated in such a shabby way; there is no British equivalent of Arlington National Cemetery, nor is there an organization as vast as the Department of Veterans' Affairs. When I was interviewing British war veterans for a documentary, every man said he was envious of the generous schemes available to American servicemen that were non-existent in Britain.

My late mother used to say that a nation's humanity could be measured by the way it treats its Jews. One ventures to say that a nation's greatness may also be measured by the way it treats its veterans in both war and peacetime.

I recall reading an article by the *Evening Standard* weekly columnist Nick Cohen about the appalling treatment of British war veterans; he mentioned the fact that Lloyd George gave all working-class men the vote after the sacrifices of the First World War. Well, I decided to do some research and discovered, as I had suspected, that the 'ghastly' and Drabble-loathed United States actually enfranchised all white men, rich and poor alike, way back in the years 1820 to 1840. In 1860, all black men were given the vote by five states. In 1870, all black men were granted the vote and, soon after, so were Native Americans. In 1920, black and white women were given the vote.

So, yet again the awful USA, about which I am browbeaten every day, actually beat Britain by a hundred years in giving all men the dignity of suffrage.

Instead of constantly condemning the United States in the media and at political party conferences, the United Kingdom might like to look to the USA for new ideas, and the first might be some way to give its struggling veterans the dignity they deserve.

SOME WONDERFUL BRITISH JOURNALISTS

It was heartening to read Rachel Halliburton, in her review of *Royal Welcome* (*Evening Standard*, 20 November 2003), actually putting tongue in cheek about the trilogy of anti-war plays at the Royal Court Theatre. In one reading that featured Vanessa Redgrave, American writer Tony Kushner's *Only We Who Guard the Mystery Shall Be Unhappy* describes the death of 650,000 children through sanctions and the bombing of Iraq. Halliburton suggests that Saddam himself would have had several rooms full of dead children to read to, without American help. One of the plays by Caryl Churchill evokes e-mails to and from Iraqis and Americans: 'I hope we nuke you and the camels you fuck with.'

* * * * *

As 2007 drew to a close and the sub-prime mortgage crisis was being mentioned every day on each and every British radio and television news discussion, the United States was now being dubbed the culprit of yet more international woe.

I really began to wonder if it could get much worse for American expatriates in Britain, as even the Northern Rock debacle – the first run on a British bank in well over a century – was blamed on irresponsible American lending. All through 2007, we had been hearing about the billions of pounds owed by British borrowers on credit cards, hire purchase and loans. Repeated interest rate rises in Britain throughout 2006 and 2007 by Chancellor of the Exchequer and Prime Minister-apparent Gordon Brown had pushed my own mortgage repayment from three to four figures a month. Thousands of Britons were finding it impossible to make ends meet and bankruptcies were at an all-time high. Was this the fault of some benighted borrowers in Texas or Arkansas?

In January 2008, elaborate explanations were offered by a stream of British pundits linking the island nation's every woe with the sub-prime disaster across the ocean. It reminded me of the many jokes in which Israel is blamed for everything – even for an Italian soccer team's bus, driven by a Swede, overturning on a road in Algiers.

It was therefore gratifying to read two pithy articles in the *Evening Standard*, one by Anthony Hilton and the other by Merryn Somerset Webb, editor of *Money Week* – both defending Americans to the hilt.

In her article in the *Evening Standard* ('Don't Blame the States for the State We're In', 8 January 2008), Merryn Somerset Webb reminds the British public that our own banks have been lending with 'gay abandon' for years, and that this fiscal gaiety had to come home to roost, not in some foreclosed turkey farm in Nebraska, but in our own repossessed backyards. She asserts that the United Kingdom had a budget surplus in 2000, but is now moving into deficit. Most significantly, she criticizes Prime Minister Gordon Brown for using the American credit crisis as a reason for a possible downturn. She quotes him having said, on a Sunday political programme hosted by the BBC's Andrew Marr, that any signs of weakness in the British economy could be tied to the 'global credit problem that started in America'. She says this verges on the dishonest.

Somerset Webb, to my relief and delight, examines the root causes of the British economic downturn with refreshing candour. She lists the removal of incentives to save, the dismantling of the manufacturing industry in favour of cheap Chinese imports, and the disorder in public finance, which she describes as a 'complete mess'. She says it is Gordon Brown's remit to come up with the cash to repair a rapidly crumbling British economy that has been in self-destruct mode for years, and she ends with a glorious: 'How exactly is that America's fault, then?'

In his *Evening Standard* article ('Mad to Attack "Our" Americans', 13 December 2007), Anthony Hilton tells of a new tax to be levied on non-domiciled workers in the UK. Americans working in Britain, whom he sees as the backbone of the explosive success of the City over the past decade, pay full tax on income earned in Britain to the British exchequer, and will now be required to pay a further £30,000 surcharge for the privilege of living in the United Kingdom.

Hilton is an established financial journalist and is not known for scare-mongering, but he asserts that the surcharge will undermine all the hard work put in by non-domiciled workers and will provoke a rapid departure of talent over the next few months. American couples would face a £60,000 surcharge, plus income tax at 40 per cent to the Inland Revenue. If they renounce their American citizenship they will, according to Hilton's source, be liable to punitive measures in the United States. He sees the exodus of Americans from the financial hub of England as a tragedy that must be reversed.

Hilton's passion in his article is a welcome change from the usual daily diet of America-hatred in the media; what is so touching is his plea to Chancellor Alistair Darling to rescind the ridiculous tax, which he says will reduce Britain's attractiveness as a place to do business and which he says 'simply beggars belief'.

CHAPTER TWENTY-EIGHT

'DIE, GLAZER, DIE!' – THE CHARMING REACTION OF BRITISH FOOTBALL FANS TO AN AMERICAN TYCOON

As I write this, most Americans will have no idea who Malcolm Glazer is, although they may get to know about him if the many Britons threatening him with death have their way.

As usual, the American media, obsessed with judicial nominations, John Bolton, *American Idol* and the Michael Jackson trial, are missing out on stories that could shake the world and explain (God forbid) the next, much worse, 9/11, Bali or Madrid.

To its credit, the Philadelphia *Evening Bulletin* put the Glazer story on its front page on 16 May 2005. It was a major event in the United Kingdom, and further illustrates the catastrophic deterioration in the 'special relationship' between the UK and the USA. Two years down the line, Manchester United is at the top of the league, but at the time of the Glazer saga one would have thought the Jewish-American tycoon was going to cause the total demise of the club.

Here is the Glazer saga.

Malcolm Glazer, a billionaire entrepreneur who owns the Tampa Bay Buccaneers football team, decided in 2005 to purchase the legendary British soccer team, Manchester United. This caused instantaneous fury and pandemonium in Her Majesty's Kingdom. Effigies of Glazer were burned in Manchester, and soccer fans across England expressed outrage that an American ('scumbag' as one fan called him) could be allowed to venture into the hallowed world of British sport. Thousands of posters of Glazer with a bull's-eye across his face proliferated across Great Britain. Even well-spoken

Britons told interviewers they were 'fucking furious' about the Glazer venture. Having been at the receiving end myself of scary vitriol from the mouths of otherwise genteel Anglos, the attitude did not surprise me.

There is something about the combination of 'American' and 'Jew' that causes paroxysms of rage in Great Britain these days. The fact that poor old Malcolm, aged 75, could provoke such malice across the British Isles is due largely to his Yank background. Interestingly enough, Russian–Jewish Roman Abramovich bought and runs Chelsea soccer team, but his purchase angered few. 'Chelski', as he is known, seems to enjoy the game and its European traditions, but Glazer had never set foot in a British footie stadium. Glazer is accused of endeavouring to attach massive debts to the assets of Manchester United, and in turn the fans are determined to boycott the turnstiles. Whatever Glazer's shortcomings and motives, the rhetoric and epithets being used to denounce him have all the hallmarks of the abuse expatriate Yanks get every day in London and other European cities. 'Piss off!' is the basic starting point.

One accusation that amused me was a British fan's comment that Glazer will bring unwanted American ways to England. Having attended countless sporting events in the United States from my early childhood in the 1950s, I cannot recall one instance in which anyone was drunk or disorderly. I attended the opening of the Washington Nationals season at Philadelphia's main stadium and then the home season opener at Robert Kennedy Stadium in the nation's capital. On both occasions, the grounds were packed to capacity, yet there was not one incident of hooliganism. Tiny children sat on their parents' laps drinking milk, and the grown-ups cried when the 'Star Spangled Banner' was sung by a beautiful African-American vocal artist. A huge American flag was unfurled by men and women of the armed forces, provoking more tears, followed by a fly-past of fighter jets. The 'Philly Phanatic' entertained the tots and a trivia quiz kept everyone occupied during the seventh inning stretch.

Such are the 'ways' Americans like Glazer would bring to alcohol-sodden, violence-ridden and wholly malevolent male yobbo-only sporting events in England. On the Metro after the Washington game, thousands of Americans of all races and backgrounds piled onto the pretty, immaculate and air-conditioned trains, and little ones chatted with their parents. Not one person was drunk, nor was there an ounce of malice between fans of opposing teams.

Malcolm Glazer may be a ruthless operator, but his actions have triggered the sort of anti-American frenzy that is not far removed from the scenes in Grosvenor and Trafalgar Squares, when the American flag was burned and used as an object of revulsion by various groups a few weeks before the 7 July bombings. Were a Briton to wish to buy an American team, one would expect excitement and the usual awe with which 'I am British' evokes on American soil. Americans have a regard, generosity of spirit and affection for Britain that is not reciprocated these days.

When Glazer was reported to have been receiving death threats, one wondered where the wave of anti-American hate would end. As it is – and if it makes the 'Die, Glazer, Die!' Mancunians happy – he had a stroke some time after this confrontation, and is now not much use to anyone. Frankly, I wish Glazer had put his millions into another American team. One British commentator, explaining to his readers who Glazer is, said he owns 'the Tampa Bay Buccaneers, whoever they may be'. Well, they ain't nothin'. If that British journalist knew anything about American sport, he would be aware of the Buccaneers' improved standing. They only happen to have won the Super Bowl.

It appears that the Jewish Yank Glazer has provoked the ugly side of the Englishman – not a pretty sight.

Before a stroke prevented him from ever travelling again, one hoped he had adequate protection when he went to Manchester. Who would have thought that in 2005 – 60 years since brave American soldiers again marched into Europe to sort out its hideous, blood-curdling disputes – an American would be threatened with death?

The Glazer episode has been shameful. Considering that Scottish football fans jeered when a moment's silence was requested for the dying Pope, one hopes the Brits might look to America for better ways of conducting sporting events.

My final word to the Manchester United fans who bombarded me with such unmitigated and sustained abuse in 2005 – and who bizarrely called my criticism of their behaviour 'racist' – is this: it should be noted that, in January 2008, the club may not have been in profit but was at the top of the league, and all were rejoicing. In May, Sir Alex Ferguson told the *Guardian* newspaper (3 May 2008) that he was flourishing under the care of the Glazers.

CHAPTER TWENTY-NINE

MAYFAIR BANS AMERICA, NOW AND FOREVER

The headline on the cover of the *Evening Standard* magazine of 13 April 2007 read: 'The US Embassy Siege'. Inasmuch as Britain had just endured the unfortunate saga of the 15 marines and sailors captured by Iran and then released with goody bags, one assumed this was a feature about the truly terrible Iranian hostage siege in 1979 that ultimately brought down the Carter administration.

However, the subtitle of the article read: 'How the Residents of W1 Saw Off the Yanks.'

Aha! This was to be yet another piece about the Americans besmirching Grosvenor Square. There has been an American presence in the square since 1786. The ambassador actually lives in Winfield House in Regent's Park, a home donated by Woolworth heiress Barbara Hutton.

The ambassador during the Second World War, John Gilbert Winant, was adored by Londoners from the East End to Mayfair to Clapham to St John's Wood. His personal generosity and solidarity with Britain during the darkest days of the Blitz endeared him to the country for a generation. One of the many legends about Winant was his insistence on distributing to Londoners sheltering in tube stations from the nightly bombings the luxury foods sent over from the USA to the embassy. After the war, when he visited London, theatregoers would run over and greet him, tears in their eyes. He was given the Freedom of various British cities. To this day, 'Winants', a group of young Americans, arrive each year to do good work in soup kitchens and shelters across Britain, in honour of his memory.

Sixty years on, the attitude of Londoners towards Americans is radically different. After 11 September 2001, the US embassy building in Grosvenor Square was supplied with large concrete barriers and bollards to ward off a car or truck bomb. Every Briton I know, old and young, from both Left and Right, fumed at me about the way 'the Americans' had ruined the look of Grosvenor Square. Armed policemen patrol day and night. Efforts were made to turn some streets into no-entry zones, but these were not successful. Animosity towards the embassy has mounted year in and year out since 9/11.

Now, after years of protests that the embassy is the number one terrorist target in the world, the Mayfair residents' association has finally succeeded in driving it from its historic residence. The US Navy Department has already moved from its beautiful offices; shortly after 9/11 a friend who had been activated to reserve duty in London told me that her uniformed colleagues were fearful of going out for a walk because several had been on the receiving end of stunning verbal abuse. This I can believe, because no sooner had 9/11 happened than I was being lectured about American support for Israel being the reason the world was in turmoil and that Yanks are such cowards. (A cab driver told me that British pilots and passengers would have seen off all four sets of hijackers.) The retired American ambassador, Philip Lader, was foot-stomped and shouted down by a hostile London audience on the BBC's *Question Time* on Thursday 13 September 2001.

So, here we are in 2007, and Mayfair residents have staged hunger strikes and mounted loud protests at meetings with representatives of the US federal government when the fate of the embassy was discussed. The reasoning presented by the Mayfair protestors was that the local residents have been in mortal danger since 9/11. Another obvious reason is the depreciation of local property and the cost of home insurance. In the end, the present ambassador, Robert Tuttle, instructed estate agents Knight Frank to put the site on the market. It is believed the embassy staff will be moved to Kensington Palace or Chelsea Barracks, if the local residents there do not go on hunger strike as well.

What is so objectionable about the fury shown by Mayfair residents is that the attitude and actions have been so hostile and, at times, so extreme. One embassy staffer is reported to have said he would welcome a transfer to Manchuria, and former Ambassador Bill Farish is reported in the *Evening Standard* to have loathed every minute of his posting, save for his moments with Her Majesty the Queen. This, the city that endured the relentless bombings and rocket attacks by Hitler night after night for years, is now furious that the presence of the Americans will make London a target. When the 7 July 2005 bombers struck, did they single out locations popular with Americans? How nice it would have been if Mayfair residents had shown generosity of spirit and solidarity with America, instead of staging ugly protests to have them removed from their environment, as if they were the Taliban or worse.

Had Britain been attacked in 2001 and then waged a war that evolved into an internationally detested conflict, it is doubtful that Washingtonians would have raised such a fuss about the British embassy in the nation's capital. If, in fact, the British embassy had been considered a top target in Washington, it is likely the authorities would have laid on extra protection.

One interesting footnote to this saga: shortly after writing this chapter I went to a tea party held by a friend I had known for some 30 years. I told the group about the imminent departure of the Americans from Grosvenor Square, and one of the guests, an otherwise elegant woman, said: 'Oh, I was thrilled to hear the CIA is leaving, although someone should have set fire to them while they were in the square, and frankly, I wish someone would blow the whole place up, preferably while everyone is working there.'

Everyone laughed. I left early.

At the end of 2007, I attended an interview with the American ambassador, Robert Tuttle, at an art gallery. He is a keen art collector and told the interviewer, a charming Newcastle businesswoman, that he also donated art to worthy causes. She was able to ask him a few questions about his life in London and his affection for artists, but when the proceedings were opened up to the mixed audience of British and American business people, all hell broke loose. Again, as I repeat often in this book, there are those who would applaud an audience that literally barracked the ambassador. Very angry questioners demanded to know his take on Guantanamo and the Iraq War. Some shouted, and one would just not sit down, delivering a lengthy discourse suggesting that the ambassador was part of a gang of callous and uncaring war criminals. A veiled Muslim journalist in the front row jumped from her seat and shouted at him as he tried to answer one of the combatants.

Yes, dear liberal reader (if you are still reading), you will think this was darned brave of that audience, but afterwards I was joined by an African-American woman who described herself as a Democrat from a long line of liberals and activists, and she was appalled by the whole event. I had never seen a foreign dignitary treated so badly since the incident involving former Ambassador Philip Lader on the BBC's *Question Time*. I found the verbal assaults on the ambassador ugly. He and his wife left in a hurry without staying for what was meant to be a post-interview reception, and I felt ashamed at the sight of his distress.

Anti-Americanism is ridiculous and it has become even nastier in Britain as this book goes to press. It is all-pervasive and creeps into the social discourse, as if picking on Americans is the new Jew-baiting. This leads me into my next chapter, the truly unbelievable story of the death threats to elderly Texan Tom Hicks and Midwesterner George Gillett, who must rue the day they ever attempted to buy Liverpool Football Club.

CHAPTER THIRTY

YOU MAY HAVE TO WALK ALONE, LIVERPOOL...BUT AVRAM GRANT WILL NEVER WALK ALONE

The hatred of 'Yanks' in widening British circles is scary and irrational. As I finish this volume, I am staggered by the level of hatred from Liverpool football fans towards the two 'bloody Yanks' who decided to make a major investment in their legendary football club and the 'Gasssss' chants at Stamford Bridge at Chelsea's Jewish coach Avram Grant, son of a Holocaust survivor.

George Gillett, owner of the fabulously successful Montreal Canadiens hockey team, has told the British media that his son and daughter-in-law in the USA were receiving threatening night-time telephone calls from England because they would not sell their Liverpool shares to the Dubai Consortium. (So Emirs are OK, but Yanks whose fathers fought alongside the Brits in Normandy are not?) Americans might know 'sweet FA' about football, but angry Britons might like to find out why it is that 99 per cent of sports events in the USA throughout the year are family outings that are free of violence. A stadium full of 100,000 people on a hot night will go home happy and sober, without one incident of loutishness. Police are rarely seen. If anything, European and British football, which often teeters on the edge of pagan bloodletting, could benefit from some 'nice potions' from the other side of the ocean.

But let's look at these football stories in detail:

George Gillett, American investor in Liverpool: 'The fans don't want him [Tom Hicks, the other American investor] to have even one share of my stake in the club... As a result of that we have received many phone calls in the middle of the night threatening our lives, death threats...my son, Foster, and daughter-in-law Lauren have received them' (*The Times*, 28 March 2008).

On Liverpool's American co-investor Tom Hicks, *The Times* (17 April 2008) wrote: 'Hicks said it was frustrating that his unpopularity with some sections of the Liverpool supporters has prevented him from bringing his whole family to Anfield to watch matches. "My family loves Liverpool. The sad thing is that right now we can't go there as a family until we get this thing sorted out."'

* * * * *

DIARY: 7 MAY 2008

Three years ago I made the grave mistake of writing about British football. Although at the time of putting pen to paper I had already spent almost 30 years in Britain, readers – including one friend who asked that I terminate the association – flooded me with abusive letters accusing me of 'writing about something you know nothing about'.

I found it amusing that people could bombard me with letters suggesting I 'knew nothing' about football when, had they taken the trouble to invite me to their towns and to buy me a drink, they would have found in my humble self one of the most sports-crazed females on earth, and that I had written huge features for *World Tennis*. My mother used to joke that I loved sport because she – a rabid baseball fan – had been glued to the World Series just before I came into this world and, in her words, had 'seen it all through my belly-button'.

There is another aspect to the rudeness of the Britons whose endless e-mails piled into my inbox when I wrote about football: in the United States, immigrants love to learn about the national sports, and in no time are cheering a local team. Did these vulgar and often obscene correspondents, whose letters were not short on threats and filth, think I had resided in Britain for three decades and been oblivious to the tremendous traditions and associated national clamour that accompany football, cricket and rugby? The *Liverpool Echo* newspaper allowed the supporters to set up a blog about me, and some of the copy was hideous. (Interesting, too, that all of the abuse was from men.)

I tend to feel anti-Americanism is manifested in the same vicious way as anti-Semitism. Russian billionaire Roman Abramovich, owner of Chelsea Football Club, decided to dispose of charismatic team manager Jose Mourinho, known as 'The Special One', and replace him with the dour Israeli Avram Grant. Fans were incensed, and columnist David Mellor was soon baying for the blood of Grant, whom he perceived as a fellow member of the faith, because Abramovich had picked a fellow Jew to run his squad. Recently Grant received a suspect parcel in the post and is reported to get considerable volumes of hate mail. A number of Anglo-Jewish journalists and non-Jewish officials have demanded that something be done about the anti-Semitic chanting and hissing (as in gas chambers) at the club's ground, Stamford Bridge.

Even when Chelsea won a phenomenal string of games in the 2007–08 season, the griping in the press about Roman Abramovich's 'co-religionist' continued, and the moment one game was lost the media were mercilessly lambasting the Israeli, who went so far as to call a press conference to ask them to stop the griping. Grant's team went on to win another string of matches and is now set to make history as one of two British teams to compete in a UEFA Champions League Final. Chelsea is also tied with Manchester United for first place in the Premier League.

Grant is by no means one of the great coaches in sport, and it must be acknowledged that Abramovich erupted into various levels of fury at the thought of his team not getting to the Moscow final of the Champions League competition; but Chelsea have got there. Having watched for 40 years miserable American baseball teams lose because of bad chemistry with a manager, I must assume that Avram Grant has instilled some degree of happiness in his men. Nothing could have been more moving than the sight of Grant, at the triumphant end of the Champions League semi-final, kneeling on the ground of Stamford Bridge, where, he later told the press, he had been saying a prayer because it was Yom Ha' Shoah (Holocaust Day) in Israel. He said he had stopped for a moment on this miraculous day to commemorate his survivor father 'burying his sister and father with his own hands' at a concentration camp 65 years ago...

The aforementioned David Mellor is a former cabinet minister–turned sports columnist in the *Evening Standard* (his image was forever embedded in the memory of Jews the world over when he bellowed and fulminated at Israeli soldiers trying to provide security for him on a visit to their country some 20 years ago). He cannot hide an obsessive revulsion towards Israeli Avram Grant. When Grant was first appointed, Mellor fumed that Abramovich was 'Israel-obsessed'. This is absurd, because at the time the Russian was, like so many modern Jews, secular and recently out of a long marriage to a non-Jew.

In an article about Chelsea's victory against Fenerbahce, Mellor says: 'Now to dear Avram Grant. Well, he won again and that will be enough for some. But not to anyone who knows about football.' Yes, David, Chelsea could have won 4–0 or 5–0 or even 6–0, but they produced a game that thrilled the fans, those blue and white flags waving like a sea of mad jumping dolphins. Mellor has to dig some more at the Israeli, calling him 'Grant, the oldest work-experience boy on the planet'. (Imagine how far Mellor's career would go after today if he were to pen 'boy' about an African–American or Latino sports figure in an American paper.)

Mellor can't let go. He reminds us that Grant is such a terrible boil on the flesh of Chelsea, adding 'the question is not whether Grant is up to it – we know the answer to that one already – but whether Chelsea's training staff can compensate for their chief's mediocrity'.

Mellor reminds me of a man named Graeme Macdonald, who was brought in by Anglia Television in 1987 to 'beef up' the most successful drama department in television history, run by Sir John Woolf, John Rosenberg and myself. When he arrived, we had had a staggering string of top-ten successes being broadcast all over the world. He was fixated on the 'tribal' closeness of Rosenberg and myself, and kept insinuating that this 'unnatural' relationship had to be brought to an end. He meant, of course, that two Americans who got on like a house on fire and had created a stunning creative partnership could simply not be allowed to flourish anymore. (Would Graeme Macdonald have pulled apart Rodgers and Hammerstein, Kander and Ebb, Lerner and Loewe and Comden and Green?) When David Mellor voiced his keen displeasure over the selection of Grant by co-religionist Abramovich, my mind raced back to the terrible years when I had to endure the Macdonald Putsch.

The point I wish to make is that Mohamed al Fayed owns Fulham Football Club, and I am sure if he appointed a fellow Egyptian – a co-religionist! – to manage the team, nobody would notice. Eggert Magnusson owns West Ham and nobody is sending him death threats. But there is something about Jews and Americans that drives an awful lot of Brits nuts.

Now we come to the bizarre situation at Liverpool and the Hicks–Gillett debacle. According to a team website, 'Liverpool made record losses of £21.9m in the financial year ending 31 July 2004... Much of the hostility was directed at chairman David Moores for the way in which he is seen to have frustrated the efforts of Steve Morgan, the third largest shareholder, in his efforts to increase his stake in the club. Indeed, it was Morgan's second wife, Didy, who stole the show at the annual meeting with an emotional appeal to the board... The club subsequently rallied round Moores.'

In the intervening years, Liverpool has had a rough time; this refers to the seemingly endless bid to build a new stadium. To a dumb American mentality like mine, if a club is doing well money-wise, it builds a new stadium. Period. In Philadelphia, we've had three new ones in my lifetime, and the Washington Nationals just got a new one – all finished and open – in the time it took me to sail back to the UK on the QM2. And now along came Americans George Gillett and Tom Hicks. Liverpool had played at Anfield stadium since the club's founding in 1892. In came the Americans, and it was agreed that work should start in Stanley Park on a new all reserved-seat stadium with a capacity of 63,000 – and possibly 80,000 – and with a completion date of 2010. Hicks and Gillett became the club's new owners on 6 February 2007. But shortly after, the rot set in. Many fans were incensed. The idea of 'two Yanks' owning the most successful club in British football history infuriated many. In recent months, the two men have fallen out after thousands of hate letters were sent to them and to their families in the United States. The men squabbled about getting out of the situation and selling their holdings to a Dubai consortium (that's OK by the fans – no 'Arabs out!' T-shirts or banners). At a recent Liverpool match, the ITV commentator remarked that the discord that had been imported by the two elderly Americans had affected everyone and this 'is not the Liverpool way'. (What IS the Liverpool way? The fans were banned from Europe for five years after the Heysel stadium tragedy.)

According to David Mellor in tonight's *Evening Standard* (7 May 2008), football clubs owned by foreigners are attracting staggering levels of debt: Manchester United, owned by the aforementioned Glazers, with £666 million, and Liverpool with less debt but still a mountain. (Mellor also mentions the Israeli–Russian Gaydamak family at Portsmouth and their 'questionable' past. Well, they may be questionable folk, but Portsmouth is having a roaring season!) Whatever the ramifications of foreign ownership of British football teams, the idea to me that middle-class and otherwise sensible Britons would stop to write death threats to two aging sports tycoons who had, after all, come here to try to bail them out and enjoy Britain, despite the appalling (for them) state of the pound sterling, is distasteful in the extreme. (It is bad enough that the credit crisis in Britain is being blamed on 'the Americans' when in fact personal debt in the United Kingdom staggers the mind, was totally self-inflicted and has little to do with 'American sub-prime'.)

I watched a match a few weeks ago in which Liverpool fans were chanting 'Yanks Out' and worse, whilst alcohol-ridden slugs passing for men shouted into the cameras their true opinions of bloody Yanks. The general feeling was that Hicks and Gillett had come in to make a quick buck. Inasmuch as these men have eaten, lived and breathed sport since they were children and have chaired some of the most successful teams of all time, it is doubtful that they would cross the ocean for a 'quick buck'. In recent weeks, as reported in all the British media, Gillett and his family have received so many death threats (and they aren't even Jewish!) that one could not imagine him continuing any business association in the United Kingdom.

There is another aspect to this sorry tale that I must put on record. Over 32 years in Britain, I have stomached many accusations against Americans. But there is one accusation that cannot be made: the behaviour of fans at sporting events. If British fans detest Americans and 'their sort' bringing their loathsome ways over here, might they not consider how the behaviour of sober, good-natured American fans could serve as an example to them instead? In Washington DC we opened a new stadium for the Nationals in no time at all, so if two Americans can deliver a beautiful, fan-friendly stadium for Liverpool for the first time since 1892, is this an act worthy of death threats?

Henry Winter, in the *Daily Telegraph* (11 April 2008), says the presence of Hicks is nothing short of a descent into Hell, and that Liverpool may end up debt-laden if he does not leave the enterprise. Fine. But my complaint is about the grotesque and childish threats that deeply offend the generous American expatriate community of Great Britain.

By the same token, if Americans are so appalling at running sports enterprises, why are so many American teams – not to mention the stunning stadium facilities from sea to shining sea – operated with such spectacular success? Why in heaven's name would clubs prefer people from countries in the Middle East to run their clubs than folks from a nation that revels in sporting success, international medals and Wimbledon crowns? If Hicks and Gillett have been successful all their very long lives, most particularly with the Stars and

Canadiens respectively, why has this British enterprise come so badly unstuck? It simply cannot be 'all the Yanks' fault'. They are quite simply too darned good at running sporting events (ever been to the US Open Tennis at Flushing Meadow?) and stadia, and at making the fans and players feel valued and cared for, for this to be the Yanks' fault.

One interesting comment made on a radio phone-in by a Liverpool fan, incandescent with rage, went something like this: 'They ought to just stop foreigners, ya know, I mean these Yanks, being allowed to do business here, they ought to pass a law stopping it once and for all.'

So I have a bit of advice for Liverpool fans. If you really hate Americans that much and do not want them to do business in Britain, and even wish death upon two millionaires who tried to bail your club out of trying times, I suggest you stop singing 'You'll Never Walk Alone' as you have done at every match for decades. I suggest you remove 'You'll Never Walk Alone' from the iron gates of Anfield. After all, the song was written by Richard Rodgers and Oscar Hammerstein – two Yanks.

CHAPTER THIRTY-ONE

THE EUROPEAN VIEW

I like to tell a story about my visit to France in June 2004, to commemorate, with a group of British Second World War veterans, the 60th anniversary of the Normandy landings.

It was impossible to find lodgings in Normandy, so I had to stay in a five-star hotel in central Paris. Although it was way beyond my budget, one blessing this brought me was air conditioning (American readers need to know that this luxury is still almost non-existent in much of Europe and the UK). The heat in France that week was considerable, and I, along with many people lining up at the Omaha Beach MASH,* had been taken ill with sun or heat stroke during the long ceremonies.

At the MASH I got into terrible trouble because I am a dual national and the military were not willing to treat me as a European citizen. As a US citizen, I needed to provide evidence of American medical insurance, because Omaha Beach is regarded as US territory. Finally, a lovely lady from the US embassy cleared me to be treated for free as a European, but by then my transport back to Paris had left. The Americans provided me with a lift back almost all the way to Paris and I was stunned by their kindness.

When I got to my room that night, I kept calling down for a bottle of water. By about 2am there was still no water, so I went downstairs. The scowling concierge (remember, this is a seriously five-star if not six-star *alberge*) ignored me as I spoke to him. I went into the bar and found a charming waiter with

* Mobile army surgical hospital.

what sounded like an American accent (he had lived in the USA for a few years). He said he would bring a bottle of water to my room, which he did a short time later. He then told me that most of the staff 'absolutely hate Americans' and that I was unlucky, because that evening's concierge on duty simply refused to send anything to the rooms of Americans.

How charming! Here it was, 6 June 2004, and the hotel was brimming with American veterans of the landings, some of whom had not been back to Europe since 1945 and were returning one last time to pay homage to their buddies whose lives were suspended at age 19 or 21, and who lie amongst the 9,500-plus crosses and stars at Omaha Beach. This is the appreciation a French hotel shows to the men – and to me, the daughter of a Second World War veteran – who liberated them from the Nazis.

European anti-whatever is characterized these days more by anti-Semitism than by anti-Americanism, though the two hate-hobbies run neck and neck. It is open season on Jews, most particularly in France, where there is a large Muslim population with the resulting tensions. Emigration of French Jews has risen in the past five years. The protracted al-Aqsa Intifadah of September 2000 onwards (which the world blames on Ariel Sharon and Israel) and the 2006 Lebanon war have fuelled the fires of Jew-hatred. Hatred of the USA is, as in the UK, intertwined with contempt for Israel; the Americans support the Zionist entity and that makes them the People from the Great Satan. Germany, despite the endless post-9/11 US-mocking covers of *Der Spiegel*, does not seem to have as bad a problem with Jews and Americans as does France.

Stories of schools and public places frequented by French and Parisian Jews being attacked have become commonplace. One is told not to wear a Star of David if visiting Paris; Marseilles, a hotbed of North African discontent, would be off limits to anyone in a *yarmulkah* or wearing a *Magen David*. Again, I blame the world media for the daily, 24/7 drip-drip feed of scenes of Israeli soldiers being belligerent with elderly or pregnant Palestinians, whilst Israel itself is never shown. European and British media would make one believe that Israel is settlers, army checkpoints and tanks patrolling the West Bank refugee camps. This, compounded by an angry print media that blames the world's ills on America (brutality to Arabs), America (greenhouse gases, as if China, India and Russia did not contribute) and America (globalization and unfair trading policies), contributes to the anger amongst the Europeans, be they elite art gallery aficionados or Muslim street vendors.

In his book *Anti-Americanism in Europe*, Russell Berman makes the apt observation: 'What provokes the anti-American is American activism: not that America plays a particular role in the world but that it is in the world at all.' Think of that! The Archbishop of Canterbury, Dr Rowan Williams, choosing the December issue of the Anglo-Muslim magazine *Emel* to denounce the United States, accuses the Great Satan of storming around the world bombing places and then cutting and running. At a recent conference in Newcastle, various fulminating delegates accused the USA of doing nothing about world poverty and AIDS, whilst 'occupying numerous countries against their will'. Thankfully, a delegate from the American State Department had a list of billion-dollar aid programmes at her fingertips to shut these critics up, but levelling accusations that 'America stands by and does nothing' or 'America should stay out of other countries' business' is a European and British pastime. Had Bill Clinton let the Balkan situation unfold without lifting a finger, there would have been an uproar; but even after NATO's noble campaign to stop the slaughter of Muslims in the region, there were still rumblings of discontent over 'American interference'.

As Russell Berman notes: 'Anti-Americanism is like a prejudice, magnifying the power and presence of its presumed opponent, turning it into a ubiquitous threat.' This is what I have said for years: anti-Americanism is the new anti-Semitism: the all-powerful Jews crush anyone else's chances and make life a misery for the rest of humanity. When I sit in a restaurant in London and my companions rail at me about the number of 'ghastly American' outlets in business just on that street alone, I ask them how quickly British firms could zip in there and replace those enterprises and employ the formidable workforce. Starbucks is particularly hated, and has caused some memorable protests in places like Primrose Hill, where the residents were successful in stopping a branch opening in their high street. There are many other noisy cafés and bistros in the street, however, but of course they are owned and operated by Poles, Greeks, Russians and others who are most welcome indeed.

Berman makes a telling point: anti-Americanism in Europe stems from an inclination to appeasement of totalitarian regimes, which is endemic in the European psyche. The concept of 'Saddam as Hitler' and 'Ahmadinejad as Hitler' resonates with many Americans, but at a lecture at the House of Commons in November 2007, I watched an audience of Britons remonstrate with the American speaker, some even shouting at him that 'dialogue' is the way to the Iranian dictator's sweet, obliging little heart. (Yes, Iran had elections, but he is still an evil despot.) European anti-Americanism channels its hatred towards the 'noble cause' mantra that has driven many a White House administration because – except for Winston Churchill as far back as 1935 – no one seems able to grasp the danger to the world posed by certain personality types.

The idea of Iran's Ahmadinejad posing an existential threat to Israel does not seem to concern anyone I speak to in Europe or Britain. In fact, the existence of Israel, to an alarming number of Europeans and Britons, appears to be of no consequence. I will venture further and say I have heard one Scotsman say he will rejoice when the Arabs finally finish off the Jewish state.

In *Uncouth Nation: Why Europe Dislikes America*, Andrei Markovits corroborates much of my narrative of the past six years; when my major feature in the *Guardian* appeared in 2004, I was flooded with letters from American expatriates saying I either imagine, concoct or exaggerate the verbal barrages I receive.

Markovits notes that there is a near-maniacal feeling amongst Europeans that American serving men are the least competent and the most cowardly in the world. I first heard this about 30 years ago from the owner of a local photographic studio: 'The Yanks always run off at the first opportunity.' He was a Tory and deeply conservative. So the fact that Tilman Fichter, a German Leftist, says 'Even a group of British boy scouts is a better military troop than today's American army' indicates that these sentiments are not the exclusive domain of any political movement. Markovits makes the wry observation that the left-wing, liberal Fichter is actually expressing a deeply racist view, inasmuch as the American armed forces are today so heavily peopled by minority groups.

The commonality of the Left and Right in Europe in their hatred of Israel and the USA is matched in the United Kingdom. One will find a Tory minister or peer on the BBC's *Question Time* screwing his face up in splenetic contortions and 'deploring the brutality of Israel and America' as vehemently as any George Galloway or Polly Toynbee.

Markovits backs up my extreme reaction when Malcolm Glazer became the new owner of the Manchester United football team. In his book, he also reports on the fury of the fans and media that an American could pollute the sacred waters of the Beautiful Game. When I reacted as I did and received a mountain of truly terrifying hate mail, even eminent Britons were fuming at me for commenting on something I 'know nothing about'. (This is another trait I find deeply painful after 32 years in Britain: how quickly individuals will accuse an American of 'knowing nothing' about a particular subject, when in my case I have spent the bulk of my life in the UK.) Markovits makes the apt observation that Roman Abramovich's takeover of Chelsea football club did not attract nearly as much opprobrium as the Glazer takeover. It was 'simply too awful' to see an American doing this. One fan wrote to me saying I should be banned from the airwaves and newspapers because I incorrectly referred to Abramovich as 'Chelski', though in fact one of the newspapers gave him exactly the same name in a huge banner headline.

I absolutely adore this comment by Markovits about the terrible 2003 heat wave: 'in France, where thousands of old and infirm people died during the traditional holiday month of August whilst they were sitting in their overheated urban apartments and neglected by their relatives at the beaches... all I heard was complaints that European weather was somehow linked to the refusal of the United States to sign the Kyoto Protocol.' As I have noted in this book, 2007 was the wettest and coldest summer in Britain in recent memory; I know because my tomato plants produced about 10 edible ones, whereas in previous years I have got 300–400. My friends in London say this is also 'global warming', as were the 10-foot snowdrifts in Buffalo and Vermont this past year.

Markovits provides a telling narrative on the subject of barely concealed European glee at the disasters of 9/11 and Hurricane Katrina, a glee I have reported on in Britain. He says that the cumulative responses of radio, television and print media to these tragedies harbour what he calls a 'not so hidden joy'. He then goes on to observe what I have said time and again: had an Air France Airbus A-300 crashed into the Eiffel Tower in 1994, as the Groupe Islamique Armée had planned, would the American media have launched a concerted and sustained verbal attack on France and its policies, suggesting even a conspiracy to perpetrate the crime in order to bring world disfavour upon Muslims? As Markovits reports, books about Mossad and Pentagon conspiracies to stage 9/11 are bestsellers in Europe. At the end of the day, it boils down to his excellent analysis: Europeans feel ruled by an entity that they have always viewed as 'their cultural and moral inferior'. He adds that a recent study by Peter Katzenstein and Robert Keohane shows:

> France has reached a stage wherein its self-perception and self-definition as an anti-America have become central to its politics and public life. Little surprise then that French teenagers at the country's elite secondary schools demonstrate nothing but contempt and hatred for the United States and Americans.

Finally, I am so glad Andrei Markovits, in his meticulously researched and very scholarly book, discusses the issue of squirrels. Yes, I have had to suffer 30-odd years of guilt over the annihilation of the poor red squirrels because of American squirrels having been introduced into Europe some years ago. He says Germans write in to their papers to lament the disappearance of red squirrels due to the 'Americanization' of the environment.

European anti-Americanism is all-pervasive, but does it matter in the great scheme of things? As this book nears completion, the 'sub-prime crisis in America' is being blamed for every catastrophe in British finance, down to the savers trying to break down the doors of Northern Rock, the Newcastle bank on which there was a billion-pound run, the likes of which had not been seen in England for 150 years. Americans wanting to do business across the ocean will find it increasingly difficult to do so with the atmosphere so poisoned by the media hysteria about the 'American credit collapse driving British banks to seek rescue bids from the Bank of England'. This is followed by reports about the 'British taxpayer' having to 'foot the bill for the American sub-prime disaster'; the media even calculating exactly £900 per taxpayer to help prop up British institutions 'ruined by the American sub-prime calamity'.

Like Markovits, I am not yet being beaten up on the streets as soon as I emerge from my home; but the constant stream of blame heaped upon America for every ill that befalls Europe and Britain, in the same way as Jews were blamed by the Third Reich for Germany's plight, does not exactly make one feel comfortable trying to do business, let alone just making friends.

But I see anti-Americanism as more than a series of causes and effects. If a sensible, well-dressed and otherwise dignified English gentleman can become nearly unhinged when discussing the awfulness of all things American, and indeed if Margaret Drabble can be consumed by, in her own words, an 'almost uncontrollable state' about Coca Cola, burgers and Disney, then one can only imagine the venom in even a 'friendly' Muslim country.

At the time of the Drabble tirade, Barbara Amiel wrote in the *Daily Telegraph* (12 May 2003) that BBC presenters now felt it was acceptable to ask an American guest: 'So, you are happy for the US to play judge, jury, prosecutor and executioner?' And she added that Europe and much of the rest of the world saw every significant movement in world events as the fault of America.

Finally, it should be noted that much anti-Americanism in Europe stems from staggering ignorance: Amiel cites Drabble's ridiculous criticism of American pilots using faces and slogans on the sides of their aircraft. The fact that Drabble thinks the entire American nation is 'insane' because of this shows how stunning is the lack of knowledge amongst those who have done their share of screaming at me until I have no choice but to flee back to the USA. That she could condemn a nation for doing something that was begun by Italian aviators in 1913, and that then became a beloved tradition of British and German pilots as well, shows how frightening America-hatred is and how much it reminds me of anti-Semitism.

In conclusion, it is significant that, in recent years, several events have unfolded that indicate a hostility felt by the American government towards Britain and Europe. The aggressive manner in which the American authorities have demanded answers on the BAE-aircraft deals with the Saudi Royal Family, and the extradition of the 'Nat West Three' to the USA (British tabloids railed about this – three Britons possibly ending up in a penitentiary), indicate a deterioration in the 'special relationship' – with a 'revenge' element tucked into the proceedings. Tensions between the United States and the rest of the world remain worrying.

How can America make itself loved? I see how angry my friends become when they see Starbucks, Disney, Kentucky Fried Chicken and McDonalds in one street. Take all of those away tomorrow and there would be a lot of unemployed people. Hating America and Americans? It is a disease that seems to have no cure; as for me, I would like to spend the rest of my life as far away from this hatred as possible, because it scares me to my core. If a mosque in London threatened to kill me in 1998 simply because I was American, at a time when Bill Clinton was president, then the present climate does not bode well.

Nebraska sounds so nice. I hope I can get there, like Dorothy when she was trapped in Oz.

I shall try clicking a pair of red shoes together and hope for the best.

CHAPTER THIRTY-TWO

MY DIARY ENTRIES...

I would like to share with readers some of my writings from the immediate post-9/11 period. I do this because, as 2008 unfolds, nothing has changed and has, in fact, got much, much worse in terms of British anti-Americanism and anti-Zionism. In fact, it is chilling to read the narratives I penned in the wake of 9/11, when one realizes that the rantings of the America-loathing and Israel-hating media occurred long before the Iraq invasion, Abu Ghraib, Guantanamo and the Lebanon War.

* * * * *

DIARY: 1 JANUARY 2003

Cartoons have been the mainstay of a free press, but in times of evil they have been used to defame ethnic groups and individuals. The repugnant Joseph Goebbels used satire to defame the Jewish people.

Conversely, Benjamin Franklin would have loved the proliferation of witty and tasteful political cartoons in this era of computer and digital technology.

Notwithstanding this, I have become increasingly worried about the nature of material used in British cartoon culture. American cartoonists have been coming up with thoughtful and usually hilarious reflections on the current White House and cabinet. One awaits with eager anticipation the many spoofs of the Bush team – even if one is a staunch supporter of the Republican administration there is fun to be had at the expense of the men and women who make up the 'War

Cabinet', just as there was mirth to be derived from the Clinton gang.

The British cartoonist has taken to parodying the Bush White House with increasing ferocity and perversity. This came to a head on 23 December 2002, when the *Guardian* published a large cartoon by Cole ('after Freud' as he calls himself) entitled 'Lap Dog', depicting a grotesque-looking President Bush in drag, lying on a couch draped in an American flag. He/she has one large breast exposed, from which is spewing milk. The milk is being lapped up by a dog lying against his/her semi-bare leg; one assumes the dog is Tony Blair. The man/woman Bush is holding a copy of the *Guardian* with the headline 'British Forces War Alert'.

As it happens, my neighbour's son had been called up to the Gulf, and the usual emotions of a departure at Christmas had affected me, even though I am not family. I found the cartoon depraved and insulting. The troops who have left for that region may not wish to go, but they are doing their duty and showing great courage. They are likely to have to endure many different injections for horrific illnesses. Meanwhile we sit and eat our Christmas turkey. This cartoon went beyond the realms of decency and lent nothing to the debate on Iraq. I cannot imagine any American newspaper depicting a British leader, no matter how despised he might be, in such a degrading context.

On Christmas Eve Day 2002, the *Independent* published a cartoon by Dave Brown, showing President Bush dressed as Santa Claus with his posterior up in the air on which is printed 'Merry Xmas'. He has a grotesque face and is carrying a sack filled with missiles and is saying 'Ho ho ho'. Again, I see nothing in this that brings humour or irony to the Iraq debate.

Though not a cartoon, the front page of the *Daily Mirror*, which throughout the year has been relentless in its attacks on America, shows President Bush holding a dog on whose head has been superimposed the face of Tony Blair. The caption is 'Warkies!' ('Let's go for a walk'). Inside is a long article by John Pilger, describing the destruction that is being wreaked upon Iraq by British and American air raids. This is acceptable in a free society – John Pilger makes some valid points – but there is never any mention of the constant harassment being endured by these same pilots from relentless Iraqi bombardment in the no-fly zones monitored by the United Nations.

So what are we trying to say here? We enjoy press freedom, but in what direction is the world going? Why is Bush the perpetual villain and not Mugabe, Gaddafi, Arafat, Saddam or Assad of Syria? Bush may not be the president many Americans and Europeans wanted, but is he the personification of evil? I think not. The ugly and sadistic websites and chat rooms that have cropped up since the accession of Bush Junior go beyond healthy debate on his foibles. They pray regularly that Bush, Cheney and Rumsfeld be 'soon drowning in pools of their own blood', but spend precious little time in debate about the appalling regimes that oppress women and children around the globe.

I abhor satire that degrades western leaders, who, even in the bumbling manner of Dubya, are trying to keep the forces of medieval extremism at bay. We beseech the editors of papers like the *Guardian* and the *Daily Mirror* to look into their hearts and re-evaluate who the real goodies and baddies are.

* * * * *

DIARY: 1 FEBRUARY 2003

This week an article about anti-Americanism appeared in the *Washington Post*, and the remarkable angle on the piece is that the author, Richard Cohen, has always expressed a liberal view of the world. He sits in Washington and is outraged, however, by the rantings of the British author John le Carre. Also this week, the *Daily Mirror* shows Tony Blair with blood on his hands, and inside is a large headline, 'BLOODY COWARDS', alongside pictures of Blair and Bush. The *Independent* last week had an appalling cartoon of a naked, leering Ariel Sharon eating a headless, bleeding infant. (Note: it went on to win a national prize.)

Is 'old Europe' sinking into its 1930s hate mode again? Frankly, I have never seen anything like the venom directed against Israel and the United States in all the years I have lived here in Britain. Neither nation is without fault, but what is so disturbing is the nearly obsessive concentration on Israeli and American evil, while some of the world's most detestable regimes go unnoticed.

Cohen writes:

> John le Carre, the author of some brilliant spy novels, writes in *The Times* of London that 'America has entered one of its periods of historical madness.' The present time is 'worse than McCarthyism' and even worse than – an odd choice – 'the Bay of Pigs.' Maybe le Carre means the Cuban missile crisis. It's possible. After all, he gets so much else wrong.

Le Carre says '88 per cent of the American people' want to go to war with Iraq. This is not true. Worrying the Bush administration is the dwindling support for an Iraq conflict, down to the high 50s at the time of writing.

Le Carre, author of *The Spy Who Came in From the Cold*, *Tinker, Tailor, Soldier, Spy* and other novels, expresses what Cohen calls 'absolute blarney'.

Le Carre's Left has, for a long time, referred to the United States as being run by the 'Bush junta', and the novelist even refers to 'poor mad little North Korea' as if the communist dictatorship is another victim of the junta.

Cohen makes the notable observation that 'le Carre's America is unrecognizable', and that one would think from reading him that Bush, not Saddam Hussein, has twice made war on his neighbours, that he has used chemical weapons on his own people and that he murders his opponents.

What is significant to those of us who live outside the United States and who still have a deep affection for that remarkable land of our birth is that Cohen has been knocked sideways by le Carre's anger. We who live in Britain have come to expect this sort of rant as soon as we go out to dinner.

Cohen continues:

> I am reminded of a documentary I saw the other night about the late civil rights leader Bayard Rustin. He was jailed in World War II for his pacifism... Rustin, a black homosexual, would have been among the first into the ovens.

Here is the crucial moment. Cohen observes what many of us have, with increasing alarm, clocked for over two years: the overwhelming number of Britons who are fascinated by Colonel Gaddafi or Yasser Arafat but who turn puce with rage when one says 'Israel', let alone 'Sharon'.

Cohen observes:

> I am tempted to say he hates Bush more than he does Saddam Hussein, but that may not be the case. It seems he's been seized by a 'historical madness' and a repugnant anti-Americanism.

Moving on to the *Daily Mirror* now: of all the venomous anti-USA, anti-Bush bile in the British papers and on TV this week – and there has been PLENTY!! – the poisonous John Pilger has written the most offensive material to date.

Here is an excerpt from his 'BLOODY COWARDS' article that appeared in the *Mirror* on 29 January 2003:

> ...in 1946, the judges at Nuremberg, who tried the Nazi leaders for war crimes, left no doubt about what they regarded as the gravest crimes against humanity. The most serious was an unprovoked invasion of a sovereign state that offered no threat to one's homeland. Then there was the murder of civilians, for which responsibility rested with the 'highest authority'... The current American elite is the Third Reich of our times...
> they have merely accelerated more than half a century of unrelenting American state terrorism: from the atomic bombs dropped cynically on Japan as a signal of their new power, to the dozens of countries invaded...

Be advised that these are not the rantings of a madman, but the journalism of one of the world's most honoured writers, read by millions of Britons and Europeans.

The cherry on my '2003 diary sundae' occurred when Nelson Mandela decided to use the forum of an international convention of women's groups in Johannesburg to issue forth with a tirade about the United States.

The Nobel Prize winner and former South African president said of President Bush:

> He is making the greatest mistake of his life by trying to cause carnage... What I am condemning is that one power, with a president who has no foresight and who cannot think properly, is now wanting to plunge the world into a holocaust. Why does the US behave so arrogantly? Their friend Israel has got weapons of mass destruction. But because it's their ally they won't ask the UN to get rid of them... Both Bush and Tony Blair are undermining [the UN]... Is this because the Secretary General [Kofi Annan, from Ghana] is now a black man? They never did that when Secretary Generals were white...

This is shameful nonsense. What European country has had a black chief of staff of the military and a senior cabinet figure who is a black woman?

Mandela even dredged up the American nuclear attacks on Hiroshima and Nagasaki:

> Because they decided to kill innocent people in Japan, who are they now to pretend they're the policeman of the world? If there is a country which has committed unspeakable atrocities, it is the US...they don't care for human beings.

Has Mr Mandela heard of Nazi Germany? Rwanda? Sudan? Cambodia?

Each year, I always stay up late in London to watch President Bush's State of the Union address. What is remarkable is the amount of time he has spent discussing the tragedy of AIDS in Africa. If we Americans, according to Mr Mandela, 'don't care for human beings', why do we send billions of dollars of aid to every Tom, Dick and Harry?

When the Japanese bombed Pearl Harbor, the admiral of the Japanese fleet said: 'This is a great victory, but I fear we have awakened a sleeping giant.' Had the Pacific War continued unabated with a land invasion of the Japanese mainland islands, the casualty figures would have been catastrophic. The bomb was a terrible weapon, but Hiroshima and Nagasaki ended what could have been a 50-year conflict. Japan is today a flourishing democracy. My aunt was based in occupied Japan and witnessed the transformation of that nation under the benign tutelage of the United States. The same may be said for post-war non-Soviet Germany – and don't let us forget the Berlin Airlift. When one considers the virtuous legacy of its involvement in the Second World War, the fact that my native country is constantly being accused of an endless litany of crimes against humanity disgusts me.

The events of 11 September were a spectacularly successful attack on the United States by well-off, well-educated young men. The relentless attacks by the well-paid media and intellectuals on America and Israel may soon reach a point where the sleeping giant will strike back – not with vengeance but with splendid isolationism.

* * * * *

IN THE SPACE OF TWO WEEKS... THREE YEARS ON...

August 2007

I decided to set aside some morsels from London's evening newspaper over a period of a fortnight in late July and early August 2007 – and sure enough I found some gems.

Michael Aspel, a television personality who is a household name to Britons of a certain age but unknown outside the United Kingdom, complained in the *Evening Standard* on

7 August 2007 that proper pronunciation has gone out of the window on the news. He says he does not expect the plummy accents of yesteryear, or 'old-style formal bulletins in dinner suits', but laments the 'Americanisation that we don't need'.

Inasmuch as many presenters on British television have such appalling command of the English language, saying, for example, 'I was sat here', I would like to know if Mr Aspel has ever listened to the beautifully spoken Brian Williams, Katie Couric or Charles Gibson? Tom Brokaw, Peter Jennings and Dan Rather, not to mention Walter Cronkite and the Huntley–Brinkley duo, were and are examples of splendid articulation. Aspel's accusation that presenters chat to one another using first names is a valid one, but to suggest that Richard and Judy annoy him because of some crime committed by Americans is absurd.

Frankly, notwithstanding the quality of BBC's *Newsnight*, and *Question Time*, there is no evening line-up on British television to match CNN USA's nightly Lou Dobbs, Paula Zahn, Larry King, Anderson Cooper and Wolf Blitzer.

Throughout my 32 years in Britain, I have been lectured in no uncertain terms about various aspects of the United States, and however much I have tried to disabuse the complainant it is to no avail. These obloquies always emanate from people who have visited the USA for two weeks and stayed in a Marriott, or else from those who have never been across the ocean at all.

The first slur I have tried in vain to dispel is the one about the American media.

Recently I attended an excellent seminar at the Institute of Contemporary Arts in London. It went well until the participants, mostly British journalists, began defaming American news programmes. How can people who work nine to five in an office in London and spend the rest of their waking hours in pubs and wine bars drinking endless pints know what is on American television in the evening?

We were reliably informed at the ICA event that American news providers are almost non-existent and that the quality of news is abysmal. I vehemently deny this. In the wake of what is being acknowledged as a 'crisis' in British television output and the 'dumbing down' of the great BBC.

I never cease to be staggered by the high quality of the news I start to watch every evening in London at 11:30pm, when the first of three American network news programmes is broadcast: first comes the liberal-leaning Brian Williams, followed by truly liberal Katie Couric and then conservative Charlie Gibson.

I often have to find out what is going on in Europe and the world from these programmes, because the BBC is obsessed with a football manager, a house of dead bodies or benefit cheats. Because I am an insomniac, I often stay up into the wee hours to follow the excellent news programmes with Larry King and Anderson Cooper. There is nothing in Britain like Hannity and Colmes or Greta van Susteren, nor does British television have anything remotely resembling the nightly brilliance of Stephen Colbert, Keith Olbermann, Gwyn Ifel, Chris Matthews, Paula Zahn, Lou Dobbs, Bill Moyers or Charlie Rose. On the Right there is a wealth to choose from: Robert Novak, Charles Krauthammer, Bill Kristol, the Beltway Boys and, of course, the legendary Bill O'Reilly. Some of the most dynamic debate programmes are *Face the Nation*, *Meet the Press* and the *McLaughlin Group*.

Lest we forget, Edward R. Murrow of CBS exposed Senator Joseph McCarthy; and a succession of brave anchormen and reporters have pursued, with brave tenacity, many a dubious man and woman of power.

In the United States, there is the remarkable C-SPAN network, all three channels of which those 'stupid' Americans I hear so much about demand from their cable providers or they refuse to subscribe. C-SPAN provides 24-hour comprehensive coverage of every aspect of national government in Washington, as well as endless literary programmes and coverage of major lectures and seminars by outstanding international and national figures in politics, science, literature, music, visual art and business. Britain has no such thing. C-SPAN is a revelation, and I grieve for it when I am in London.

A friend once told me that she went to Chicago and had never read such 'rubbish' as the 'American newspapers'. I asked her what she meant, and she said she had looked at a local paper and could see why 'Americans know nothing about anything'. She then said she had glanced at the *New York Times*, which she also dismissed as 'dreadful'. This evaluation of American newspapers has been thrown at me for all the years I have lived in Britain. Again, I ask: if a person lives in the UK for 50 weeks of the year and reads the British papers, how can they know with such alacrity that American daily newspapers are abysmal? To me, reading the Sunday *New York Times* is still an education. The *Los Angeles Times*, *Washington Post*, *Boston Herald* and *Philadelphia Inquirer* can also educate, as well as enrage and amuse. Investigative journalists on the Left and Right, of the monumental influence of Seymour Hersh, Bob Novak and Bob Woodward, have come from those roots. Yes, Britain has John Pilger, Robert Fisk and Max Hastings, but America also has its great journalists. The Joseph Pulitzer Prize is a testament to the high standards of American journalism.

The dynamism of the American media has been demonstrated time and again with coverage of Hurricane Katrina, the Abu Ghraib and Guantanamo issues, global warming (Seymour Hersh, Al Gore and Michael Moore are American, not British) and the outing of CIA agent Valerie Plame. When Americans voted to oust the Republicans from Congress and the Senate in November 2006, they were responding to the information imparted by a dynamic press. Had the British media spent less time on whether Wayne Rooney would play in the World Cup and whether the tattooed and mini-skirted WAGS* of the football stars would travel to Germany, and more time on the election issues, perhaps those who wanted Labour ousted would have had their wish in May 2005.

The *Evening Standard* Londoner's Diary of August 2007 observed how 'different' (code for dumb) 'our American

* Wives and girlfriends.

cousins are' because the New York Public Library has bought 1,484 copies of the new Harry Potter book, *Harry Potter and the Deathly Hallows*. All are already out on loan, with 1,500 on the waiting list. The point was made that the London Library has bought just one copy. For some reason, this is meant to show how daft Americans are. Well, I have an explanation: the New York Public Library, funded by the fabulously generous Astor heiress, serves an enormous city and community. Many of its citizens cannot afford to buy books, but having a chance to borrow from the library is next best. I like to think that an inner-city youth who might otherwise have gone out and committed a crime might instead be wrapped up in a book. And that makes the huge supply bought by the New York library a good thing. Americans are mad about things British, and this is a factor in the popularity of Harry Potter for book borrowers.

I am reminded of a story told to me by a train conductor on Amtrak last year. He made amusing and often lyrical announcements to passengers, and on my journey told them that I was onboard – 'a visitor from the land of John Keats'. It transpired that he was a member of the Keats Society in the United States. But that was not the end of the story: he told me he had been a 'good-for-nothing' delinquent, hanging around the houses of wealthy folks and waiting for them to die so he and his fellow gang members could take goods from outside the houses of the deceased when the house-clearance people appeared. One day he took a box of books, but, instead of selling them, he started to read them. Soon he was a Keats devotee. He said: 'One old lady dying changed my life; one box of books led me to become a decent guy.' He made me promise I would pay homage to Keats in Hampstead when I was back in London. He said that one day, perhaps in retirement, he would make it to England to pay his own homage.

So, dear 'Londoner's Diary', Americans may, in your eyes, be odd; but if a book that a library holds in plentiful supply for its local community inspires a deprived child to lead an honourable life, long may the New York Public Library prosper.

* * * * *

In the *Evening Standard* of 31 July 2007, in an item entitled 'Dubya's Latest Caddie', Will Self makes the following observations: 'Sickening to see our latest "Great Leader" visiting Dubya'. Yes, a huge majority of Americans feel nothing but loathing for Bush-43 at this point in the summer of 2007, but I never cease to be niggled by the contempt that the British press so readily shows for any event concerning him. Let's face it, Will, Prime Minister Brown has to meet the American president. I still find these meetings infinitely less alarming than the sight of Hugo Chavez and Mahmoud Ahmadinejad, or our London mayor calling a Jewish newspaper reporter a 'Nazi concentration camp guard'.

Self goes on to say that Tony Blair was 'that well known poodle'. What is so objectionable about this kind of journalism is that it is immature. Countless cartoons of Blair as Bush's poodle have proliferated in Britain since 9/11, but the reality of world affairs is that the great powers have to talk to each other.

Self continues with the usual mantra that many feel is true: 'Don't make me laugh. It's the Bush regime's disastrous Iraq adventure that has promoted global terror.' Readers need not be reminded that World Trade Center 1993, the terrible attacks on the American embassies in Tanzania and Kenya in 1998, and the attack on the USS *Cole* in 2000 – and for that matter 9/11 – occurred well before the Iraq entanglement. Self concludes with an analogy between Brown and a golf caddie. Again, I would rather caddie for Bush than for Ahmadinejad, Mugabe or Chavez.

* * * * *

July 2007 was a fertile time for anyone writing about anti-Americanism in Britain.

In the *Guardian* (where else?) at various times in 2006 and 2007, former Labour minister David Clark infuriated Jewish readers – even moderate David Hirsh of the Zionist left-wing *Engage* – with articles critical of Israel; in one segment on the newspaper's 'Comment is Free' website, he asked: 'Will the Brown government make it clear that the US unwillingness to put serious pressure on Israel is the main obstacle to a two-state solution?' Has Mr Clark not thought it might be an idea to put pressure on Hamas and Hezbollah as well?

* * * * *

In the *Evening Standard* of 27 July, the eminent London-based historian Felipe Fernandez-Armesto makes some interesting observations, based on his viewing of the new *Simpsons* movie and the classic television series. Considering he was badly roughed up by traffic police in Washington DC for jay-walking earlier in 2007, he ought to be more anti-American than most Britons, but he makes the following point:

> ...maybe the rest of the world, which hates, resents or even envies the United States, can also endorse the show as gratifyingly anti-American...yet American viewers recently voted it the programme they would be most likely to record. In a country where self-respect is a cult and self-deprecation almost unknown...it seems amazing that people should love to watch themselves being demonised.

Notwithstanding the article's inclination towards a grudging affection for American culture, Dr Fernandez-Armesto misses the point about the mocking tone of the *Simpsons*. The programme and the film are devised by Americans. The genre would be less loved were it generated by Europeans or Britons. One of the most endearing aspects of *What's Cooking?*, the 2001 film directed by Gurinder Chadha, is her unconditional love for the November tradition of Thanksgiving Day and her depiction of five families from diverse backgrounds celebrating the national observance with passion and occasional family rancour. Had the film been a mocking critique of American patriotism and eccentricity, it would have been less of a success. It was released just after 9/11, and I recall weeping as the opening sequence showed a mother shopping for a turkey with a jazzed-up version of the 'Star Spangled Banner' playing against the credits. Even though a friend who saw it with me less than a week after 9/11 said 'I do not know why you people are making such a fuss about 11 September – we got far worse in the Blitz', I still felt nourished by this film, made by an Anglo-Indian woman who obviously loved the American culture she had been visiting.

* * * * *

On a more sombre note, Joshua Walker in the *Jerusalem Post* (15 July 2007), in an article entitled 'Truly Democratic – and Anti-American', writes: 'Turkey has slid from opposing US policy to opposing all the US stands for.' This could be said of scores of countries in 2007. I am reminded of my Pakistani neighbours, who leapt out of their car on 11 September 2001 excited and breathless, shouting to me: 'Well, Carol, you lot finally got it in the neck, and about time, too!'

The fact that Turkey – in recent years an ally of sorts to Israel and possibly of least concern to western powers in terms of an Islamic fundamentalist insurgency – is now simmering with hatred of the United States is a worrying phenomenon. If my otherwise charming, well-read English friends simmer with hatred of the United States and Israel, the level of hatred in Muslim and US-loathing Christian countries – for example, Venezuela – is no doubt palpable. The big difference between my perception of this phenomenon and that of much of the British and European media is that America has done nothing except try to bring stability to turbulent societies whose festering chaos is spilling out into the West and causing death and terror. It will be argued that Abu Ghraib and Guantanamo have nothing to do with spreading western values to turbulent societies. My argument is that

Abu Ghraib was an aberration rather than the norm, and that Guantanamo is a waste of American taxpayers' money. The terrorists 'scooped up' by Donald Rumsfeld should have been dealt with swiftly. It is my belief that even without the two prisons, anti-Americanism would have been as high as ever across the world. All major terror attacks against American interests, going back as far as the Khobar Towers atrocity and the singling out of Americans on airplanes hijacked by the PLO in the 1970s and 1980s, unfolded long before Abu Ghraib and Gitmo.

In his article, Joshua Walker notes that the Pew Global Attitudes Project's 47-nation survey, released on 11 July 2007, reports that it is not Venezuela, the Palestinians or Pakistan that is most anti-American, but Turkey. Only 2 per cent of Turks feel American Middle East policy is balanced. Look at a dinner party in London: if I so much as dare to wax lyrical about Israel, the dark looks of anger will be universal around the table. Imagine the fury in Turkey. According to the article, Turkey has the lowest Pew rating for supporting the war on terror. Walker observes that anti-Americanism in Turkey stems from the dangers in the country due to increased PKK terrorists entering from Northern Iraq. The USA is perceived as doing nothing about this, and Turks now regard Americans as duplicitous. Walker asserts: 'Hating America and Americans is a disturbing trend that requires serious attention and prolonged engagement.'

One is inclined to wish Joshua Walker good luck in the proposed prolonged engagement and serious attention; but my conclusion is that no matter what the United States of America does or does not do, it is hated to the depths of its core. Had Al Gore taken the presidential oath and been fiercely isolationist after 9/11, earnestly trying to engage with the forces who hate America, there would not have been a hugely unpopular Iraq War, but the Jihadists would have carried on as before and there would have been more attacks on American interests around the world. If Britons who think 7/7 was caused by the Iraq War, all they need do is read the leaflets being produced by radical groups inside the UK long,

long before the time of Bush-43. I know, because I was threatened with death in 1998 by local Muslims in my sleepy, leafy London suburb, when Bill 'shake hands with Arafat' Clinton was in office.

America will always be hated. I love America and most everything about it. Call me nuts, but I can't help it. I cannot understand how anyone can hate its good-natured soul. And yet millions, indeed billions, hate it in perpetuity, as do their children and grandchildren. World without end, amen...

CHAPTER THIRTY-THREE

'GO BACK TO AMERICA!' SAID THE (MOST LIKELY ILLEGAL) IMMIGRANT TO ME

Reports in early September 2007 that Germany had foiled a massive terror plot emphasized that the perpetrators had expressed a 'profound hatred of Americans'.

Now, this is an interesting piece of phrasing. They have not said they 'hate America'. They have not said they 'hate American foreign policy' or 'American support for the Zionist entity'. They hate *Americans*.

This item of news would not have resonated so much with me had I not had a disturbing few weeks trying to live quietly in central London, where I have resided for 32 years.

Recently I went into a well-known coffee chain in Edgware Road, near Marble Arch. As I waited to be served, I noticed that the café was crowded but that I was the only female customer. Men in various permutations of Middle Eastern garb, including several in full head-to-toe *keffiyah* and robe, stared at me.

When I sat down and opened my bottle of apple juice, I noticed that it was fizzing. I called the waitress over and told her that the juice had fermented. 'No – English', she said, throwing her arms up in despair. Another waitress came over and asked me what the problem seemed to be. I told her the juice had fermented and that they needed to check their fridge. She looked at the other woman and they shrugged.

I have to confess that I have a short fuse about non-English people populating what seems to be 99 per cent of every job in London and the Home Counties. I am spoilt because I have been to the USA several times in recent years, and I marvel at the stupendous service provided by young college students and other Americans who possess perfect English and are obliging beyond anyone's expectations.

So, I became exasperated and said: 'Is there no one working here who speaks English? This is Paddington – this is still a London neighbourhood.'

A well-dressed man said: 'I speak English.' I thought he was going to intervene on my behalf, but instead he came out with this astonishing observation: 'You are a racist! You are a racist ape! Look at you – you are an ape!'

I was dumbfounded. I came to London 32 years ago to soak up the culture of Dr Johnson and Chaucer and Milton, and in the autumn of my life am called an ape by a man from, well, perhaps Egypt, perhaps Palestine, perhaps Saudi Arabia.

Shocked, I glared at him, but he had to finish things off: 'You want them to speak Hebrew, don't you?'

I got up from my seat, went over to him and, at the top of my voice, said I would be proud to speak Hebrew if I could, it being the language of the Torah and of an ancient culture going back 6,000 years.

He then embarked on a tirade about the '5 million Indians' slaughtered in genocide in America. Meanwhile, the men in the café were hooting with laughter at me, and exhibiting great admiration for him.

Believe it or not, the waitress had, in the meantime, brought me a fresh juice, which I calmly drank with my very un-Hebrew ham and cheese sandwich. And then I left. I wandered over to the flower shop and found myself commiserating with what seemed to be two Englishwomen who lived in a permanent state of fear in a neighbourhood they had called their own for generations. They told me I must have been mad going into that shop, as 'all the establishments in Edgware Road are off limits to us now'. They told me there was one small café that was safe for a western woman. (I had a private giggle about this, considering how appallingly rudely I had been treated by the cockney publican in the Green Man Pub in Edgware Road. I can't win.)

For those of you who think I invite these mishaps, be assured that wherever I go in Philadelphia, New York,

Washington DC, Vermont and other American destinations, I seem to attract names like 'sugar pie' and 'doll face' from waiting staff, bus drivers, train conductors and others in service to the public; so, as the saying goes, it can't be me.

In the context of the aforementioned arrests in Germany of a terror cell of men (two German-born converts to Islam) who 'profoundly hate Americans', the hatred the man in the café had for me in his eyes was palpable. This is not some sort of paranoia; some of the other men in the café looked as if they would be glad to do me in or watch him do the deed.

Moving on to the weekend, I went to a little bakery and café in Abbey Road to ask for a refund for some very, very stale rolls my friend had asked me to collect the night before. She had held a splendid dinner party with some very illustrious guests, and I had stayed overnight at her beautiful home. I was on a high from the civilized and enlightened conversation of the dinner party the night before, but was brought down to a new low when the bakery proprietor, whom I understand to be Iranian, glowered at me and literally refused to talk to me. I must have stood there for an eternity until I was able to tell him my story of the stale rolls. He walked away and did not answer. It was as if I did not exist, or was too inferior a being to be given the time of day. Finally, in a totally foul manner – as if I was a piece of human garbage – he snarled at me that I should have known the night before when I brought my friend the rolls that they would be stale, and he said he could not buy the story anyway, as I had returned only one roll. Thinking of a swap, perhaps, rather than a refund, I asked him how much chicken wings were. He refused to talk to me.

I stood there for a while, wondering what to do and he gave me 50 pence. My blood boiled. Again, when my buttons are pressed these days in a country where men used to tip their hats and call me 'madam', I turned around and told him that in the USA a regular customer would receive a refund and even a complimentary item to take home.

He shouted, in front of a café full of customers: 'GET OUT OF MY SHOP! NOW! GO BACK TO AMERICA!'

Well, that is a red rag to a bull; though I fully intend very soon to go back to America, I resent a (most likely) illegally working immigrant to Britain telling me to go back home.

I thundered at him about my dignity and how proud I am of being an American, etc., etc., but afterwards I felt a right fool. What was I doing justifying myself?

I never used to be filled with anger as I am these days. I see a country that had an exceptionally unique and gracious way of doing things disintegrating into a morass of multiculturalism that has no place in the land of Shakespeare, Keats, Milton and Chaucer.

CHAPTER THIRTY-FOUR

INTERLUDE – ON A LIGHTER NOTE...

There are certain things that have not changed one iota in my 32 years in Britain. For a bit of comic relief, and at the risk of overly lightening the tone of this book, here they are, provided with the greatest affection:

1. Why is it never possible to get hot water from a tap in most public places or even in homes?

2. Why is it never possible to get once-over-lightly fried eggs?

3. Why do all Japanese restaurants in the USA serve the exquisite Yo-kan for dessert, but in Britain, where I have tried in vain to get it served, no one will take up my suggestion, from Wagamama to Nobu?

4. Why do Chinese restaurants all across the USA serve those gorgeous dry noodles for free and end one's meal with fortune cookies, but not in the UK? And why are Chinese waiters so rude in London but such dolls in the USA?

5. Why is it never possible to get a glass of water when one sits down in a British eatery? And why did *New York Magazine* name London culinary capital of the world? Doh?

6. Why are there no steak sandwiches like Geno's or Pat's in Britain?

7. Why is it impossible to get chocolate sorbet in the UK? (It is served and sold everywhere in North America.)

8. Why are there sealed mailboxes all over the place in England, with never any explanation?

9. Why are post offices being closed down across Britain? I think my local one in Philadelphia has been in continuous existence since around 1812. Who closes post offices?

10. Why are the floors always so dirty in London eateries, even five-star ones?

11. Why does British public transport not offer tokens or bus transfers, as we enterprising Philadelphians have had since, as the saying goes, Market Street was a prairie?

12. Why is there never anything to eat at functions to which one goes after work?

13. Why do British companies still insist that customers stay in from 8am to 6pm to receive a repairman?

14. Why do people who look at my home (which has been on the market for a year now) with a string of grumpy estate agents ask me why I have so many 'things on the wall' and why do people ask me to 'get rid of books'? This is the land of Chaucer and Milton.

15. Why is shellfish so horrendously expensive in a country surrounded by water?

CHAPTER THIRTY-FIVE

DEAR ARCHBISHOP OF CANTERBURY – WHY I STILL ADORE AMERICA

OK, the simple fact of the matter is that I loved every bloody minute of my upbringing in the United States. So, when the Archbishop of Canterbury, Dr Rowan Williams, gives an interview to the Muslim lifestyle magazine *Emel* in December 2007 and slams the United States as a violent, ruthless, uncaring and ungenerous empire of people who think they are 'chosen', I would like to stop and explain to him the simple things that make the America he so detests special.

I loved going for Carvel ice cream with my father and practising my baseball pitching until his poor catching hand was red. I loved trips to the Philadelphia Orchestra children's concerts with my mother; the Free Library; the Franklin Institute; the Settlement Music School (nothing to do with Israeli settlers, by the way, you Zionist-obsessed *Guardian* readers); the Betsy Ross House; and Phillies games. I loved eating out at the Stenton Diner with my family and going to my friends' lively houses. And, despite a year confined with scarlet and rheumatic fever, I loved chatting to the gentle paediatrician, Dr Abe Perlman, who attended me with such kindness. I loved reading and watching those marvellous television programmes with erudite hosts: Jack Paar, Edward R. Murrow, John Cameron Swayze, Harry K. Smith, Eric Sevareid...

I loved going to the farmers' markets and to Pennsylvania Dutch country, and the holidays to Vermont, where we ate silver dollar pancakes with maple syrup. I loved trips to Atlantic City and Cape May and walks along the Boardwalk. And though, at times, I dreaded the company of some of my teachers, I loved Dr Samson Friedman, who wanted me to pursue a career in science, but who was tragically murdered by a fellow seventh-grade student. I loved the brilliant English teachers Dr Meixner and Mrs Johnston ('Oh, Charles!' she used to exclaim to the ghost of Dickens); looking back even further I loved Mr Musicant, who gave us a sixth-grade year of breathtaking history of the Mayas, Incas and Aztecs; and I adored Mrs Singer, my first teacher after my long confinement. Then there were the legion of splendid professors at Temple University – from Gillian Speeth to Ben Schoenfeld to Annette Levitt – where I also had a wonderful time as a Phi Beta Kappa scholar. The American year is full of events that make one's heart leap as one looks at the calendar. It is difficult to explain to my British friends the excitement of 4 July, Thanksgiving and the Macy's and Mummers' Parades. Dr Rowan Williams, who laments the drop in a moral path of the world, ought to see how packed American churches are every Sunday. His interview was granted to Sarah Joseph, who at a conference in Newcastle had suggested that allied airmen were of the same cloth as suicide bombers.

Dr Williams said that millions of Christian Zionists in the USA are following the 'chosen nation myth' of Americans. Well, Archbishop, I was born there, as were my parents, and I know nothing of a 'chosen nation myth'; but perhaps you are confusing Americans with that loathsome Zionist tribe you berate in the *Emel* article. (What is interesting about Archbishop Williams is that he says humans are here for the glory of God, 'so that God's light may be reflected and God's love diffused'. He then goes on to list the world's faiths and omits Judaism. Nice.)

What is stunning about the archbishop's attack on Americans in the article is his suggestion that the United States temporarily releases itself from some sort of problem by committing international violence. Though some people would agree with this, it is appalling that he seems to be referring to 9/11 as 'some sort of problem'. When Britain was being bombed back to the Ice Age by the Luftwaffe, would Rowan Williams have suggested a period of quiet reflection? He also accuses Americans of seeking global hegemony, which he sees as 'the worst of all worlds'. He slams the Israeli separation fence as causing huge human suffering, but has he ever thought of advising the Palestinians to find an inspiring leader? (Considering the huge rifts in the Anglican Episcopal 'Union' he is hardly a shining example...)

Dr Williams suggests that America start repairing the damage it has done to the world by giving aid to the less fortunate. Just what does he think successive administrations have done, going back to the time of Woodrow Wilson or Harry Truman's Berlin Airlift? Who right now is at the forefront of Darfur aid? Mia Farrow and George Clooney. Has he heard of Warren Buffett and the Bill and Melinda Gates Foundation? The generosity of the United States over the past century has been notable.

So, Archbishop, notwithstanding the Evil Empire of America that you paint for the benefit of the Muslim readership of *Emel*, even now, three decades on, I get breathless with excitement at the prospect of being able to spend the many annual commemorations that are unique to America there, in the USA. John Pilger's poisonous diatribe about the evil United States in the *Daily Mirror* of 4 July 2002, with its hateful front page, was so hurtful to me that it was one of many events in Britain post-9/11 that made me think about returning to the United States. It is these things that inspired this book.

Sometimes in London I am asked why I am interested in so many things. Why do I not 'wind down at 50?' How does one answer this? Like so many Americans, I grew up in a society that simmers with excitement and innovation and newness. The idea that the USA is some sort of evil wasteland infuriates me because my childhood was spent being exposed to the likes of the aforementioned Eric Sevareid, Ed Murrow, Dick Cavett and Jack Paar, and the wonders of the Philadelphia Orchestra concerts conducted by Eugene Ormandy.

The first thing I do when I go to the USA is to eat at Little Pete's in the centre of Philadelphia and reacquaint myself with the warm and lovable characters who frequent it – the sort of people one finds across the great and varied expanse of America.

The Archbishop of Canterbury ought to drop his pompous presence into a diner and meet some of his Episcopalian flock, instead of accusing them of being myth-driven nutters, filled with some divine notion of 'chosenness'. It is to the credit of the American Episcopal Church that it is tolerant of homosexuals, appoints female bishops and has now ordained a woman, Katharine Schori, as the head of the American Episcopal Church. It is the legacy of Rowan Williams that the huge rift in the Church has unfolded, and that his Church is playing to empty houses in England. I am proud of the originality and tolerance of the large American church community and suggest that he should try to find out why it has full houses before he devotes any more time to denigrating America. I bet that, if the United States had taken the reactionary route and refused to ordain Gene Robinson and Mrs Schori, the British media and clergy, and the BBC *Question Time* panels, with their foot-stomping audiences, would have been up in arms about the right-wing Americans bringing down the world Anglican Communion!*

The other day, I stopped at a newspaper vendor's stand in Charing Cross. I noticed that the newspaper bill board had changed, and that its message differed from the headline on the front page of the paper I had purchased an hour before. I went to look at the fresh newspaper and he grabbed it. I said: 'Is there a new edition?' He shouted at me: 'What do you think it is? And don't touch it! Buy it but don't touch!' I gave him a pound as he continued to scowl at me and he gave me 10 pence back. I told him he had short-changed me and he literally growled back, handing over the extra 40 pence. A few days later, I told a woman in my local newsagent that I was

* Notwithstanding several 'how dare you?' tirades from British friends, I am pleased that Bishop Gene Robinson of New Hampshire has taken a stand in 2008 and told the Archbishop of Canterbury how damaging his views on homosexuals and women bishops have been; instead of encouraging the African Church to accept these forward-looking changes with grace, Dr Williams has fuelled the fires of discord, not to mention fuelling the fires of discord in Britain with his speeches about bringing in a limited form of Sharia law.

not pleased that her child was coughing on everyone and not covering her mouth (I was recovering from pneumonia). This elicited a stream of invective from the woman that would have made Gordon Ramsay blush. Of course, she had to interject epithets about my Jewishness – and even the newsagent's Arab origins. When I told her it was unfortunate that her child had to listen to the F-word so many times, she unleashed a further torrent of abuse.

The other day, I went out for a walk, despite the torrential rain. As I reached the exit of my mews, I saw a cascade of fluid spewing out. I walked on and, as I did, I realized the cascade was attached to a raised penis: a man was walking calmly along urinating, an umbrella in his other hand. I am reminded of my elegant American Boston blue-blood friend Bob Neer, who was shocked to leave his hotel in Edinburgh to find men urinating against the wall of the building next door. These are things I will not miss! I will not miss the London cabbie who railed at me for the whole journey – for no reason whatsoever – on 14 February 2007, on my first night out after breast surgery. I was attending a Valentine's night concert given by two of my closest friends. As the driver continued to spew abuse at me for everything under the sun, I decided to open my coat and lift up my sweater to expose my red, still swollen and scarred breast for a split second (it still hurt like hell even to touch it) and threw the money at him. I recall screaming incoherently at him about surviving an operation. He was speechless. Whether he saw what I exposed is immaterial. He turned a cheerful, grateful survivor into a screaming shrew. I still hate him. They don't make people like that in the USA.

This is why I still adore America: maybe I have been lucky, but whenever I cross the ocean I am treated like the respectable lady that I am – and frankly, it isn't the mustard pretzels and hot dogs: being treated like a *mensch* still means everything to me.

PS: And one more thing, while I am extolling the wonders of America the Beautiful: for 32 years, I have been asking bemused friends why there are no street signs for blocks and blocks of city and rural roads in London and all around Britain. There is not a corner in the whole of the USA where one will get lost: those wonderful green street signs are there at every corner, from sea to shining sea. Little things like that make it shine, even on the darkest day.

CHAPTER THIRTY-SIX

BOOING THE 'STAR SPANGLED BANNER' – AND PUMPKIN PIE!

As 2007 was coming to an end, an incident occurred in Las Vegas that brought anti-Americanism to even newer horizons.

It is unlikely that the men who were behaving like fourth-century pagans in the Nevada desert are *Guardian* or *Independent* readers who harbour a litany of grudges against American environment-spoilers, Zionist neocons, serial racists and genocidal murderers, but the despicable behaviour of the English fans at the Ricky Hatton fight on 7 December must be included in this book.

The events of 7 December need to be examined on several levels. The fans of undefeated Mancunian welterweight boxer Hatton arrived in Las Vegas in their thousands – one estimate places the figure at 18,000 – to cheer their hero on, he having been pitted against the supremely fit Floyd 'Pretty Boy' Mayweather Jr. It was a match I had felt weeks before was doomed to be a humiliation for the (I thought) physically vulnerable British boxer.

The Hatton fans spent serious money in Las Vegas and were generous patrons of every amenity the Strip had to offer. They brought thousands of pounds sterling to the city and were an object of bemusement, as they strutted around in the loud, crass style one associates with football fans in Europe.

Some had spent a chunk of their savings to travel thousands of miles to see Hatton fight; the hype before the match was, to me, silly, because the mismatch was so glaringly obvious. I felt there was a foolish Walter Mitty-ism bordering on arrogance amongst some British commentators. In the *Daily*

Mail of 10 December, Paul Hayward felt this was Hatton playing golf with the Tiger, tennis against Federer or participating in a singing competition against Tom Jones. One felt the cards were already on the table when 'Mayweather UK' fans reminded the media that 'UK' stands for 'Undefeated King'. I cringed when I saw the two fighters meet in their prematch facedown, Hatton pale and almost sickly looking, and Mayweather the picture of vitality and brute strength.

And so it was to transpire that, on the night of the big fight at the MGM Grand Garden Arena, Tom Jones sang 'God Save the Queen' to a silent and reverent 95 per cent American audience; but when it came time for the host country's 'Star Spangled Banner' national anthem to be sung, all hell broke loose. As the song began, the large crowd of British fans booed and jeered, drowning out the anthem altogether; when the introductions were being made, the British fans once again booed and jeered.

When I first heard about this in the early hours of Sunday 8 December, I thought I was imagining things. It was being discussed on a news programme broadcast before the Sunday political shows. I was stunned and disgusted; imagine how Britons would feel if a large crowd of Americans jeered the national anthem?

Soon the incident became a national talking point, and many commentators were setting aside time to write and talk about it. On the night itself, the fighter Sugar Ray Leonard was incandescent with rage when his country's anthem was trashed. 'They crossed the line,' he fumed. Interestingly enough, a British friend asked me why an African-American boxer would care if the national anthem 'of such a racist country' was drowned out, and I explained to her that a significant majority of Americans, whatever their ethnic origin, feel the 'Star Spangled Banner' must be heard with reverence, as, one assumes, Britons would expect of their own anthem.

It was also reported that the referee, Joe Cortez, was well beyond incandescent when the anthem was drowned out by the deafening roar of jeers, boos and verbal garbage spewing from the British crowd. The head of the MGM Grand attempted to speak but gave up, throwing the mike away.

Hatton lost the fight and, in the replay I watched, barely escaped with his life; but his 'Sorry' afterwards was as much an apology to the Americans as to his disappointed fans. Paul Hayward in the *Daily Mail* remarked that an HBO documentary about the fight included a boxing saying: 'In the ring, the truth will eventually find you.' The *Guardian*'s Richard Williams referred to the match as Hatton being 'broken by the hands of a master' and 'comprehensively dismantled'. John Rawling in the *Guardian* wrote at length about the deluded arrogance of the British media in hysterically promoting the Hatton phenomenon, when the sum total of the event could be described thus: 'football standards reached the MGM Grand as Hatton's hordes booed and whistled through the American national anthem'.

After the bout, Mayweather reminded a supporter that respect must be shown to Hatton in defeat. Hayward added in his column: 'Pity respect was a one-way street between Mayweather, America and the English anthem wreckers.'

It is interesting that so many commentators wrote about this aspect of the big fight, and with considerable shame and disgust. Bloggers who had returned to England from Las Vegas in the days after protested that it had all been in good fun, and that Americans should be glad they had spent a fortune on the gaming tables, in hotels and in the bars of the Strip. Others reminded readers that the American Ryder Cup team had offended British fans and golfers three years before.

It is doubtful that the Hatton fans jeered the American anthem because they were outraged by Abu Ghraib or Guantanamo, but the all-pervasive denigration of all things American has so permeated British society at all levels that Britons think it can be open season on Yanks wherever they may find them. This should not have been manifested by guests in the host country, and during the singing of the national anthem.

When my virulently anti-Bush and anti-war marching family is outraged by the behaviour of the Hatton fans, then

I know my instinct is correct. It was an ugly and unnecessary moment; it was not 'good fun' but illustrates the facility with which so many around the world will ostracize America, when Americans behave impeccably in similar circumstances.

* * * * *

Now we move on to the gentler subject of pumpkin pie, which emerged as an issue as the 2007–08 holiday season drew to a close.

There are many things I have been told about America and Americans over the years by my well-meaning British friends and colleagues. On most occasions I have let them lecture me or otherwise talk down to me about the 'appalling', 'ghastly' and 'dreadful' Americanisms that offend them. The ones I find particularly amusing are the people who have never set foot inside any of the 50 states, but who have definite sentiments about things American. One whole chapter in this book is devoted to an evening in which I nearly expired from near-cardiac arrest defending the honour of *academia Americana*.

One recent event that encapsulated the views on America occurred on 26 December 2007, when Miles Kington wrote a long discourse in the *Independent* ('Steamed for Mrs Cratchit – with a washing-day smell') about the horrors of pumpkin pie. Now, you may ask, why would you spend time and money reading in my book, which you thought would be deeply absorbing and enlightening, a chapter about pumpkin pie? My response is that it is these long discourses, filled with sarcasm and contempt, that characterize the bigger picture: whether it is pie or Zionists or American prison warders or Mummers strutters, many Britons think it is open season on a culture they will never, ever understand.

Miles criticized the custom of Americans having pumpkin pie for dessert. How the editor of the *Indy* let this article pass is beyond me, because it is written with considerable lack of knowledge about American traditions, but the next stage of this story comes from across the pond; Miles Kington uses a

New York Times editorial by Kate Colquhoun ('A Dessert with a Past', 24 December 2007) about Christmas pudding as a benchmark for slamming 'pumpkin pie at Christmas'. Kate, though British, is at least kind to the Americans, reminding us that pumpkin was introduced into Tudor England by the French. She even compliments the 'frontier spirit' of colonial settlers, who recognized the simplicity of pumpkin-derivative foods. Christmas pudding was more complicated to devise and not as easy on the digestion.

Kington's article starts out as an amusing piece about traditional British Christmas pudding, also known as plum pudding, and the loathing so many Britons have of this dessert (yet will not admit to). Where he goes horribly wrong is his contention that the only thing worse than Christmas pudding is American pumpkin pie. From what one can deduce from both articles, the authors seem to think Americans indulge in pumpkin pie at Christmas.

I decided to canvass my American friends, and discovered that – from Maryland to Philadelphia to Los Angeles to wee Barton, Vermont – they had traditional British-style plum pudding or German Stollen cake for Christmas dessert. What irked me about the two editorials is that they ignored the fact that pumpkin pie is dessert at Thanksgiving, not Christmas. Miles Kington is likely paid a great deal for his column inches, as is Kate of the *New York Times*. They fail in their homework, because pumpkins are not widely harvested after Thanksgiving and so pumpkin pie cannot possibly be the traditional country-wide dessert for Christmas.

Miles Kington, who, one assumes, did not grow up in the USA and who, one also assumes, does not live year in and year out in an American setting, spends a considerable amount of time denouncing the disgusting pumpkin mixture and wheeling out Italian relatives who suggest the use of pumpkin in a sweet pie is an insult to the fruit, which is meant only for savoury ravioli fillings. The amount of space devoted to criticizing American taste in desserts borders on the ludicrous.

So as not to waste the reader's time any further on this eccentric topic, I will move on to more pithy subject matter, but will admonish British journalists to do their homework before seeking to condemn something American. Pumpkins are for Halloween and Thanksgiving, not Christmas.

And by the way, before European writers assert that Americans have done nothing with the tomato except make ketchup, tell that to the national group that more than any other has passed through Ellis Island – Italian Americans – and try telling Geno and Pat in South Philly what Americans can and can't do with a tomato.

CHAPTER THIRTY-SEVEN

AMERICANS 'POISON' BRITISH SOLDIERS – AND I FINALLY GET WHACKED!

Thank goodness my dear, patient publishers have allowed me a few extra weeks to put the final touches to this manuscript, because in that precious extra time it finally happened – someone actually hit me!

This arose from a 24-hour British news cycle on 9/10 January 2008, in which headlines like 'BLOODY DISGRACE!' (*Sun*, 10 January) peppered the public discourse. Radio, television and print media had begun to obsess over a story about American troops giving British soldiers contaminated blood. The nation was gripped when it was revealed that the Pentagon had warned Allied forces that some blood sent to the war front for emergency transfusions may not have been properly screened.

This is an appalling story, but the manner in which it was reported and discussed had that tinge to which expatriate Americans have become so familiar: that the incompetent, uncaring Yanks had donated blood to dying British soldiers without checking it for AIDS, syphilis and hepatitis.

Coverage of this story included, at the very extreme end of the spectrum – in the *Sun* – quotes from senior British army officers asserting that this was a scandal that outdid the 'friendly fire' death of Matty Hull, killed by American airpower. In the *Sun*, an article by General Sir Anthony Walker does question the British policy of taking blood from American sources, suggesting it was cost-cutting and bad forward planning on the part of the British side that made it necessary to source blood from the United States. He asks why the USA did not check 100 per cent the safety of the blood, calling the episode an 'absolute disgrace'.

Headlining the *Sun*'s feature article is the powerful concept of 18 soldiers, now all deployed elsewhere or demobilized, walking around with incurable diseases. It asks the 18 soldiers to call the *Sun* news desk. The *Sun*'s chief reporter, John Kay, says American blood for the troops was sourced from 'banged-up convicts' given financial reward.

One military spokesperson made the point that the British field hospitals must use other supplies when they run out of screened British blood, but that this did not excuse the Americans for not properly screening blood for the battlefield. Emma Morton, the *Sun*'s health editor, adds that blood that was meant to save lives may now have disseminated death sentences.

A nasty story, but in the 24-hour news cycle in those dark days of early winter it kept a loud presence. So, when I went into my local bank to ask for information and had to queue for what seemed an eternity, I decided to strike up a conversation with a man elbowing his way to stand alongside me, and not behind me, telling him how long the wait was. He was well dressed and promptly cuffed me with his newspaper, saying: 'Oh, shut up.' I said: 'What??' And he said: 'Bloody Americans, thought you'd stopped coming here.' I thought: 'That is actually assault and battery.' But I decided to leave him in peace. Obviously he had been exposed to the 24-hour news cycle drumming into the great British public the image of 18 brave veterans falling like flies.

I suppose I have been lucky: the United States is depicted as a house of horrors, and my accent elicits hostility (lest I forget the miserable woman at the Bagel of the North shop in Newcastle, who could barely contain her hatred of me; I honestly decided not to buy a coffee for fear of arsenic being poured into it). It surprises me that I have not been whacked before.

A few days after the incident in the bank, a group of young presenters produced a poignant one-hour special on British television about Omaha Beach. It was a searing tableau of carnage and a handful of aging survivors were interviewed. Sixty-three years on, these elderly men wept as they spoke of the guilt and emotional torment they still experience, having survived when thousands of their fellow soldiers died after only just reaching the beach. Richard Hammond and Simon Trew, the presenters, young enough to be their grandsons, were deeply moved by the staggering level of fatalities amongst the Americans on D-Day. Their programme did not assuage the daily abuse I and many expatriate Americans receive, but one hopes it put into perspective for the watching public the sacrifices made by North American troops to stop Hitler's advance and conquest of all Europe and Great Britain.

The old man in the bank may wish Americans would stop coming, but the waves of Yanks who relieved the shattered French forces in the Great War, and those further waves of men and women who poured into England in the Second World War, changed the course of history. When I visited Madingley Cemetery in Cambridge and saw how many Americans had lost their lives or been declared missing – close to 9,000 – from as early as the beginning of 1942, I felt the United States had made as much effort as it could to help its ally, and that two European wars had left tens of thousands of American teenagers buried in the soil of Europe and Britain, or lost protecting its waters.

I will never understand hatred of Americans. One of my most congenial work colleagues, now retired, has a pathological hatred of my compatriots and accuses them of 'knocking people over in Harrods' and being the 'most vile of all tourist groups'. She simply loathes anyone from the United States, and even avoids most films because she 'cannot bear to listen to those appalling accents'. When I ask her why she does not hate me, she says I have 'cultivated' myself over the years.

What is so sad is that my last few years in Britain have been characterized by reactions ranging from scowls to unbridled fury when my accent is detected. I like to think that all of the British soldiers supposedly infected by tainted blood will be tested and revealed to be in the clear. I like to think that the men, facing death, were saved by resourceful Americans in the field of battle, offering life-saving supplies to their comrades in arms. Just as millions of Christian and Muslim Jew-haters around the world gratefully accept the Salk vaccine, developed by a Jew, to rid their communities of polio, so one hopes Europeans and Britons who love to hate Americans will one day acknowledge that their redeeming features far outweigh whatever it is that makes them so hated, and that no one will tread on Yanks anymore.

EPILOGUE

AMERICA BECKONS ONCE MORE

Lately my thoughts have been turning to my great-grandparents, whose images adorn my wall here in London. I have only one photograph of them and that is it. All I know is that their family name was Karash and that the bearded, sad man in the photo was a great rabbi in Bialystok. Like so many with Jewish ancestry, I do not have a family tree, unlike my British friends, some of whom can trace every ancestor back to 1066 and the Battle of Hastings.

It is odd that I ended up in Europe after the struggle my ancestors endured to find their way to the United States. Now that I am embroiled on a daily basis in the anguished 'anti-Boycott Israel' movement in Britain, and feeling less and less welcome in a much-loved land I thought would be my permanent home, I am feeling a strong kinship with those Jews who left Europe a hundred years ago to escape pogroms and conscription into the Tsar's army.

But how, you may ask, could England possibly be mentioned in the same breath as the pogroms or the Pale of Settlement? Here is my answer: the anger and hatred I have felt in the past year from many people here have made me understand the despair of my great-grandparents and their children, who begged, borrowed and bartered to get passage to the United States.

Right now, I am trying to work out an economical way to ship my worldly goods to the USA, and though I am not on the receiving end of beatings and rape (as used to be customary in Tsarist Russia), that feeling of 'I have to get out of here' has hit me for the first time in the 32 years I have resided in Britain, a nation I had tried to take into my soul as my own. I understand how my ancestors felt, and I am counting the days until I can see the Statue of Liberty, as they did a hundred years ago.

It caused me profound shock in late 2007 to hear that the combined Protestant and Catholic Irish Congress of Trade Unions, representing 800,000 members in both Ulster and the Irish Republic, had united in condemnation of Israel and had passed a resolution in the week of 16 July 2007 calling for an all-out boycott of all things Israeli.

Considering that it is only a few months since Martin McGuinness and Ian Paisley, the leaders of the IRA and the Ulster Unionists, respectively, finally shook hands after almost a century of Protestant–Catholic bloodletting, it is a disturbing turn of events to see the Irish workers' union uniting against Israel.

As was reported in the *Jewish Chronicle* of 20 July, the resolution was proposed by the Belfast and District Trades Council and Derry Trades Council. Ulster's largest union, the Northern Ireland Public Service Alliance, had already taken the decision to boycott Israeli goods in the manner of the boycott during South African apartheid.

The combined Irish resolution urges complete disinvestment in Israeli companies and pension and investment funds, and urges union members to encourage colleagues in all walks of life to follow suit.

What is going on here?

I have a theory. European countries are not engaging in boycotts. In fact, the Seventh Research Framework Programme of 2007 links Israel and the EU in well-funded academic cross-fertilization. The reason why I think Britain and Ireland are at the forefront of these punitive measures against the Jewish state is that – despite the Blitz – mainland Britain was never occupied by Germany and its citizens were not forced to live under the jackboot of the Third Reich. Ireland was not occupied, and neither country watched its Jews being marched off to death camps.

Europe was occupied by the Nazis, and still fresh in the minds of many of its citizens is the genocide committed against its Jewish population. Likewise, Europeans are less likely to engage in the condemnatory rhetoric being used in Britain to characterize Israeli policies. It is interesting, too, that Britain has such a small Jewish community – less than 300,000 – and yet the aggressive language being used by the media, politicians and trade unionists borders on the anti-Semitic. France has a much larger Jewish population but boycotts are not proliferating.

There is deep bitterness amongst many Britons, even so many decades on, about the lynching of British soldiers and the bombing of the King David Hotel by the Irgun and other Jewish resistance groups in post-war Palestine. For 32 years I have heard over and over again at dinner parties the stories of British soldiers and sailors being terrorized by the Stern Gang, and the mantra: 'You people invented terrorism!'

Notwithstanding this, the anger directed towards me in social situations these days goes beyond British bitterness over an episode in Jerusalem 60 years ago. I find it disturbing and unsettling that I am spending more and more time alone, blessedly away from a fulminating population; on the rare occasions when I socialize, it is with two Jewish friends, both expatriates and both also now planning to return to their native countries after many, many decades in Britain.

As I, like my ancestors, try to scrape together the resources to ship myself and my belongings to the USA, my thoughts return to my Bialystok family, which found a home in Philadelphia, away from the hatred they had left behind in a festering Europe.

Like them, I long for the day, very soon, when I, with my one-way ticket in my hand, can pass Lady Liberty and watch her lift her lamp beside the golden door.